AN AMERICAN IMPERATIVE:

Higher Expectations for Higher Education

An Open Letter to Those Concerned
about the American Future

Report of the
Wingspread Group on Higher Education

Library of Congress Cataloging in Publication Data
Wingspread Group on Higher Education
An American Imperative

ISBN 0-9639160-0-9
Library of Congress Catalog Card Number 93-061441
1. Education, Higher—United States.

An electronic version of the report of the Wingspread Group on Higher Education is available on INTERNET through anonymous ftp at the University of Wisconsin—Milwaukee. To locate the report, ftp to csd4.csd.uwm.edu, change directory to pub/wingspread/report.txt. If you have questions, call 414-229-6151 or send E-mail to help@csd4.csd.uwm.edu.

Contents

Chairman's Preface

The world our children inhabit is different, radically so, than the one we inherited. An increasingly open, global economy requires—absolutely requires—that all of us be better educated, more skilled, more adaptable, and more capable of working collaboratively. These economic considerations alone mean that we must change the ways we teach and learn.

But an increasingly diverse society, battered (and that is not too strong a term) by accelerating change, requires more than workplace competence. It also requires that we do a better job of passing on to the next generation a sense of the value of diversity and the critical importance of honesty, decency, integrity, compassion, and personal responsibility in a democratic society. Above all, we must get across the idea that the individual flourishes best in a genuine community to which the individual in turn has an obligation to contribute.

None of us is doing as well as we should in this whole business. We are all part of the problem, if only because we acquiesce in a formal education system that is not meeting our needs.

We must not forget that no nation can remain great without developing a truly well-educated people. No nation can remain good without transmitting the fundamental values of a civil society to each new generation. No nation can remain strong unless it puts its young people at the forefront of its concerns. America is falling short on each of these counts. It has much to do.

Believing these things, I was very pleased when in January 1993 the president of The Johnson Foundation suggested that I chair a working group sponsored by four leading private foundations—The William and Flora Hewlett Foundation, The Johnson Foundation, Inc., Lilly Endowment Inc., and The Pew Charitable Trusts—to examine the question: "What Does Society Need from Higher Education?"

The foundations assembled a working group of talented and experienced men and women (Appendix C) and provided us with a remarkable collection of essays written for our use by 32 individuals representing diverse social, professional, and economic perspectives. Indeed, we found the essays so helpful that we have appended them to this report for the benefit of others (Appendix D). The Johnson Foundation made the magnificent setting of its Wingspread facilities and, more importantly, the talents of its staff available to us. We were encouraged to define our own agenda and to begin our work.

Some of what we have to say in the attached open letter will not be easy reading for our friends and colleagues in higher education. We understand that; some of it was not easy writing, either. We have, however, tried to avoid finding fault and pointing fingers. Our comments should be understood as an effort by close and affectionate friends to express concern and to offer suggestions to colleagues whose labors we respect and badly need.

An additional point: there is no single silver bullet cure. Much as it would simplify our national task, no single act will transform the incredibly diverse world of higher education into an enterprise routinely producing graduates with all of the qualities, competences, and attitudes we would hope for them.

Rather, our suggestions and our questions will require of each institution—campus by campus—honest introspection and some very hard and even controversial new thinking about its roles and responsibilities, principles, and priorities.

I want to express our gratitude to all those who have assisted our work in so many thoughtful and gracious ways, beginning with the four sponsoring foundations. I should note that their support and the assistance of others (including the scores of individuals from education, business, public life, and philanthropy who offered helpful comments on a preliminary draft of this document) does not impl that any of them subscribe to the conclusions we have reached or the challenges we advance.

Finally, I think it only fair to point out that although every member of our group supports the major themes of our open letter, none of us necessarily subscribes to every detail. That should be little surprise. The Wingspread Group was composed of 16 accomplished, thoughtful individuals, all with strongly held views On the big questions—the conviction that American education faces serious problems, the belief that we need to develop new ways of thinking about higher education, and the conclusions and challenges in this document—we are unanimous.

We hope this open letter to those of our fellow Americans who share our concern for the future will stimulate the national debate about higher education that we consider essential.

William E. Brock
Chairman

An American Imperative:

Higher Expectations For Higher Education

*Everything has changed but our ways of thinking, and if these
do not change we drift toward unparalleled catastrophe.*

Albert Einstein

A disturbing and dangerous mismatch exists between what American society
needs of higher education and what it is receiving. Nowhere is the mismatch
more dangerous than in the quality of undergraduate preparation provided on
many campuses. The American imperative for the 21st century is that society must
hold higher education to much higher expectations or risk national decline.

Establishing higher expectations, however, will require that students and
parents rethink what too many seem to want from education: the credential without the content, the degree without the knowledge and effort it implies.

In the past, our industrial economy produced many new and low-skill jobs
and provided stable employment, often at high wages, for all. Now the nation
faces an entirely different economic scenario: a knowledge-based economy with a
shortage of highly skilled workers at all levels and a surplus of unskilled applicants scrambling to earn a precarious living. Many of those unskilled applicants
are college graduates, not high school dropouts.

Like much of the rest of American education, the nation's colleges and universities appear to live by an unconscious educational rule of thumb that their
function is to weed out, not to cultivate, students for whom they have accepted
responsibility. An unacceptably high percentage of students leaks out of the system at each juncture in the education pipeline. This hemorrhaging of our human
resources occurs despite the low standards prevalent in American education and
the existence of a wide diversity of institutions offering many options for students.
It is almost as though educators take failure for granted.

Education is in trouble, and with it our nation's hopes for the future.
America's ability to compete in a global economy is threatened. The American
people's hopes for a civil, humane society ride on the outcome. The capacity of
the United States to shoulder its responsibilities on the world stage is at risk. We
understand the explanations offered when criticisms are leveled at higher education: entrants are inadequately prepared; institutional missions vary; we are
required by law to accept all high school graduates; students change their minds
frequently and drop out of school; controlling costs is difficult in the labor-
intensive academy; cutting-edge research consumes the time of senior faculty. All
of these things are true.

But the larger truth is that the explanations, no matter how persuasive they
once were, no longer add up to a compelling whole. The simple fact is that some
faculties and institutions certify for graduation too many students who cannot
read and write very well, too many whose intellectual depth and breadth are
unimpressive, and too many whose skills are inadequate in the face of the
demands of contemporary life.

These conclusions point to the possibilities for institutional decline given that an increasingly skeptical public expresses the same sense of sticker shock about college costs that is now driving health care reform. The withdrawal of public support for higher education can only accelerate as students, parents, and tax-payers come to understand that they paid for an expensive education without receiving fair value in return.

The seeds for national disaster are also there: the needs of an information- and technology-based global economy, the complexities of modern life, the accelerated pace of change and the growing demands for competent, high-skill performance in the workplace require that we produce much higher numbers of individuals—whether high school, community college or four-year graduates— prepared to learn their way through life. Most Americans and their policymakers concerned about the quality of pre-collegiate education, take heart in the large numbers of Americans who receive associate's and bachelor's degrees every year. The harsh truth is that a significant minority of these graduates enter or reenter the world with little more than the knowledge, competence, and skill we would have expected in a high school graduate scarcely a generation ago.

What does our society *need* from higher education? It needs stronger, more vital forms of community. It needs an informed and involved citizenry. It needs graduates able to assume leadership roles in American life. It needs a competent and adaptable workforce. It needs very high quality undergraduate education producing graduates who can sustain each of these goals. It needs more first-rate research pushing back the important boundaries of human knowledge and less research designed to lengthen academic résumés. It needs an affordable, cost-effective educational enterprise offering lifelong learning. Above all, it needs a commitment to the American promise—the idea that all Americans have the opportunity to develop their talents to the fullest. Higher education is not meeting these imperatives.

A Changing America and a Changing World

American society has never been static, but now change is accelerating. The United States is becoming more diverse: by the year 2020, about one-third of Americans will be members of minority groups, traditionally poorly served by education at all levels. New information and technologies are accelerating change with a half life of less than five years, they are reshaping the way the world lives, works, and plays. Our society is aging: in 1933, 17 Americans were employed for every Social Security recipient; by 2020, the ratio will have dropped from 17-to-1 to 3-to-1. In 1950, the Ford Motor Company employed 62 active workers for every retiree; by 1993, the ratio dropped to 1.2-to-1. These statistics are a stark reminder of our need to assure that American workers are educated to levels that maximize their productivity and, hence, our collective economic well-being.

A generation ago, Americans were confident that the core values which had served our nation well in the past could guide it into the future. These values were expressed in homey statements such as: "Honesty is the best policy"; "Serve your country"; "Be a good neighbor." Today we worry that the core values may be shifting and that the sentiments expressed are different: "Don't get involved";

"I gave at the office"; "It's cheating only if you get caught." Too many of us today worry about "me" at the expense of "we."

A generation ago, our society and its institutions were overseen by white males. Immigration policy favored peoples from Northern Europe. The television images of "Ozzie and Harriet" were thought to reflect the middle-class American family. Almost all of that has changed as women and members of minority groups increasingly have assumed their place at the table, and immigrants and refugees from once-distant lands have remade the face of the United States.

A generation ago, computers took up entire rooms; punch cards for data processing were the cutting edge of technology; operators stood by to help with transatlantic calls; many families watched the clock each afternoon until local television stations began their evening broadcasts. Today, microprocessors, miniaturization, and fiber optics have made information from the four corners of the world instantaneously available to anyone with a computer, transforming the way we manage our institutions, the way we entertain ourselves, and the way we do our business.

A generation ago, our society was affluent, richer than it had ever been, with the prospect that its wealth would be more widely and deeply shared than ever before. The American economy—our assembly lines, our banks and farms, our workers and managers—dominated the global economy. Ours was the only major economy to emerge intact from World War II. Trade barriers limited global competition. Our industrial plant and national infrastructure were the envy of the world. As a people, we believed we could afford practically anything, and we undertook practically everything.

Those days are behind us. Global competition is transforming the economic landscape. Fierce competitors from abroad have entered domestic markets, and one great American industry after another has felt the effects. We have watched with growing concern as our great national strengths have been challenged, as the gap between rich and poor has widened, and as the nation's economic energy has been sapped by budget and trade deficits. We have struggled—so far unsuccessfully—to set the country back on the confident, spirited course we took for granted a generation ago.

We can regain that course only if Americans work smarter. Otherwise, our standard of living will continue the enervating erosion that began two decades ago. Individual economic security in the future will depend not on job or career stability, but on employability, which itself will be a function of adaptability and the willingness to learn, grow, and change throughout a lifetime.

Americans may be aware of all of this, but we are prisoners of our past. Our thinking and many of our institutions, including our educational institutions, are still organized as though none of these changes had occurred.

The 3,400 institutions of higher learning in America come in all shapes and sizes, public and private. They include small liberal arts institutions, two-year community colleges, and technical institutions, state colleges and universities, and flagship research universities. In each of these categories, models of both excellence and mediocrity exist. Despite this diversity, most operate as though their focus were still the traditional student of days gone by: a white, male, recent high school graduate, who attended classes full-time at a four-year institution and lived on campus. Yesterday's traditional student is, in fact, today's exception.

There are more women than men among the 13.5 million students on today's campuses. Forty-three percent of today's students are over the age of 25, including 300,000 over the age of 50. Minority Americans now make up about 20 percent of enrollments in higher education. Almost as many students attend part-time and intermittently as attend full-time and without interruption. More college students are enrolled in community colleges than in four-year institutions. And there are more students living at home or off-campus than there are in dormitories. Fixed in our mind's eye, however, the image of the traditional student blocks effective responses to these new realities.

These demographic, economic, and technological changes underscore the mismatch between what is needed of higher education and what it provides. Because we are now a more diverse people, society needs a much better sense of the things that unite us. Because the global economy has had such a profound effect on American standards of living, individuals in our society and the economy as a whole need to be much better prepared for the world of work.

In short, we need to educate more people, educate them to far higher standards, and do it as effectively and efficiently as possible.

Warning Signs

Institutions, like organisms, must respond to changes in their environment if they are to survive. Not surprisingly, given higher education's slow adaptation, real problems shadow the real successes of the nation's colleges and universities.

Crisis of Values. The nation's colleges and universities are enmeshed in, and in some ways contributing to, society's larger crisis of values. Intolerance on campus is on the rise; half of big-time college sports programs have been caught cheating in the last decade; reports of ethical lapses by administrators, faculty members and trustees, and of cheating and plagiarism by students are given widespread credence.

From the founding of the first American colleges 300 years ago, higher education viewed the development of student character and the transmission of the values supporting that character as an essential responsibility of faculty and administration. The importance of higher education's role in the transmission of values is, if anything, even greater today than it was 300 or even 50 years ago. The weakening of the role of family and religious institutions in the lives of young people, the increase in the number of people seeking the benefits of higher education, and what appears to be the larger erosion of core values in our society make this traditional role all the more important.

In this context, it is fair to ask how well our educational institutions are transmitting an understanding of good and bad, right and wrong, and the compelling core of values any society needs to sustain itself. While there is a paucity of concrete data, enough anecdotal evidence exists to suggest that there is too little concerted attention, on too many campuses, to this responsibility.

In the final analysis, a society is not simply something in which we find ourselves. Society is "we." It is our individual and collective integrity, our commitment to each other and to the dignity of all. All of the other accomplishments of higher education will be degraded if our colleges and universities lose their moral compass and moral vocation.

The Costs of "Weeding." Few thoughtful observers believe that our K-12 schools are adequate for today's needs. About half our high school students are enrolled in dead-end curricula that prepare them poorly for work, life, or additional learning. Too many of the rest are bored and unchallenged. Too few are performing to standards that make them competitive with peers in other industrialized countries. Half of those entering college full-time do not have a degree within five years. Half of all students entering Ph.D. programs never obtain the degree. In short, our education system is better organized to discourage students—to weed them out—than it is to cultivate and support our most important national resource, our people.

The Uneducated Graduate. The failure to cultivate our students is evident in a 1992 analysis of college transcripts by the U.S. Department of Education, which reveals that 26.2 percent of recent bachelor's degree recipients earned not a single undergraduate credit in history; 30.8 percent did not study mathematics of any kind; 39.6 percent earned no credits in either English or American literature; and 58.4 percent left college without any exposure to a foreign language. Much too frequently, American higher education now offers a smorgasbord of fanciful courses in a fragmented curriculum that accords as much credit for "Introduction to Tennis" and for courses in pop culture as it does for "Principles of English Composition," history, or physics, thereby trivializing education—indeed, misleading students by implying that they are receiving the education they need for life when they are not.

The original purpose of an undergraduate education, the development of a broadly educated human being, prepared, in the words of Englishman John Henry Cardinal Newman, "to fill any post with credit", has been pushed to the periphery. That purpose, restated, was the essential message of a commission convened by President Harry S Truman 45 years ago. According to the Truman Commission, higher education should help students acquire the knowledge, skills, and attitudes to enable them "to live rightly and well in a free society." The 1992 transcript analysis cited above suggests that educators need to ask themselves how well their current graduates measure up to the standards of Newman and the Truman Commission, and to the needs of American society for thoughtful citizens, workers, and potential leaders.

For without a broad liberal education, students are denied the opportunity to engage with the principal ideas and events that are the source of any civilization. How then are they to understand the values that sustain community and society, much less their own values? Educators know better, but stand silent.

There is further disturbing evidence that graduates are unprepared for the requirements of daily life. According to the 1993 National Adult Literacy Survey (NALS), surprisingly large numbers of two- and four-year college graduates are unable, in everyday situations, to use basic skills involving reading, writing, computation, and elementary problem-solving.[*]

---

[*] Results of the NALS survey, conducted by the Educational Testing Service for the U.S. Department of Education, were released in September 1993. The largest effort of its type ever attempted, the survey offers a comprehensive analysis of the competence of American adults (both college- and non-college-educated) based on face-to-face interviews with 26,000 people. We note with concern that the 1993 survey findings reflect a statistically significant decline from those of an earlier survey conducted in 1985.

The NALS tasks required participants to do three things: read and interpret prose, such as newspaper articles, work with documents like bus schedules and tables and charts, and use elementary arithmetic to solve problems involving, for example, the costs of restaurant meals or mortgages. The NALS findings were presented on a scale from low (Level 1) to high (Level 5) in each of the three areas. The performance of college graduates on these scales is distressing:

- in working with documents, only eight percent of all four-year college graduates reach the highest level;
- in terms of their ability to work with prose, only 10 percent of four-year graduates are found in Level 5; and
- with respect to quantitative skills, only 12 percent of four-year graduates reach the highest level.

In fact, only about one-half of four-year graduates are able to demonstrate intermediate levels of competence in each of the three areas. In the area of quantitative skills, for example, 56.3 percent of American-born, four-year college graduates are unable *consistently* to perform simple tasks, such as calculating the change from $3 after buying a 60 cent bowl of soup and a $1.95 sandwich. Tasks such as these should not be insuperable for people with 16 years of education.

Growing Public Concern. Opinion polls leave no doubt that Americans have a profound respect for higher education. They consider it essential to the nation's civility and economic progress, and to advances in science, technology, and medicine. Americans are convinced that an undergraduate degree is as important to success in today's world as a high school diploma was in yesterday's.

But, simultaneously, the polls reveal deep public concern about higher education. The public is overwhelmed by sticker shock when it considers college costs. According to the polls, the overwhelming majority of the American people believes that colleges and universities—both public and private—are overpriced and lie increasingly beyond the reach of all but the wealthy. Public confidence in the "people running higher education" has declined as dramatically with respect to education leaders as it has with respect to the leadership of medicine, government, and business.

While the public is most interested in achievement, costs, and management, it believes that the academy focuses instead on advanced study and research. Several of the essays written for our study echo a number of the conclusions of the 1992 report of the President's Advisory Council on Science and Technology. Both remind us that the academic culture and rewards system too frequently encourages graduate education and research at the expense of undergraduate education. What emerges is a picture of academic life which only grudgingly attends to undergraduate learning, and to the advice, counseling, and other support services students need. The dominant academic attitude, particularly on large campuses enrolling most American students, is that research deserves pride of place over teaching and public service, in part because many senior faculty prefer specialized research to teaching, and in part because institutions derive much of their prestige from faculty research. Indeed, the ideal model in the minds of faculty members on campuses of all kinds is defined by what they perceive to be the culture and aspirations of flagship research universities.

Three Central Issues

It is hard not to conclude that too much undergraduate education is little more than secondary school material—warmed over and reoffered at much higher expense, but not at correspondingly higher levels of effectiveness. The United States can no longer afford the inefficiencies, or the waste of talent, time, and money, revealed by these warning signs. Indeed, the nation that responds best and most rapidly to the educational demands of the Age of the Learner will enjoy a commanding international advantage in the pursuit of both domestic tranquillity and economic prosperity. To achieve these goals for our country, we must educate more people, and educate them far better. That will require new ways of thinking.

Given the diversity of American higher education, there can be no single formula for change common to all, but we do believe that there are at least three fundamental issues common to all 3,400 colleges and universities:

- **taking values seriously;**
- **putting student learning first;**
- **creating a nation of learners.**

The nation's colleges and universities can respond to the agenda defined in this open letter. They can do so by reaffirming their conviction that the moral purpose of knowledge is at least as important as its utility. They can do so by placing student learning at the heart of their concerns. They can do so by working toward what educator John Goodlad has called "a simultaneous renewal" of higher education and the nation's K-12 schools as one continuous learning system.

To focus what we hope will be a vigorous, widespread national debate, we have distilled the results of six-months' work and discussion into a compact document designed to make our line of reasoning as clear as possible. Our purpose is not so much to provide answers. Rather, we hope to raise some of the right questions and thus encourage Americans and their colleges and universities to consider and adopt a new direction. That is why we close this document not with a set of recommendations, but with a set of challenges for American higher education, for the public, and for its representatives.

We begin our discussion in the pages that follow with an argument for putting first things first: the need for a rigorous liberal education that takes values seriously and acknowledges that value-free education has proven a costly blind alley for society.

Taking Values Seriously

*The Holocaust reminds us forever that knowledge divorced
from values can only serve to deepen the human nightmare;
that a head without a heart is not humanity.*

President Bill Clinton

Democratic societies need a common ground, a shared frame of reference within which to encourage both diversity and constructive debate about the common good. A free people cannot enjoy the fruits of its liberty without collaborative efforts in behalf of community. Higher education has a central obligation to develop these abilities.

There are some values, rooted in national experience, even defined in the Constitution, that Americans share. These "constitutional" values have evolved into a set of civic virtues:

- respect for the individual and commitment to equal opportunity;
- the belief that our common interests exceed our individual differences;
- concern for those who come after us;
- support for the freedoms enunciated in the Bill of Rights, including freedom of religion, of the press, of speech, and of the right to assemble;
- the belief that individual rights and privileges are to be exercised responsibly;
- respect for the views of others; and
- the conviction that no one is above the law.

If values are to be taken seriously, the place to start is by reaffirming the primacy of the visions of Newman and the Truman Commission: liberal education is central to living "rightly and well in a free society." We do not believe that a history major needs to know as much chemistry as a forest management major, that an engineering major needs to know as much literature as an English major. But every student needs the knowledge and understanding that can come only from the rigors of a liberal education. Such an education lies at the heart of developing both social and personal values. If the center of American society is to hold, a liberal education must be central to the undergraduate experience of all students. The essentials of a liberal education should be contained in a rigorous, required curriculum defined on each campus.

We believe, too, that every institution of higher education should ask itself—*now*—what it proposes to do to assure that next year's entering students will graduate as individuals of character more sensitive to the needs of community, more competent in their ability to contribute to society, and more civil in their habits of thought, speech, and action.

We are also convinced that each educational institution must, openly and directly, begin the kinds of discussions that promise to build campus consensus on the civic virtues it most treasures. The questions concluding this section, and repeated in Appendix A, define some of the issues that need to be addressed.

What do these issues mean in practice? Several implications appear obvious: campuses must model the values they espouse; they must help students experience society and reflect on it as an integral part of their education; they must act on their understanding that matters of the spirit reflect such a profound aspect of the human condition that they cannot be ignored on any campus.

With respect to modeling values, a former president of Yale University, A. Bartlett Giamatti, once said: "[A]n educational institution teaches far, far more, and more profoundly, by how it acts than by anything anyone within it ever says." Mr. Giamatti was echoed by one of our essayists, Robert Rosenzweig, who wrote, "American society needs colleges and universities to be active exemplars of the values they have always professed...." In both statements, the critical emphasis is on *acting* and *exemplifying*, not simply proclaiming. On campus, as elsewhere, the dictum "Do as I say, not as I do" is an invitation to cynicism among our citizens, particularly students.

We want also to stress that society's needs will be well served if colleges and universities wholeheartedly commit themselves to providing students with opportunities to experience and reflect on the world beyond the campus. Books and lectures provide an intellectual grounding in the realities of the marketplace and of the nation's social dilemmas. But there is no substitute for experience. Academic work should be complemented by the kinds of knowledge derived from first-hand experience, such as contributing to the well-being of others, participating in political campaigns, and working with the enterprises that create wealth in our society.

Last but not least, we want to suggest that matters of the spirit have a far more important role to play in institutions of higher education than has been encouraged in recent years. We do not argue for one system of belief or another, one denomination or another, or for compulsory religious observance of any kind. Certainly we understand that campuses must be dedicated to free inquiry, ungoverned by either faddish orthodoxy or intolerant ideology. But we do argue that faith and deep moral conviction *matter* in human affairs. Because they do, they must matter on campus.

We believe that the concept of a value-free education is a profoundly misleading contradiction in terms, a blind alley with very high costs to personal life, community, and even workplace. A campus community whose members cannot readily give answers to the following questions is a campus without a purpose:

- What kind of people do we want our children and grandchildren to be?
- What kind of society do we want them to live in?
- How can we best shape our institution to nurture those kinds of people and that kind of society?*

---

* Questions taken from Howard Bowen, *The State of the Nation and the Agenda for Higher Education*. San Francisco: Jossey-Bass, 1982.

Initiating and sustaining discussions and initiatives of the sort suggested above will be difficult on large campuses, but not impossible. Organizing and sustaining community service programs for large numbers of students both inside and outside the classroom is difficult, but not impossible. Encouraging collaborative learning is perhaps more difficult than grading on the curve, but it is not impossible. Yet activities such as these both model and teach the skills of community.

The questions raised in the realm of values may, on occasion, be deeply troubling. In our view that is all to the good. If the journey is too comfortable, the right questions are probably not being asked, and asking the right questions is essential if higher education is to rise to Pericles' standards:

> Pericles knew that any successful society must be an educational institution. However great its commitment to individual freedom and diversity, it needs a code of civic virtue and a general devotion to the common enterprise without which it cannot flourish or survive.

> It must transmit its understanding of good and bad and a sense of pride, admiration, and love for its institutions and values to its citizens, especially the young.*

It is fashionable to decry the quality of American leadership, public and private. Yet virtually all our leadership emerges from one institution of higher education or another. As students are groomed on campus, so shall they live and lead. Pericles understood. Do we?

* Donald Kagan, *Pericles of Athens and the Birth of Democracy.* New York: Simon & Schuster, 1991.

Taking Values Seriously

- How does our educational program match the claims of our recruiting brochures, and where is it falling short?

- How does our core curriculum of required courses respond to the needs of our students for a rigorous liberal education enabling them to "live rightly and well in a free society?" Where does it fall short?

- In what ways does our institution model the values and skills expected in our community? Where and how are we falling short?

- What steps might we take to improve the general climate of civility on our campus?

- How comprehensive and effective is the code of professional conduct and ethics for our faculty and staff? When was it last reviewed?

- In what ways does our institution and its educational program promote the development of shared values, specifically the civic virtues listed below, among our students?

  - respect for the individual and commitment to equal opportunity in a diverse society;

  - the belief that our common interests exceed our individual differences;

  - support for the freedoms enunciated in the Bill of Rights, including freedom of religion, of the press, of speech, and of the right to assemble;

  - the belief that individual rights and privileges are accompanied by responsibilities to others;

  - respect for the views of others; and

  - the conviction that no one is above the law.

- What moral and ethical questions should we be putting to the student groups and organizations we sanction on campus? What standards of conduct do we expect of these groups? How have we made these standards clear?

- How do the activities of our athletic programs square with our institution's stated values, and where do they fall short?

- What steps will we take to assure that next year's entering students will graduate as individuals of character more sensitive to the needs of community, more competent to contribute to society, more civil in their habits of thought, speech, and action?

- What other related questions should we address at our institution?

Putting Student Learning First

The future now belongs to societies that organize themselves for learning.

Ray Marshall and Marc Tucker

If it is time to take values seriously on campus, it is also time to redress the imbalance that has led to the decline of undergraduate education. To do so, the nation's colleges and universities must for the foreseeable future focus over-whelmingly on what their students learn and achieve. Too much of education at every level seems to be organized for the convenience of educators and the institution's interests, procedures and prestige, and too little focused on the needs of students.

Putting students at the heart of the educational enterprise requires that we face a difficult truth: academic expectations and standards on many campuses are too low, and it shows. Institutions that start with learning will set higher expecta-tions for all students, then do a much more effective job of helping them meet those expectations, points to which we return below.

Putting learning at the heart of the enterprise means campuses must:

- understand their mission clearly and define the kinds of students they can serve best;
- define exactly what their entering students need to succeed;
- start from where the students begin and help them achieve explicitly stated institutional standards for high achievement;
- tailor their programs—curriculum, schedules, support services, office hours—to meet the needs of the students they admit, not the convenience of staff and faculty;
- systematically apply the very best of what is known about learning and teaching on their campuses;
- rigorously assess what their students know and are able to do in order to improve both student and institutional performance; and
- develop and publish explicit exit standards for graduates, and grant degrees only to students who meet them.

Interestingly, steps such as these are among the recommendations recently advanced by some of this nation's most distinguished African-American leaders.* As they note, their recommendations for improving the learning environment for minorities will inevitably work to the advantage of all students, including dis-advantaged *majority* learners. We were struck by how congruent their analysis and recommendations are to our own.

---

* John Hope Franklin, et al., *The Inclusive University: A New Environment for Higher Education.* Washington: Joint Center for Political and Economic Studies, 1993.

Putting learning at the heart of the academic enterprise will mean overhauling the conceptual, procedural, curricular, and other architecture of postsecondary education on most campuses. For some students this will mean greater independence. For others, the academic experience may change little outwardly; internally it will be far more challenging and exciting. For many others—particularly those whose learning needs are being served poorly now—academic life will be more directive, more supportive, and more demanding. It will be more directive on the assumption that institutions are responsible for evaluating and responding to the learning needs of students. It will be more supportive because it will be focused on what students need in order to succeed. It will be far more demanding because it will be aimed at producing graduates who demonstrate much higher levels of knowledge and skills.

Skills. Traditionally, the acquisition of skills essential to life and work has been considered a by-product of study, not something requiring explicit attention on campus. We know of only a handful of the nation's colleges and universities that have developed curricular approaches similar to, for example, the list of critical skills developed by the Secretary of Labor's Commission on Achieving Necessary Skills (SCANS—see Appendix E). But skills such as these—written and oral communication, critical analysis, interpersonal competence, the ability to obtain and use data, the capacity to make informed judgments, and the skills required in community life—are essential attributes of a liberal education when they are accompanied by discipline-based knowledge. These skills can be learned. If they are to be learned, however, they must be taught and practiced, not merely absorbed as a result of unplanned academic experience. We believe that the modern world requires both knowledge *and* such skills and competences. Neither is adequate without the other.

Student Achievement. There is growing research evidence that all students can learn to much higher standards than we now require. When they do not, the flaw is most likely to be in the system, not the individual. We agree with those who make the important point that the truly outstanding educational institution graduates students who achieve more than would have been predicted on entry. (This is a standard, incidentally, that challenges even the most prestigious of our great universities and small liberal arts colleges, the institutions routinely enrolling the best secondary school graduates.)

There is a growing body of knowledge about learning and the implications of that knowledge for teaching. What is known, however, is rarely applied by individual teachers, much less in concert by entire faculties. We know that teaching is more than lecturing. We know that active engagement in learning is more productive than passive listening. We know that experiential learning can be even more so. We know we should evaluate institutional performance against student outcomes. We know all of this, but appear unable to act on it. It is time to explore the reasons for our failure to act.

No group has a greater stake in the new evidence relative to student achievement than socially and economically disadvantaged students, particularly disadvantaged minority Americans. At the elementary and secondary levels, the achievement gap separating minority and majority students is slowly closing. These results appear to reflect a combination of factors including minimum competency standards, on-going assessment, and programs to provide the special support many of these young Americans need. These were vitally important steps, but we share the distress of many Americans, including educators, that they have not gone far enough: minimum competency is not enough. Many minority Americans are still being left behind by an education system that is not serving their needs.

We also know that support services work. From a host of small experiments it is clear that when students—particularly those less advantaged in life—know their institution is unambiguously committed to their success, performance rises dramatically. Yet too few campuses have done much more than offer perfunctory, often inconvenient, student-support services. Too few have created one-stop "success centers" where students can find assistance with the full range of their concerns when they most need help—which is frequently before 9 a.m. and after 5 p.m. In the most impressive of these centers, a student enters into a relationship with a single individual who becomes an advocate for the student, responsible for marshaling all of the institution's assets and focusing them on the student's success.

Assessment. Finally, our vision calls for new ways of thinking about assessing what students know and are able to do. In medicine, testing and assessment are used to define the best course for future action. They provide data for both doctor (the teacher) and patient (the student) as to what steps to take to improve the individual's health (learning). In contemporary colleges and universities, however, such use of assessment is rare.

Examinations in educational institutions (including elementary and secondary schools) normally establish competitive rankings and sort students. They rarely diagnose strengths and weaknesses, examine needs, or suggest what steps to take next. In almost no institution are a student's skills systematically assessed, developed, and then certified. This assessment issue transcends the needs of learners. In an institution focused on learning, assessment feedback becomes central to the institution's ability to improve its own performance, enhancing student learning in turn.

New forms of assessment should focus on establishing what college and university graduates have learned—the knowledge and skill levels they have achieved and their potential for further independent learning. Only a few scattered institutions have instituted exit assessments.

The sad fact is that campuses spend far more time and money establishing the credentials of applicants than they do assessing the knowledge, skills, and competences of their graduates.

Indeed, the entire system is skewed in favor of the input side of the learning equation: credit hours, library collections, percentage of faculty with terminal degrees, and the like. The output side of the equation—student achievement—requires much greater attention than it now receives. That attention should begin by establishing improved measures of student achievement, measures that are credible and valued by the friends and supporters of education, by testing and accrediting bodies, and by educational institutions themselves.

We understand that the changes we suggest will be difficult and demanding. We recognize that they will require new attitudes on the part of faculty and institutions and, most critically, new skills and ways of doing business. There will be costs associated with these changes—though relatively modest costs in the context of overall institutional budgets—notably for staff development and student support services. We believe it reasonable to suggest that campuses devote a greater percentage of revenues to these needs.

Finally, we want to stress that responsibility in a learning institution is a two-way street. Students, at any level of education, are the workers in the educational process. They have a major obligation for their own success. Too many students do not behave as though that were the case, apparently believing (as do many parents) that grades are more important for success in life than acquired knowledge, the ability to learn throughout a lifetime, and hard work on campus. Educational institutions, having accepted students and their tuition, have a positive obligation to help these students acquire the knowledge, skills, competences, and habits of intellectual self-discipline requisite to becoming productive citizens and employees. Students, parents, and community leaders will have to be willing to support the high expectations and hard work that superior student achievement will require.

Too many campuses have become co-conspirators in the game of "credentialism." Many campuses still do not offer the guidance and support all students require to reach the higher levels of achievement contemporary life requires. Too few are sufficiently engaged in effective collaboration with other learning institutions, notably K-12 schools, to assure that students arriving on campus are prepared intellectually and are received in ways which enhance their prospects for success. Institutions of higher education must reach out much more effectively to colleagues elsewhere to help create a nation of learners and reduce the barriers to their learning.

Putting Student Learning First

- How recently have we reviewed our program offerings to assure that they match our mission and the needs and goals of the students we admit?

- In what ways could we do a better job of helping our students to attain higher levels of both knowledge and skills?

- What steps should we take to establish or improve a rigorous curriculum requiring core knowledge and competences of our students?

- How have we tried to integrate curricular offerings for the benefit of students and faculty? Is "course sprawl" contributing to our budgetary problems and making it more difficult for students to register in courses required for graduation? What might be done?

- To what extent are our educational programs, class schedules, registration, and other administrative and support services organized around the needs of learners rather than the convenience of the institution? What improvements can we make?

- How do we encourage and assist students to develop the basic values required for learning, e.g., self-discipline, perseverance, responsibility, hard work, intellectual openness?

- In what ways are we assessing learning to diagnose needs and accomplishments? How could we improve feedback to students and faculty on student performance in order to enhance both teaching and learning?

- How does our institution assure that students have demonstrated a high level of achievement, consistent with our published standards for acquiring both knowledge and skills, as a basis for receiving our degrees or certificates? Can we raise our standards?

- In what ways are we applying what is known about learning to the teaching practices of our faculty and graduate students? How do our pedagogical approaches enhance learning, and where do they fall short?

- How do we support faculty initiatives to improve learning and teaching? In particular, is our faculty well grounded in the available research concerning adult learning? If not, what will we do to improve our record?

- How could we do a better job of helping students learn at lower overall cost to our institution? How would we reinvest the savings?

- What other related questions should we address at our institution to improve the quality of learning?

Creating A Nation Of Learners

*The fixed person for the fixed duties, who in older societies
was a blessing, in the future will be a public danger.*

Alfred North Whitehead

We must redesign all of our learning systems to align our entire education enterprise with the personal, civic, and workplace needs of the 21st Century.

In the last generation, higher education has been swept up in the tide of social and economic change. The horizons and aspirations of women and members of minority groups have expanded. Older students have arrived on campus, many for the first time, seeking help to improve their skills, develop career prospects, and respond to new developments in technology. Family mobility is on the rise, and with it mobility from campus to campus. The modern workplace, open to global competition, requires levels of knowledge and skills beyond anything we have aspired to in the past, and well beyond what our schools and universities are now producing.

These changes demand that American education transform itself into a seamless system that can produce and support a nation of learners, providing access to educational services for learners as they need them, when they need them, and wherever they need them.

This is not an argument for merger or homogeneity. But colleges and universities need to understand that their business is *all* of education—learning. They can no longer afford to concern themselves exclusively with *higher* education. They must address themselves much more effectively to the other key pieces of the education enterprise. Americans and their educators are now handicapped by an education legacy from the past when what they need is a solution for the future. Our current educational institutions worked reasonably well in a society that had little need for large numbers of educated adults. Why question that structure when 90 percent of the population left school after 8th grade (the turn of the century); when only 50 percent of the population graduated from high school (1940); or even when only one-third of high school graduates enrolled in higher education (1950)? Now the need has changed. There can be no justification for such a system in today's world with its growing demand for better-educated people.

In this new environment many more educators must be prepared to say: "All of us, from pre-school to post-graduate, are in this together. It is not enough to complain about each other's failings. It is time to stop addressing the problem piecemeal. We must begin to work collaboratively on the system as a whole." It is no longer tolerable for so many in higher education to complain about the quality of those they admit, but do nothing to set higher standards and work with colleagues in K-12 schools to help students attain those standards. Our education system is in crisis; business-as-usual is a formula for national disaster.

Assessment and achievement are critical components of an enhanced education system. Experts today are thinking about the need for summary educational documents, not just grades, attendance records, and test scores, but data representing genuine learning achievements across a lifetime of educational and training experiences. The Educational Testing Service, the American College Testing program, and the American Council on Education are already piloting initiatives of this kind—Work Link, Work Keys, and the External Diploma Program respectively—which aim to revise quite radically how we think about and use assessment. These efforts deserve encouragement from everyone interested in improving the quality of learning, and in particular from the American business community. They will increasingly assure that learning, wherever it occurs, is valued and given credit; they will, in and of themselves, help to create a national culture encouraging life-long formal and informal learning.

We are aware that a number of institutions work with local schools, and that some are very serious and effective in these efforts. But as one of our essayists put it, "the sum of it all adds up to considerably less than a response to an urgent need that is grounded in both self-interest and national interest."

We join others in calling for a simultaneous renewal of both higher education and the nation's K-12 schools. A serious, sustained dialogue should start by identifying shared needs and problems:

- a clear public definition of what students should know and be able to do at each educational level;
- standards of entry *and exit* for higher education;
- increasing the use of assessment to diagnose learning needs and enhance student achievement;
- improving both the theory and practice of teaching and learning;
- recruiting and educating more effective teachers at all levels;
- bringing education's resources to bear on issues of character and its development;
- reducing the barriers to inter-institutional transfer among institutions of higher education; and
- exploring the implications for college admissions practices of the six National Education Goals established in 1989, and the potential for collaboration with K-12 schools.

The entire education establishment has a self-evident interest in this kind of collaborative dialogue and action. If a community college has developed an outstanding student support system, even the most prestigious research university should consider it as a benchmark. If a public school system has created a successful school-within-a-school to relieve the negative impact of size on students, public mega-universities should consider the possibility that they have something to learn from it. Any educational institution should want to practice existing, innovative, research-based approaches for applying to teaching what is known about learning. Where innovations in self-paced and distance learning are succeeding, any institution concerned about productivity and cost containment should examine them carefully as potential contributors to its own efficiency and effectiveness. Every campus has an interest in emulating those colleges and universities that have extended a collaborative hand to elementary and secondary education. Such collaboration can enhance course content and standards across the board, and raise the motivation and confidence of students who might otherwise not be considering postsecondary education.

Nor is the opportunity to learn from others restricted to the traditional world of education. Where a corporation has developed effective educational innovations, campuses should investigate the implications for their own work. Many museums are currently developing innovative and effective approaches to teaching and learning about science, history, and art. But all of these advances—and many others—are taking place independently of each other at a time when America needs a more collaborative, cost-effective and better-articulated way of responding to the lifelong learning needs of growing numbers of its citizens.

Creating A Nation Of Learners

- In what ways have we organized our programs to develop and support a capacity for lifelong learning among our students?

- How might we provide the same level of service and support to "non-traditional" students, and students in non-traditional learning programs, as we do for traditional full-time students? Within our mission, when have we examined alternative, more flexible, and student-oriented ways to provide for student learning?

- How often do we survey employers of our recent graduates—and the graduates themselves—to discover how and under what circumstances graduates succeed or fall short? How can that process be improved?

- In what ways do we work with K-12 systems to enlarge our understanding of their difficulties, encourage teachers and administrators to see us as resources, and enlarge our own competences? In what ways have we relegated this effort to our school of education? How have we tried to involve the entire campus?

- How are we working with high schools and other educational institutions both to communicate to them the knowledge and skills that students will need to be successful in higher education and to help students meet those requirements?

- How do our departments provide graduate students and professors with training in how people learn and what that means for teaching? What needs to be done to make this institution-wide and to set institution-wide standards?

- How is our campus working with local schools and other colleges and universities to bring teaching and learning to state-of-the-art standards from kindergarten through the undergraduate years? What more can we do?

- How might we bring our teacher recruitment and teacher education programs into better alignment with the real needs of both society and students? What are our benchmarks?

- What provisions might a statewide compact contain if we wished to ease student transfer between institutions?

- In what ways are we organized to make use of educational achievements from non-traditional organizations and settings?

- What other related questions should we address in an effort to reduce the institutional barriers to learning and to make our institution more responsive to the needs of others, e.g., K-12 education, employers, and other institutions of higher education?

First Steps: Challenges For Higher Education

*For every right that you cherish, you have a duty which you
must fulfill. For every hope that you entertain, you have a
task that you must perform. For every good that you wish to
preserve, you will have to sacrifice your comfort and your
ease. There is nothing for nothing any longer.*

Walter Lippmann

Our wake-up call places a heavy burden on the shoulders of the men and
women in higher education. It will require rethinking the assumptions of the
education enterprise and reinventing many of its ways of doing business.
Educators, particularly faculty members, must demonstrate that they have noted
the warning signs, understand the potential for institutional and national decline,
and are ready to act.

Solutions for the problems we have described will require vigorous, creative,
and persistent leadership on campus, in the community, in state capitols, and in
Washington. On the other hand, the problems of undergraduate education cannot
effectively be addressed by bold strokes of state or national public policy. They
can best be solved campus by campus with the active involvement of faculty,
staff, students, trustees, and their friends and supporters off campus including,
notably, state legislators. Hence, our solutions are cast not as recommendations
for policymakers to impose from on high, but as challenges to be taken up on
each of the nation's 3,400 campuses. Diversity and autonomy are among the great
strengths of American higher education, as they are of American society itself.
They are strengths to be respected and drawn upon as each institution decides for
itself how it will respond.

As first steps in what will be a long journey, we issue five challenges.
For colleges and universities:

- **We challeng**e you to evaluate yourselves against the questions in the
  attached "Self-Assessment Checklist," and to commit yourself publicly
  to an institutional plan that builds on the strengths and remedies the
  deficiencies you identify.
- **We challenge** you to define and publicly state your standards of entry
  and exit in terms of the knowledge, skills, and abilities you expect
  from both applicants and graduates, and to put in place measures to
  assure student and institutional attainment of those standards by a
  fixed date.
- **We challenge** you to develop a curriculum that will assure all
  graduates—our future citizens, employees, and leaders—the benefits
  of a liberal education.
- **We challenge** you to assure that next year's entering students will
  graduate as individuals of character more sensitive to the needs of
  community, more competent to contribute to society, and more civil in
  habits of thought, speech, and action.

For trustees, regents, legislators, alumni, and funders in particular:
- **We challenge** you to respond to institutions that take up the first four challenges by giving them the regulatory and financial flexibility they need to get the job done. Institutional creativity, not micro-management, is the essential precondition to change. But we do urge you to urge them on. One of the best ways to do so is to insist that the campuses for which you have stewardship responsibility undertake the attached self-assessment.

We understand that some institutions will believe it unnecessary to respond to the challenges above. Perhaps they are correct, although we suggest that even the best can be better. Institutions hesitant to undertake a comprehensive self-assessment might consider administering the National Adult Literacy Survey instrument to a representative sample of graduating seniors. By permitting comparison of institutional performance with a nationwide sample of graduates of either two- or four-year institutions, the NALS instrument can provide a minimally acceptable performance benchmark for any institution. No campus has anything to lose by turning to NALS, and it is difficult to imagine that most would not want to know where they stand. Some may be satisfied with the results, but many will be surprised.

Finally, we issue a challenge to the broader public, specifically to students, parents, employers, and citizens. This agenda for higher education is ambitious. It will not be accomplished easily or soon; nor can it bear fruit without your participation and support. All of us have contributed to the situation in which higher education today finds itself; we too must play our part in responding to the imperatives of the future. Every American must accept the fact that in an open, global economy, education is a critical national resource.

A generation ago, we told educators we wanted more people with a college credential and more research-based knowledge. Educators responded accordingly. Now we need to ask for different things. Students must value achievement, not simply seek a credential. Students (and parents) should look to the value added to their lives, not simply to the prestige of the institutions they attend. Employers must make clear to educators what they value in new employees. Without new public attitudes, higher education will find it difficult to persevere in the task ahead.

One of these difficulties is financial. Higher education's claim on public and private funds increasingly competes with a growing list of other compelling claims. One consequence is that after rising every year since the end of World War II, total state support for public higher education declined for two successive years as the 1990s began, and there is little reason to expect net new resources for the foreseeable future.

Since at least World War II, higher education's growth has been made possible by an expanding national economy. However, the post-World War II surge in productivity which fueled remarkable growth in our national wealth will not repeat itself unless educational institutions make a determined, successful effort to enhance the knowledge and skills Americans bring to the workplace. Thus, higher education's best financial hope rests on helping itself by helping expand the nation's wealth, by providing the knowledgeable and highly skilled workforce that can enhance our productivity, revitalize our communities, and rebuild our sense of "we."

We are convinced that those colleges and universities that demonstrate that they are doing more with what they have—those doing the best job of preserving strong, core programs and eliminating the less essential—will find not only that they have freed up resources to reinvest in themselves, but they will also have made a compelling case for additional external support. We also believe that institutions that defer change until new resources are available will find themselves waiting for a very long time. Financial salvation will begin on the campus, or it will probably not begin at all. But as campuses begin to respond to the kinds of challenges we issue, there must be solid public and financial support for higher education. It *is* a critical national resource.

Finally . . .

Higher education and the society it serves face a fork in the road. Either educators and other Americans raise their sights and take the difficult steps described in this open letter, or we all face the certain and unpleasant prospect of national decline. No one can look squarely at the quality of our undergraduate education, and its graduates, and come to a more optimistic conclusion.

We are guardedly hopeful that higher education will respond positively to the kinds of change we believe essential to our national well-being. That hope rests on the active participation of faculty members, administrators, and the public, many of whom understand the need for change and are working to effect it.

That hope rests on the fact that so many Americans understand how critical a productive and affordable system of higher education is to the American future. Even the most severe critic of higher education understands its importance and wishes it well.

Most significantly, there is hope, because when the nation has called on colleges and universities to adapt in the past, higher education has always responded.

We cannot believe it will hesitate now.

Appendix A

A Self-Assessment Checklist

All those with an interest in higher education—faculty, academic leadership, trustees and regents, students, parents, state legislators, public officials, and others—will find the questions on the following pages helpful in assessing the educational institutions in which they have an interest. Additional questions and issues will, of course, arise on each campus.

Conducting this kind of self-assessment is the first step in any effort to think in different ways about the nation's colleges and universities. Each institution will want to conduct its self-assessment in its own way, but we believe committed, persistent, straightforward leadership at the institutional level, including participation by trustees and regents, is essential to a candid and useful outcome.

We also believe that each institution should develop and publish an action plan to respond to both the positive and negative conclusions of its self-assessment.

A Postscript version of this Appendix is available on INTERNET for those institutions with Postscript printing capability and wishing to reproduce large quantities of the entire Appendix. To locate the Appendix, anonymous ftp to csd4.csd.uwm.edu, change directory to pub/wingspread/checklist.ps. If you have questions, call 414-229-6151 or send E-mail to belp@csd4.csd.uwm.edu.

A detachable, single-copy version is located following page 40 in this document.

First Questions

Responses to the following three questions will provide a helpful context in which to assess one's institution.

- **What kind of people do we want our children and grandchildren to be**

- **What kind of society do we want them to live in?**

- **How can we best shape our institution to nurture those kinds of people and that kind of society?***

Our campus's response to these questions includes the following major points:

* Questions taken from Howard Bowen, *The State of the Nation and the Agenda for Higher Education.* San Francisco: Jossey-Bass, 1982.

Taking Values Seriously

- How does our educational program match the claims of our recruiting brochures, and where is it falling short?

- How does our core curriculum of required courses respond to the needs of our students for a rigorous liberal education enabling them to "live rightly and well in a free society?" Where does it fall short?

- In what ways does our institution model the values and skills expected in our community? Where and how are we falling short?

- What steps might we take to improve the general climate of civility on our campus?

- How comprehensive and effective is the code of professional conduct and ethics for our faculty and staff? When was it last reviewed?

- In what ways does our institution and its educational program promote the development of shared values, specifically the civic virtues listed below, among our students?

    - respect for the individual and commitment to equal opportunity in a diverse society;

    - the belief that our common interests exceed our individual differences;

    - support for the freedoms enunciated in the Bill of Rights, including freedom of religion, of the press, of speech, and of the right to assemble;

    - the belief that individual rights and privileges are accompanied by responsibilities to others;

    - respect for the views of others; and

    - the conviction that no one is above the law.

- What moral and ethical questions should we be putting to the student groups and organizations we sanction on campus? What standards of conduct do we expect of these groups? How have we made these standards clear?

- How do the activities of our athletic programs square with our institution's stated values, and where do they fall short?

- What steps will we take to assure that next year's entering students will graduate as individuals of character more sensitive to the needs of community, more competent to contribute to society, more civil in their habits of thought, speech, and action?

- What other related questions should we address at our institution?

Putting Student Learning First

- How recently have we reviewed our program offerings to assure that they match our mission and the needs and goals of the students we admit?

- In what ways could we do a better job of helping our students to attain higher levels of both knowledge and skills?

- What steps should we take to establish or improve a rigorous curriculum requiring core knowledge and competences of our students?

- How have we tried to integrate curricular offerings for the benefit of students and faculty? Is "course sprawl" contributing to our budgetary problems and making it more difficult for students to register in courses required for graduation? What might be done?

- To what extent are our educational programs, class schedules, registration, and other administrative and support services organized around the needs of learners rather than the convenience of the institution? What improvements can we make?

- How do we encourage and assist students to develop the basic values required for learning, e.g., self-discipline, perseverance, responsibility, hard work, intellectual openness?

- In what ways are we assessing learning to diagnose needs and accomplishments? How could we improve feedback to students and faculty on student performance in order to enhance both teaching and learning?

- How does our institution assure that students have demonstrated a high level of achievement, consistent with our published standards for acquiring both knowledge and skills, as a basis for receiving our degrees or certificates? Can we raise our standards?

- In what ways are we applying what is known about learning to the teaching practices of our faculty and graduate students? How do our pedagogical approaches enhance learning, and where do they fall short?

- How do we support faculty initiatives to improve learning and teaching? In particular, is our faculty well grounded in the available research concerning adult learning? If not, what will we do to improve our record?

- How could we do a better job of helping students learn at lower overall cost to our institution? How would we reinvest the savings?

- What other related questions should we address at our institution to improve the quality of learning?

Creating A Nation Of Learners

- In what ways have we organized our programs to develop and support a capacity for lifelong learning among our students?

- How might we provide the same level of service and support to "non-traditional" students, and students in non-traditional learning programs, as we do for traditional full-time students? Within our mission, when have we examined alternative, more flexible, and student-oriented ways to provide for student learning?

- How often do we survey employers of our recent graduates—and the graduates themselves—to discover how and under what circumstances graduates succeed or fall short? How can that process be improved?

- In what ways do we work with K-12 systems to enlarge our understanding of their difficulties, encourage teachers and administrators to see us as resources, and enlarge our own competences? In what ways have we relegated this effort to our school of education? How have we tried to involve the entire campus?

- How are we working with high schools and other educational institutions both to communicate to them the knowledge and skills that students will need to be successful in higher education and to help students meet those requirements?

- How do our departments provide graduate students and professors with training in how people learn and what that means for teaching? What needs to be done to make this institution-wide and to set institution-wide standards?

- How is our campus working with local schools and other colleges and universities to bring teaching and learning to state-of-the-art standards from kindergarten through the undergraduate years? What more can we do?

- How might we bring our teacher recruitment and teacher education programs into better alignment with the real needs of both society and students? What are our benchmarks?

- What provisions might a statewide compact contain if we wished to ease student transfer between institutions?

- In what ways are we organized to make use of educational achievements from non-traditional organizations and settings?

- What other related questions should we address in an effort to reduce the institutional barriers to learning and to make our institution more responsive to the needs of others, e.g., K-12 education, employers, and other institutions of higher education?

Appendix B

Resources and Documentation

A Changing America and a Changing World

Those interested in exploring social, economic, and demographic change and its educational implications will find the following helpful:

Bureau of the Census. *Money Income and Poverty Status in the United States, 1988* (Current Population Reports, Consumer Income Series P-60, No. 166). Washington: U.S. Department of Commerce, 1989.

Business-Higher Education Forum. *America's Competitive Challenge: The Need for a National Response.* Washington: Business-Higher Education Forum, 1983.

Carnevale, Anthony P., and Leila J. Gainer and Ann S. Meltzer. *Workplace Basics: The Essential Skills Employers Want.* San Francisco: Jossey-Bass, Inc., 1990.

Handy, Charles. *The Age of Unreason.* Cambridge: Harvard University Press, 1991.

Hodgkinson, Harold L. *The Same Client: The Demographics of Education and Service Delivery Systems.* Washington: Center for Demographic Policy, September 1989.

Institute on Education and the Economy. *Education and the Economy: Hard Questions, Hard Answers* (Conference Background Papers). New York: Teachers' College, Columbia University, 1989.

Marshall, Ray, and Marc Tucker. *Thinking for a Living.* New York: Harper Collins, 1992.

Morrison, Catherine and E. Patrick McGuire and Mary Ann Clarke. *Keys to U.S. Competitiveness.* Washington: The Conference Board (Research Report No. 907), 1988.

Moulton, Harper W. and Arthur A. Fickel. *Executive Development: Preparing for the 21st Century.* New York: Oxford University Press, 1993.

Phillips, Kevin. *The Politics of Rich and Poor.* New York: Random House, 1990.

Reich, Robert B. "The Real Economy," *The Atlantic Monthly,* February 1991.

Scott, Bruce R. and George C. Lodge (eds.). *U.S. Competitiveness in the World Economy.* Cambridge: Harvard Business School Press, 1985.

Spencer, Gregory. *Projections of the Population of the United States by Age, Sex and Race: 1988 to 2080.* (Current Population Reports, Consumer Income Series P-25, No. 1018). Washington: Bureau of the Census, 1989.

Informative data and analyses of campus change can be found in:

American Council on Education. *Investing in the American Future: College Attendance, Costs, and Benefits.* Washington: American Council on Education, 1992.

Benjamin, Roger, Stephen Carroll, Maryann Jacobi, Cathy Krop, and Michael Shires. *The Redesign of Governance in Higher Education.* Santa Monica: RAND Corporation, 1993.

Commission on Minority Participation in Education and American Life. *One-Third of a Nation*. Washington: American Council on Education and Education Commission of the States, May 1988.

Duffey, Joseph D. "What's Ahead for Higher Education: The Future Isn't What It Used To Be," *Educational Record* (Fall 1992).

Eaton, Judith (ed.). *Financing Nontraditional Students: A Seminar Report*. Washington: American Council on Education, 1992.

Franklin, John Hope, et. al. *The Inclusive University: A New Environment for Higher Education*. Washington: Joint Center for Political and Economic Studies, 1993.

Hauptman, Arthur M. *The Economic Prospects for American Higher Education*. Washington: Association of Governing Boards and American Council on Education, 1992.

Levine, Arthur (ed.). *Higher Learning in America, 1980-2000*. Baltimore: Johns Hopkins University Press, 1993.

O'Keefe, Michael and P. Michael Timpane (eds.). *American Higher Education: Purposes, Problems and Public Perceptions*. Queenstown, Md.: The Aspen Institute, 1992.

National Center for Education Statistics. *The Condition of Education, 1991* (Volume 2: Postsecondary Education). Washington: U.S. Department of Education, 1991.

National Center for Education Statistics. *Digest of Education Statistics, 1991*. Washington: U.S. Department of Education, November 1991.

National Center for Education Statistics. *Projections of Education Statistics to 2002*. Washington: U.S. Department of Education, 1991.

President's Council of Advisors on Science and Technology. *Renewing the Promise: Research-Intensive Universities and the Nation*. Washington: President's Council of Advisors on Science and Technology, December 1992.

SHEEO. *Building a Quality Workforce: An Agenda for Postsecondary Education*. Denver: State Higher Education Executive Officers, 1992.

Crisis of Values

Thoughtful discussion of the need to renew higher education's commitment to values, and data shedding light on that need, can be found in:

Bellah, Robert N. and Richard Madsen, William M. Sullivan, Ann Swidler and Steven M. Tipton. *The Good Society*. New York: Alfred A. Knopf, Inc., 1991.

Dey, Eric L. and Alexander W. Astin and William S. Korn. *The American Freshman: Twenty-Five Year Trends*. Los Angeles: Higher Education Research Institute, 1991.

Dey, Eric L. and Alexander W. Astin, William S. Korn and Ellyne Riggs. *The American Freshman: National Norms for Fall 1992*. Los Angeles: Higher Education Research Institute, 1992.

Knight Foundation Commission on Intercollegiate Athletics. *Keeping Faith with the Student-Athlete: A New Model for Intercollegiate Athletics*. Charlotte: Knight Foundation Commission on Intercollegiate Athletics, March 1991.

Mentkowski, M. "Paths to Integrity: Educating for Personal Growth and Professional Performance." In S. Srivastva & Associates (eds.). *Executive Integrity: The Search for High Human Values in Organizational Life*. San Francisco: Jossey-Bass, 1988.

Swift, John S., Jr. *Social Consciousness and Career Awareness: Emerging Link in Higher Education*. Washington: The George Washington University's ERIC Clearinghouse on Higher Education, 1992.

Wilcox, John R. and Susan L. Ebbs. *The Leadership Compass: Values and Ethics in Higher Education*. Washington: The George Washington University's ERIC Clearinghouse on Higher Education, 1992.

The Costs of "Weeding"

A variety of sources led the Wingspread Group to the conclusion that an unconscious rule of thumb guides American education:

Bowen, William G. and Neil L. Rudenstine. *In Pursuit of the Ph.D.* Princeton: Princeton University Press, 1992.

Carroll, C. Dennis. *College Persistence and Degree Attainment for 1980 High School Graduates: Hazards for Transfers, Stopouts, and Part-Timers*. Washington: National Center for Education Statistics, January 1989.

Ries, Paula and Delores H. Thurgood. *Summary Report 1991: Doctorate Recipients from United States Universities*. Washington: National Academy Press, 1993.

Tuckman, Howard and Susan Coyle and Yupin Bae. *On Time to the Doctorate: A Study of the Increased Time to Complete Doctorates in Science and Engineering*. Washington: National Academy Press, 1990.

National Center for Education Statistics. *The Condition of Education, 1993* (Volume 1, Elementary and Secondary Education & Volume 2, Postsecondary Education). Washington: U.S. Department of Education, 1993.

National Center for Education Statistics. *Digest of Education Statistics, 1993*. Washington: U.S. Department of Education, 1993.

William T. Grant Foundation Commission on Work, Family and Citizenship. *The Forgotten Half: Non-College Youth in America*. Washington: William T. Grant Foundation Commission on Work, Family and Citizenship, January 1988.

The Unprepared Graduate

Indicators of the low levels of knowledge and skills possessed by significant numbers of two- and four-year graduates were drawn from the following:

Adelman, Clifford. *Tourists in Our Own Land: Cultural Literacies and the College Curriculum*. Washington: U.S. Department of Education, October 1992.

Kirsch, Irwin S. and Ann Jungeblut, Lynn Jenkins and Andrew Kolstad. *Adult Literacy in America*. Princeton: Educational Testing Service, September 1993.

Growing Public Concern

Interest in public perceptions of higher education has been quite high for the past four years. Readers interested in pursuing this topic might consult:

Harris, Louis. "Planning to Get Real," Remarks at the March 1992 Annual Meeting of the American Association for Higher Education. (Summarizes Harris Poll findings from 1966 on public confidence in national leaders.)

Harvey, James and John Immerwahr. "Goodwill and Growing Worry: Public Perceptions of Higher Education." (January 1993 Briefing for the Board of the Directors, American Council on Education.)

Harvey, James and John Immerwahr. *Data Book on Public Perceptions of Higher Education.* Washington: James Harvey & Associates, January 1993.

John Immerwahr and Steve Farkas. *The Closing Gateway: Californians Consider Their Higher Education System.* San Jose: The Public Agenda Foundation and the California Higher Education Policy Center, September 1993.

For comments on the academic culture, see the following essays elsewhere in this volume:

Brown, Eileen Moran, President, Cambridge College.

Griffiths, Phillip A., Director, Institute for Advanced Study.

Hernandez, Antonia, President and General Counsel, Mexican American Legal Defense and Educational Fund.

Katz, Stanley N., President, American Council of Learned Societies.

Meisel, Wayne, Executive Director, the Corella and Bertram F. Bonner Foundation. *See also:*

Boyer, Ernest L. *Scholarship Reconsidered: Priorities of the Professoriate.* Princeton: The Carnegie Foundation for the Advancement of Teaching, 1990.

Levin, Henry. "Raising Productivity in Higher Education," *Higher Education Extension Review* (Summer 1993).

Smith, Page. *Killing the Spirit: Higher Education in America.* New York: Viking Press, 1990.

Taking Values Seriously

Of the Wingspread Group's essayists, 20 brought up the need for higher education to engage more intensively the issue of values addressed in this report. The following four confined themselves largely to problems of values and responsibility

Atwell, Robert, President, American Council on Education.

Bosworth, Stephen W., President, U.S.-Japan Foundation.

Johnson, Geneva B., President, Family Service America.

Meisel, Wayne, Executive Director, the Corella and Bertram F. Bonner Foundation. *See also:*

Ramirez, Blandina Cardenas. "Can We ALL Get Along? Examining Our Capacity for Diversity," *Educational Record* (Fall 1992).

Newman, Frank. *Higher Education and the American Resurgence.* Princeton: The Carnegie Foundation for the Advancement of Teaching, 1985.

Spitzberg, Irving J., Jr. and Virginia V. Thorndike. *Creating Community on College Campuses.* Albany: State University of New York Press, 1992.

Putting Student Learning First

Many of the contributed essays focused on the need to put learning at the center of the higher education enterprise. The following contained particularly thoughtful comments:

Brown, Eileen Moran, President, Cambridge College.

Featherman, David L., President, Social Science Research Council.

Mahoney, Margaret E., President, The Commonwealth Fund.

Stanley, Peter W., President, Pomona College.

See also:

Becker, Lovice. "Report on Reports: What They Say about Teaching at the College Level," *College Teaching* (Vol. 35, No. 4, Fall 1987)

Cardozier, V. Ray (ed.). *Important Lessons from Innovative Colleges and Universities.* San Francisco: Jossey-Bass, 1993.

College Board. *Reaching Each Student: National Challenge and Organizational Commitment.* (Addresses to the College Board National Forum, October 31-November 2, 1990). New York: College Board, 1991.

Goodsell, Anne, Michelle Maher, Vincent Tinto, Barbara Leigh Smith and Jean McGregor. *Collaborative Learning: A Sourcebook for Higher Education.* State College: National Center on Postsecondary Teaching, Learning and Assessment, 1992.

Johnston, William B. and Arnold E. Packer. *Workforce 2000: Work and Workers for the Twenty-first Century.* Indianapolis: Hudson Institute, June 1987.

Richardson, Richard C. *Creating Effective Learning Environments.* Denver: Education Commission of the States, 1992.

Secretary's Commission on Achieving Necessary Skills (SCANS). *Learning a Living: A Blueprint for High Performance.* Washington: U.S. Department of Labor, April 1992.

Sheckley, Barry G., Lois Lamdin and Morris Keeton. "Employability: Today's Problems, Tomorrow's Solutions," *Educational Record* (Fall 1992).

Solomon, Robert C. and Jon Solomon. *Up the University: Re-Creating Higher Education in America.* Reading: Addison-Wesley, 1993.

Spille, Henry. "Curriculum Must Teach Work Skills." Paper presented to DANTES Conference, Tacoma, Washington, September 1993. (Work skills and the liberal arts college). Available from American Council on Education.

A Nation of Learners

The contributed essays drew the Wingspread Group's attention to the poorly articulated nature of the American education enterprise, notably:

Griffiths, Phillip A., Director, Institute for Advanced Study.

Magrath, C. Peter, President, National Association of State Universities and Land-Grant Colleges.

Rosenzweig, Robert M., former President, Association of American Universities.

Stewart, Donald M., President, The College Entrance Examination Board.

Woodson, Robert L., Sr., President, National Center for Neighborhood Enterprise.

For additional insights into the practical problems standing in the way of creating a nation of learners see:

Adelman, Alan and Patricia Somers. "Exploring an Academic Common Market in North America," *Educational Record* (Fall 1992).

American Council on Education. *Setting the National Agenda: Academic Achievement and Transfer.* (Policy Statement and Background Paper about Transfer Education.) Washington: American Council on Education, 1991.

Carnegie Council on Adolescent Development. *Turning Points: Preparing American Youth for the 21st Century.* New York: Carnegie Corporation of New York, June 1989.

College Entrance Examination Board. *Academic Preparation for College: What Students Need to Know and Be Able to Do.* New York: The College Entrance Examination Board, 1983.

Eaton, Judith S. (ed.). *Faculty and Transfer: Academic Partnerships at Work.* Washington: American Council on Education, 1992.

Greenberg, Arthur R. *High School-College Partnerships: Conceptual Models, Programs, and Issues.* Washington: George Washington University, 1991. (ERIC Report No. 5, 1991).

Hodgkinson, Harold L. *All One System: Demographics of Education, Kindergarten through Graduate School.* Washington: Institute for Educational Leadership, June 1985.

Houghton, Mary J. *College Admission Standards and School Reform: Toward a Partnership in Education.* Washington: National Governors' Association, 1993.

Lillard, A. Lee and Hong W. Tan. *Private Sector Training: Who Gets It and What Are Its Effects?* Santa Monica: The RAND Corporation, 1986.

National Association of Independent Colleges and Universities. *Independent Institutions in Partnership: Sharing Educational Responsibility.* Washington: National Association of Independent Colleges and Universities, 1991.

National Education Goals Panel. *The National Education Goals Report: Building a Nation of Learners.* Washington: National Education Goals Panel, 1991.

National Council on Education Standards and Testing. *Raising Standards for American Education.* Washington: National Council on Education Standards and Testing. January 1992.

National Governors' Association. *New Frontiers for Lifelong Learning. Redefining the Possible: Achieving the National Education Goals.* Washington: National Governors' Association, 1992.

Pelavin, Sol H. and Michael Kane. *Changing the Odds: Factors Increasing Access to College.* New York: College Entrance Examination Board, 1990.

Quality Education for Minorities Project. *Education that Works: An Action Plan for the Education of Minorities.* Cambridge: Quality Education for Minorities Project, January 1990.

Assessment

With respect to assessment issues, the American Council on Education's Center on Adult Learning and Educational Credentials is an excellent clearinghouse. The center conducts several programs awarding secondary school and undergraduate credit for experience in life, work, and the military including the following:

Army/American Council on Education Registry Transcript System (AARTS) provides enlisted soldiers and members of the National Guard with transcripts of military education and training, helping academic institutions award academic credit and assisting employers in making hiring decisions.

The Credit by Examination Program evaluates national standardized tests and professional licensure/certification examinations for college credit recommendations.

General Educational Development Testing Service (GED) provides a testing service that permits about 400,000 Americans annually to obtain a high school equivalency diploma.

External Diploma Program is an innovative assessment-based system to encourage adults to earn a high school credential by assessing their workplace skills against defined competences.

Military Evaluations Program evaluates formal military training and occupations for college credit examinations.

Program on Noncollegiate Sponsored Instruction (ACE/PONSI) evaluates formal training offered by business, industry, government, labor unions, and professional associations for college credit.

Also with regard to assessment, see the following:

Adelman, Clifford (ed.). *Signs and Traces: Model Indicators of College Student Learning in the Disciplines.* Washington: U.S. Department of Education, 1989.

Astin, A.W. *Assessment for Excellence: The Philosophy and Practice of Assessment and Evaluation in Higher Education.* New York: Macmillan, 1991.

Erwin, T. Dary. *Assessing Student Learning and Development: A Guide to the Principles, Goals, and Methods of Determining College Outcomes.* San Francisco: Jossey-Bass, 1991.

Ewell, P. (ed.). *Assessing Educational Outcomes: New Directions for Institutional Research.* San Francisco: Jossey-Bass, 1985.

Ewell, P. *Benefits and Costs of Assessment in Higher Education: A Framework for Choicemaking.* Boulder: National Center for Higher Education Management Systems, 1991.

Haney, W. and G. Madaus. "Searching for Alternatives to Standardized Tests: Whys, Whats, and Whithers." *Phi Delta Kappan,* May 1989.

Loacker, G. and E. Palola (eds.). *Revitalizing Academic Disciplines by Clarifying Outcomes: New Directions for Experiential Learning.* San Francisco: Jossey-Bass, 1981.

Mentkowski, M. "Creating a Context Where Institutional Assessment Yields Educational Improvement," *Journal of General Education,* 1991, vol. 40.

Pascarella, E.T. and P.T. Terenzini. *How College Affects Students: Findings and Insights from Twenty Years of Research.* San Francisco: Jossey-Bass, 1991.

Shulman, L.S. *Assessing Content and Process: Challenges for the New Assessments.* Washington: AAHE Assessment Forum, 1987.

Spille, Henry. "Beyond the Rhetoric: Toward a System of Learning and Credentialing for Adults." (Paper submitted to National Governors' Association for conference on A More Productive Workforce.) Available from ACE.

Taking Values Seriously

- How does our educational program match the claims of our recruiting brochures, and where is it falling short?

- How does our core curriculum of required courses respond to the needs of our students for a rigorous liberal education enabling them to "live rightly and well in a free society?" Where does it fall short?

- In what ways does our institution model the values and skills expected in our community? Where and how are we falling short?

- What steps might we take to improve the general climate of civility on our campus?

- How comprehensive and effective is the code of professional conduct and ethics for our faculty and staff? When was it last reviewed?

- In what ways does our institution and its educational program promote the development of shared values, specifically the civic virtues listed below, among our students?

  - respect for the individual and commitment to equal opportunity in a diverse society;

  - the belief that our common interests exceed our individual differences;

  - support for the freedoms enunciated in the Bill of Rights, including freedom of religion, of the press, of speech, and of the right to assemble;

  - the belief that individual rights and privileges are accompanied by responsibilities to others;

  - respect for the views of others; and

  - the conviction that no one is above the law.

- What moral and ethical questions should we be putting to the student groups and organizations we sanction on campus? What standards of conduct do we expect of these groups? How have we made these standards clear?

- How do the activities of our athletic programs square with our institution's stated values, and where do they fall short?

- What steps will we take to assure that next year's entering students will graduate as individuals of character more sensitive to the needs of community, more competent to contribute to society, more civil in their habits of thought, speech, and action?

- What other related questions should we address at our institution?

"First Questions"

Responses to the following three questions will provide a helpful context in which to assess one's institution.

- **What kind of people do we want our children and grandchildren to be?**

- **What kind of society do we want them to live in?**

- **How can we best shape our institution to nurture those kinds of people and that kind of society?***

Our campus response to these questions includes the following major points:

_____

_____

_____

_____

_____

_____

_____

_____

_____

_____

_____

_____

_____

* Questions taken from Howard Bowen, _The State of the Nation and the Agenda for Higher Education._ San Francisco: Jossey-Bass, 1982.

Putting Student Learning First

- How recently have we reviewed our program offerings to assure that they match our mission and the needs and goals of the students we admit?

- In what ways could we do a better job of helping our students to attain higher levels of both knowledge and skills?

- What steps should we take to establish or improve a rigorous curriculum requiring core knowledge and competences of our students?

- How have we tried to integrate curricular offerings for the benefit of students and faculty? Is "course sprawl" contributing to our budgetary problems and making it more difficult for students to register in courses required for graduation? What might be done?

- To what extent are our educational programs, class schedules, registration, and other administrative and support services organized around the needs of learners rather than the convenience of the institution? What improvements can we make?

- How do we encourage and assist students to develop the basic values required for learning, e.g., self-discipline, perseverance, responsibility, hard work, intellectual openness?

- In what ways are we assessing learning to diagnose needs and accomplishments? How could we improve feedback to students and faculty on student performance in order to enhance both teaching and learning?

- How does our institution assure that students have demonstrated a high level of achievement, consistent with our published standards for acquiring both knowledge and skills, as a basis for receiving our degrees or certificates? Can we raise our standards?

- In what ways are we applying what is known about learning to the teaching practices of our faculty and graduate students? How do our pedagogical approaches enhance learning, and where do they fall short?

- How do we support faculty initiatives to improve learning and teaching? In particular, is our faculty well grounded in the available research concerning adult learning? If not, what will we do to improve our record?

- How could we do a better job of helping students learn at lower overall cost to our institution? How would we reinvest the savings?

- What other related questions should we address at our institution to improve the quality of learning?

A Self-Assessment Checklist

All those with an interest in higher education—faculty, academic leadership, trustees and regents, students, parents, state legislators, public officials, and others—will find the questions on the following pages helpful in assessing the educational institutions in which they have an interest. Additional questions and issues will, of course, arise on each campus.

Conducting this kind of self-assessment is the first step in any effort to think in different ways about the nation's colleges and universities. Each institution will want to conduct its self-assessment in its own way, but we believe committed, persistent, straightforward leadership at the institutional level—including participation by trustees and regents—is essential to a candid and useful outcome.

We also believe that each institution should develop and publish an action plan to respond to both the positive and negative conclusions of its self-assessment.

This insert can be detached and duplicated as a whole.

A Postscript version of this Appendix is available on INTERNET for those institutions with Postscript printing capability and wishing to reproduce large quantities of the entire Appendix. To locate the Appendix, anonymous ftp to csd4.csd.uwm.edu, change directory to pub/wingspread/ checklist.ps. If you have questions, call 414-229-6151 or send "E-mail" to help@csd4.csd.uwm.edu.

Creating A Nation Of Learners

- In what ways have we organized our programs to develop and support a capacity for lifelong learning among our students?

- How might we provide the same level of service and support to non-traditional students, and students in non-traditional learning programs, as we do for traditional full-time students? Within our mission, when have we examined alternative, more flexible, and student-oriented ways to provide for student learning?

- How often do we survey employers of our recent graduates—and the graduates themselves—to discover how and under what circumstances graduates succeed or fall short? How can that process be improved?

- In what ways do we work with K-12 systems to enlarge our understanding of their difficulties, encourage teachers and administrators to see us as resources, and enlarge our own competences? In what ways have we relegated this effort to our school of education? How have we tried to involve the entire campus?

- How are we working with high schools and other educational institutions both to communicate to them the knowledge and skills that students will need to be successful in higher education and to help students meet those requirements?

- How do our departments provide graduate students and professors with training in how people learn and what that means for teaching? What needs to be done to make this institution-wide and to set institution-wide standards?

- How is our campus working with local schools and other colleges and universities to bring teaching and learning to state-of-the-art standards from kindergarten through the undergraduate years? What more can we do?

- How might we bring our teacher recruitment and teacher education programs into better alignment with the real needs of both society and students? What are our benchmarks?

- What provisions might a statewide compact contain if we wished to ease student transfer between institutions?

- In what ways are we organized to make use of educational achievements from non-traditional organizations and settings?

- What other related questions should we address in an effort to reduce the institutional barriers to learning and to make our institution more responsive to the needs of others, e.g., K-12 education, employers, and other institutions of higher education?

This detachable foldout is taken from "An American Imperative: Higher Expectations for Higher Education." If you wish to obtain a copy of the full report, call 414-554-2434 or write

The Johnson Foundation, Inc.
P.O. Box 2029
Racine, WI 53404.

An American Imperative

Higher Expectations for Higher Education

Report of the
Wingspread Group on Higher Education

Appendix C

Members of the Wingspread Group on Higher Education

Patricia Aburdene
Author
Megatrends, Limited
Washington, DC

Patricia Aburdene is an author and social forecaster. She co-authored four books in the "Megatrends" series, most recently *Megatrends for Women*. She lectures to business and university audiences throughout North America, Europe, and Asia and serves as a Public Policy Fellow at Radcliffe College, Cambridge, Massachusetts.

Gilbert F. Amelio
President and Chief Executive Officer
National Semiconductor Corporation
Santa Clara, CA

Prior to joining National Semiconductor in 1991, Dr. Amelio was President of Rockwell Communication Systems and Rockwell Semiconductor Products Division. In his 25 years in the semiconductor industry, Dr. Amelio has 16 patents held alone or jointly. He holds a bachelor's and master's degree from Georgia Tech, and was awarded a doctorate in 1968.

Michael E. Baroody
President
National Policy Forum
Washington, DC

Michael E. Baroody became President of the National Policy Forum: A Republican Center for the Exchange of Ideas on July 1, 1993, after serving for 3 ½ years as Senior Vice President for Policy and Communications at the National Association of Manufacturers. Over the previous two decades, he held a variety of political and governmental positions including service on President Reagan's White House staff and as Assistant Secretary for Policy at the U.S. Department of Labor.

William E. Brock
Chairman
The Brock Group, Ltd.
Washington, DC

William E. Brock is Chairman of The Brock Group, a Washington, DC-based consulting firm specializing in international trade, strategic planning, investment strategy, and human resource development. A former congressman, senator, Chairman of the Republican Party, United States Trade Representative, and

Secretary of Labor, he initiated the landmark study, *Workforce 2000*. Senator Brock was a member of President Bush's Education Policy Advisory Committee and Chairman of the Secretary's Commission on Achieving Necessary Skills, Co-Chair of The Commission on The Skills of the American Workforce and its report, *America's Choice, High Skills or Low Wages,* and Chairman of the Center for Learning and Competitiveness.

Martha Layne Collins
President
St. Catharine College
St. Catharine, KY

Martha Layne Collins, President of St. Catharine College, was Governor of Kentucky from 1983-87, achieving historic success in education reform and industrial development. She was a Fellow at the Harvard University John F. Kennedy School of Government and Executive in Residence at the University o Louisville School of Business. Her current board positions are: R.R. Donnelley & Sons, Bank of Louisville, Eastman Kodak Co., and Norfolk Southern Corporatio She has chaired the Democratic Convention and served as keynote speaker.

Robben W. Fleming
President Emeritus
University of Michigan
Ann Arbor, MI

Robben W. Fleming, President Emeritus and Professor of Law Emeritus of the University of Michigan, former Chancellor of the University of Wisconsin, and former President of The Corporation for Public Broadcasting, has served as boa member and chairman of a number of national organizations, including The Carnegie Foundation for the Advancement of Teaching, the American Council c Education, the Association of American Universities, the National Academy of Arbitrators, and the National Institute for Dispute Resolution. He has been a trustee of The Johnson Foundation.

Mitchell S. Fromstein
Chairman and Chief Executive Officer
Manpower, Incorporated
Milwaukee, WI

Mitchell S. Fromstein has been Chief Executive Officer of Manpower, Incorporat since 1976 following 25 years as an advertising executive. During his tenure, worldwide sales have increased tenfold to $4 billion annually. He is known for I innovative approaches to the development of human resources technologies, particularly in the areas of employee selection, skill measurement, training techniques, and job placement. He is a director of Public/Private Ventures in Philadelphia.

Roger W. Heyns
Retired President
The William and Flora Hewlett Foundation
West Olive, MI

Roger Heyns graduated from Calvin College in 1940 and holds a Ph.D. in psychology from the University of Michigan. He served in the U.S. Air Force in World War II. Subsequent positions included Professor of Psychology, Dean of The College of Literature, Science and The Arts, and Vice President for Academic Affairs at the University of Michigan, 1948-65; Chancellor, University of California, Berkeley, 1965-71; President, American Council on Education, 1971-77; President, The William and Flora Hewlett Foundation, 1977-92.

Robert H. McCabe
President
Miami-Dade Community College District
Miami, FL

President of the Miami-Dade Community College District in Miami, Florida, since 1980, Robert McCabe has been active in local, state, and national organizations; most recently he served as Chair of the College Board. He is the recipient of many awards, including a MacArthur Fellowship in 1992, the 1991 Harold W. McGraw, Jr. Prize in Education, and *The Miami Herald* Spirit of Excellence Award in 1988.

Constance Berry Newman
Under Secretary
The Smithsonian Institution
Washington, DC

Constance Berry Newman became Under Secretary of The Smithsonian Institution in July 1992. She was Director of the U.S. Office of Personnel Management from June 1989 to June 1992. Her other major management positions have included: Assistant Secretary of the U.S. Department of Housing and Urban Development; Director of VISTA; President of the Newman & Hermanson Company; and Commissioner and Vice-Chairman of the Consumer Product Safety Commission.

Sr. Joel Read
President
Alverno College
Milwaukee, WI

In *The Many Lives of Academic Presidents,* by Clark Kerr and Marian L. Gade, Read was named one of a handful of college presidents who have broken new educational ground in the past 100 years. She has served as President of the American Association for Higher Education and on the boards of the American Council on Education, Association of American Colleges, Educational Testing Service, and Foundation of Independent Higher Education. She is a member of the American Academy of Arts and Sciences.

Albert Shanker
President
American Federation of Teachers
Washington, DC

Albert Shanker, educator, labor leader, and author, is President of the American Federation of Teachers and a vice president of the AFL-CIO. He is a member of the National Board for Professional Teaching Standards, the National Academy of Education, and the Competitiveness Policy Council and numerous other groups. Since December 1970, he has written a weekly column, "Where We Stand," on education, labor, economic, and human-rights issues, which appears in the "New of the Week in Review" section of *The New York Times*.

Peter Smith
Dean
School of Education and Human Development
The George Washington University
Washington, DC

Peter Smith has combined careers in higher education and elective politics. Currently Dean of the School of Education and Human Development at The George Washington University, he is a graduate of Princeton University, and holds an M.A. and a Doctorate of Education in Administration Planning and Social Policy from Harvard's Graduate School of Education. Lieutenant Governor of Vermont from 1982 to 1986, Congressman-at-Large from Vermont, member of the House Education and Labor Committee. Director of a facility for drop-outs in the Montpelier School System, founder and first President of the Community College of Vermont, Senior Fellow with the American Council on Education, and Executive Director of the National Commission on Responsibilities for Financing Postsecondary Education, Smith served on the Executive Committee of the Education Commission of the States and as a board member of the Carnegie Forum for Education and the Economy.

Adrienne K. Wheatley
Student, John F. Kennedy School of Government and
Trustee, Princeton University
Cambridge, MA

Adrienne K. Wheatley is a 1992 *magna cum laude* graduate of Princeton University. She was recently elected to serve a four-year term as a Princeton University Trustee by nearly 5,000 alumni and undergraduates. Ms. Wheatley is pursuing a master's degree in public policy from the John F. Kennedy School of Government at Harvard University and will begin studying at the Harvard Law School in September 1994.

Blenda J. Wilson
President
California State University, Northridge
Northridge, CA

Dr. Wilson is the third president of California State University, Northridge (CSUN), one of the largest CSU campuses, with a student population of 29,000. As Chancellor of the University of Michigan, Dearborn, she was the first woman to preside over a public higher educational institution in the state. Her higher education administration career began at Rutgers University, proceeded at the Harvard University Graduate School of Education, and continued at the Colorado Commission on Higher Education, where she was executive director and served as an officer in the governor's cabinet. She is the current Chair of the American Association for Higher Education.

Joe B. Wyatt
Chancellor
Vanderbilt University
Nashville, TN

Joe B. Wyatt has been Chancellor of Vanderbilt University in Nashville, Tennessee, since June 1982. He served previously as Vice President for Administration at Harvard University and also as Senior Lecturer in computer science. He has until recently served as Chair of the Association of American Universities and is a director of Ingram Industries; Sonat, Inc.; Advanced Network and Services (ANS); The Reynolds Metals Company, and the Public Agenda Foundation. He is also a member of the Government University Industry Research Roundtable (GUIRR).

* * * * *

The Wingspread Group wishes to acknowledge the contributions to its work of David R. Gergen, who participated in the Group before resigning to assume a White House position as Counselor to the President.

Appendix D

Table of Contents for Contributed Essays

What Does Society Need from Higher Education?

Robert H. Atwell
President, American Council on Education

Most contemporary discussions of society's requirements of higher education begin with economic considerations—most often, the need for colleges and universities to prepare students to work and compete in the global economy of the twenty-first century. We often hear a similarly instrumental approach advocated for university research, that it should be the source of scientific advances and technological developments that improve the nation's health and contribute to the strength of its economy.

I take no exception to either of these views, and to one degree or another have argued them myself. However, for purposes of this brief paper, I want to distinguish between what society *wants* from higher education—a list that seems to expand daily and one that includes many legitimate expectations—and what at base society *needs*. In the latter category I place a set interrelated roles and functions: the teaching of citizenship and values; the academy as an independent critic of society; and higher education as an agent of social change.

As valuable as theses roles and functions are, many members of society would not view them as self-evidently desirable, and some might actively oppose them. Nonetheless, I would maintain that if higher education fails to fulfill theses roles and functions, it will undermine both our democratic society and the support on which it depends for its continued vitality.

Teaching Citizenship and Values

Higher education is not value neutral. The essence of liberal learning—what distinguishes higher education from vocational training—is the communication of a basic set of values, including tolerance, understanding, a love of learning, and a devotion to free inquiry and free expression. Debates over the core curriculum or the canon often miss the point that liberal learning is fundamentally expansive and inclusive. Much as we might like to reach agreement on a set of facts, ideas, and works, familiarity with which would define an individual as educated, accomplishing such a goal is a hopeless—and perhaps pointless—task. Insistence on its realization often springs from the spirit of ideology rather than inquiry, and runs the risk of establishing a totalitarian academic regime with little tolerance for new ideas.

Indeed, in an age when the quantity of information is expanding exponentially, and coming at us in ever more forms, the importance of inculcating the values named above is greater than ever. Without them, it is impossible for a society to sort through its political, economic, and social dilemmas effectively, or humanely. The apportionment of health care, the application of technology, the complexities of international relations—these are but some of the challenges we face now, and will for the foreseeable future, that will test our capacity for rigorous analysis, informed judgment, moral rectitude, and devotion to democratic principles. As daunting and divisive as these challenges are, unless we approach them in this fashion our society risks a Yugoslavia of the soul.

The job of colleges and universities, then, is to prepare students to be citizens who can make wise choices and exercise leadership in all spheres of society. Citizenship is not identical to patriotism—at least not the narrow notion of it that we hear expressed too often, and that makes it "the last refuge of scoundrels." Citizenship requires active participation in society, in the solution of its problems, what we often now call "service." This concept of citizenship is the basis of President Clinton's call for a national service program; it should be no surprise that it has drawn an enthusiastic response from the nation's youth, as well as many of their elders. It also is behind the explosion of community service activities at colleges and universities through such programs as Campus Compact. These programs are valuable for the benefits they provide to society and to the student's understanding of society. They form an important base on which any national effort should build.

Higher Education as an Independent Critic of Society

Colleges and universities often are at their best when they are most annoying, when they stand a little apart from the daily life of society and point out its flaws. Indeed, faculty tenure needs no better defense than the necessity for this critical role to continue despite the hue and cry it often generates from those who benefit most from the status quo.

Universities can be catalytic in bringing about positive change. In Eastern Europe, the universities and their students were important engines of the fall of communism in 1989. In our own country, whatever else one might want to say about the 1960s on college campuses, I would argue that universities and their students played a fundamental role in exposing the flaws of American foreign policy and certainly helped to bring about the end of our involvement in Vietnam.

Higher education has a major role to play in raising the national consciousness above the selfishness and divisiveness that have characterized our national life in recent years. No institution is better positioned to define our common stake. It is no coincidence that President Clinton, both before and since the election, has chosen college campuses as the primary sites to articulate his campaign for "change"—in economic and foreign policy and in attitudes toward service for society. Nor is it surprising that he has drawn an inordinate number of advisers and appointees from academe, where they have been afforded the opportunity to analyze social and economic trends, develop new policy proposals, and subject them to analysis and criticism by other scholars. No doubt, most of the analysis—and criticism—of this administration's policies in turn will emanate from the nation's campuses.

In a larger sense, however, it seems to me that universities have failed in their roles as critics of society. Derek Bok has pointed out that in teaching and research, universities are responsive to what society chooses to pay for, not what it needs the most. Obviously, our institutions do and will serve society. But I believe more must be done to encourage faculty members and students to assume a critical stance, to use the knowledge and resources assembled on the campus—and the time available to them—to perform this function. Criticism may not be what most citizens and office-holders want to hear, but it is essential to social progress and the functioning of a democratic society.

Higher Education as an Agent of Social Change

Transmitting values and taking a critical stance together constitute a formula for social change. There is no avoiding the fact that colleges and universities have assumed a central position in our society; the positions taken and activities engaged in by academic leaders, faculty members, and students have an impact far beyond the boundaries of the campus. I believe all these actors should recognize this fact and act on it for the betterment of society and their own institutions.

On numerous occasions in the past I have encouraged higher education leaders to speak out on broader social issues and not limit themselves only to educational matters. But I have also tried to make it clear that in advocating that we become agents of social change, I am not urging university leaders and administrators to politicize their institutions. Rather, I have tried to posit a true test of academic leadership, what should be an exciting challenge to reshape and redirect colleges and universities to better serve their students and our society—and ultimately those leaders themselves.

The trick in all this is how simultaneously to be agents of change while avoiding the partisanship and politicization in which such agents often find themselves entrapped. This isn't easy. It requires that we negotiate some difficult shoals, and resolve what often appear to be conflicting demands. As I implied earlier, we must resist the tyranny of both the left and the right, the effort to impose narrowly drawn, uniform systems of thought and values on the curriculum, on classroom teaching, on interactions between members of the campus community. We must meet the constitutional imperative of free expression and the demands of academic freedom. At the same time, we must find ways to diversify and incorporate into the educational process new knowledge and new perspectives.

The university's critical stance can be unproductive and even indefensible when it takes the form of mindless carping by those more interested in asserting their own anti-establishment credentials than in bringing about change. But just as unproductive, and just as indefensible, are the complaints of those so threatened or offended by change that they retreat into apocalyptic warnings that the end of the academic world is near.

Colleges and universities become agents of social change through both their internal and their external activities. Let me cite two examples: diversity and internationalization. By making our campuses—and that includes the curriculum—more inclusive and welcoming to minorities, women, and others who historically have been excluded or neglected, we foster change both within the institution and outside it. Similarly, emphasizing the study of foreign languages and cultures, promoting increased student exchange, and developing stronger international ties among institutions changes both the campus and the broader society. Again, this is a tricky process, and difficulties along the way are inevitable, especially with regard to diversity. But when those difficulties occur, we must resist the rush to regulation, the temptation to believe we can solve all problems by drafting codes and imposing punishments. At the same time, we must be prepared to argue that requiring students to learn about things, ideas, places, and people with which they are unfamiliar is not a penalty but an essential part of a liberal education.

Given the resources it has invested in higher education, society needs to harness the intellectual horsepower available principally in colleges and universities to deal with the many manifestations of our current social deficit. In fact, it is difficult to imagine a problem confronting society, from the state of public education to the need for better health care to environmental degradation, that colleges and universities could not or should not play a big part in solving. This is not a role that higher education should embrace reluctantly, but one toward which it should aspire.

Perhaps John Masefield said it best: "There are few earthly things more splendid that a University. In these days of broken frontiers and collapsing values, when the dams are down and the floods are making misery, when every future looks somewhat grim and every ancient foothold has become something of a quagmire, wherever a University stands, it stands and shines; wherever it exists, the free minds of men [and I would add women], urged on to full and fair enquiry, may still bring wisdom into human affairs." ✦

Stephen W. Bosworth
President, United States – Japan Foundation

I have thought long and hard about the Foundation's project and the question it poses: What does society need from higher education? The question has been featured in a number of recent dinner parties, long conversations with my wife, several discussions with our children, a recent lunch with the former provost of Harvard University, a long house-bound weekend during the Blizzard of '93 with the Chairman of the Physics Department at Temple University and a lot of reflective noodling.

Alas, I have not found the Rosetta stone, that single, simple concept that goes to the heart of what is obviously an extremely complex question. A major problem here is of course that the question requires as much or more examination of society as it does of the institution of higher education. Our society itself is undergoing great change, and it is not at all clear what it will look like a decade or two from now. More importantly, there is not even the beginnings of a consensus as to what we want it to look like.

Perhaps the best way around this dilemma is to ensure that change in higher education—a process which is already underway—takes place within a broad social context. We need to lay out the structure, purposes and content of higher education as part of an even broader examination of our societal goals. Clearly, our institutions of higher education must themselves provide leadership as we try to develop a common vision of what our society should be and how we can get there.

Society has traditionally looked to higher education for two tasks: to increase knowledge and to teach. The performance of these two tasks has never been easy. They have always involved difficult choices by higher education and by society at large. What knowledge? Who will benefit? And who will pay? Who will be taught, what will be taught, and who will pay?

In the United States, these questions are complicated further by the fact that our society grew from egalitarian roots. In higher education, as in so many other aspects of our society, our broad choices must take account of the tension between efficiency and equity. But while our founding fathers may have argued that all men are created equal, they did not contend that all men (and women) are equal in terms of potential, and they expected that American national leadership would be drawn from a relatively small reservoir of talent. The particularly American distinction was that the early leaders of the country believed in the existence of a "natural aristocracy" based on talent and virtue, as opposed to what were seen as the "artificial aristocracies" of Europe based on birth and inheritance.

From the very beginning of the United States, this faith in a natural aristocracy led to an emphasis on the broad diffusion of knowledge through public education. Thomas Jefferson, for example, argued in his correspondence with John Adams that "that form of government is the best, which provides the most effectually for a pure selection of these natural aristocrats into the offices of government."

For much of our national existence, public education was pretty much confined to primary and secondary schools. Other than the training of teachers in normal schools, higher education was generally limited to the private colleges and universities of the Eastern United States, and entrance to these elite institutions was not generally accessible to more than a small minority drawn principally from the upper echelons of the society. On the other hand, higher education itself was not a requirement for individual achievement. There was an expectation that the natural aristocracy would advance toward their individual potential through self-study and self-improvement. In this regard, it is interesting to note how many of our early leaders pursued the study of natural science through their own resources.

This all began to change somewhat in the middle of the nineteenth century with the creation of land-grant universities. At about the same time, the development of modern scientific methodology began to close off major areas of knowledge from all but the specialists who were, increasingly, the product of higher education. But even then the American society tended to rely on a drive for individual self-improvement to lift people beyond secondary education, and graduation from an institution of higher education was by no means seen as necessary to professional accomplishment or personal fulfillment.

It was not until after World War II that higher education became truly accessible to large numbers of Americans and thus began to constitute a broad line of economic and social demarcation within the society. The GI Bill provided access to higher education for hundreds of thousands of returning veterans, leveraging them, their children, and their grandchildren up into a rapidly expanding American middle class.

The result was revolutionary. Access to higher education began to be perceived as part of the American birthright. Regardless of family circumstances, some type of higher education became accessible to virtually all Americans who wanted it. There were corresponding structural changes in higher education itself as new demand brought new supply into the market. Community colleges proliferated; state universities expanded and opened new campuses.

All of this worked fairly well through at least the 1960s. True, one could question the quality of education received in some parts of higher education. Some of the locally supported colleges and even state institutions reached down to meet the needs and abilities of lower echelons of high school graduates. Many state institutions, supported largely through public funds, imposed only minimal standards for admission. But the net result was that a large segment of the population received more education—and probably more knowledge—than would otherwise have been the case. In the meantime, with middle class family incomes rising and more and more private and public tuition assistance available, the members of Jefferson's natural aristocracy tended to find their way into the higher quality—and higher cost—institutions.

Over the last twenty years, however, the system has come under increasing strain. Beginning in the early 1970s the unprecedented growth of family income flattened out for most Americans. Today, for example, median family income is no higher than in 1973. In fact, only a dramatic increase in the employment of women has prevented a substantial decline in median family income. At the same time, all levels of government began to experience severe budgetary problems as revenues grew less rapidly and the political process was less and less able to allocate conflicting demands for public funds in a rational fashion against some agreed set of societal goals.

As a consequence, public institutions of higher education began to increase tuition rates to cover the gap between rising costs and declining support from state legislatures. Looked at in isolation, such increases may seem small. However, when one remembers that roughly 80 percent of all students now enrolled in higher education attend schools with an annual tuition of $2,000 or less and 16 percent attend institutions with tuition of less than $10,000, it is clear that increases which seem small in absolute terms in fact constitute a rising barrier to higher education for large numbers of students.

The strain on the elite private institutions is no less severe. One of the hallmarks of these institutions through much of the post-World War II period has been a policy of need-blind admission. Of the 4 percent of total students of higher education in these schools, approximately half receive some form of financial assistance. Stagnant family income makes it difficult for all but the most richly endowed of the private schools to continue to admit the best applicants regardless of their ability to pay. These institutions are in a vicious circle as they have to increase tuition to cover the rising cost of financial aid and thereby place more applicants in the zone where financial aid is required.

The overall effect of all this is that access to higher education, one of the basic cements of American society for the past several decades, is beginning to be severely restricted. For several generations of Americans, higher education has been key to their ability to get a piece of the American dream. Moreover, by introducing more and more Americans to the world of ideas, higher education has been critical to the building of a national value system within which individuals can make personal choices and civic judgements.

Unfortunately, the weakening of higher education as an institution of national unification comes at a time when the society is undergoing the most profound change in ethnic composition in nearly a century. Just when we need a strong system of higher education to help forge a set of national goals and values, the system is in crisis. Just when we need a broadly accessible system of higher education as a counterweight to an increasingly skewed distribution of national income, access to higher education threatens to become far more restricted.

Our national task is further complicated by the rapid loss of our national auton-omy. Americans no longer have the luxury of making—or not making—decisions on our national agenda and priorities in isolation from the world around us. To a degree still not fully realized, our national well-being depends on our ability to compete with the rest of the world. Our size and geography will not shield us from the consequences of an inability to compete in a global economy.

In order to compete effectively, we of course need the political talent and economic and social dynamism of well-educated leaders. The ability to educate our most talented citizens is still, as Jefferson argued, a key test of effective government. Even more, it is a key test of a healthy society. But in an increasingly globalized economy, where the ability to develop and apply technology is ever more critical to success, we also need a broad base of educated, trained managers and workers. American workers now compete not just with Germans and Japanese but also with Mexicans and Chinese. Inevitably and inescapably, American wages and family incomes and our national standard of living depend on how we do in this competition.

It is not reasonable or realistic to expect that higher education by itself can meet all these needs. It cannot, for instance, compensate for a broad failure of secondary education in the society. Neither can it substitute for more effective worker training and apprenticeship programs, though it can certainly be an important source of support for those programs.

On the other hand, none of our efforts at national renewal will succeed if our system of higher education deteriorates in quality and shrinks in terms of accessibility. It must teach more things, more effectively, to more people, and at a cost which the society can afford. Society as a whole will have to continue to struggle to balance equity with efficiency. In the end, this will mean more money: more money from tax payers for state institutions and more scholarship funds from public and private sources.

At the same time, we should remember that education is in the end largely an individual experience. We are unfortunately far beyond the era of a student and a teacher sitting on opposite ends of a log. But we should not concentrate so exclusively on teaching young Americans how to work in an increasingly complex, technologically driven world, that we neglect to teach them how to live in such a world.

My own father was not a veteran of World War II and did not benefit from the GI Bill. He and his family were, however, beneficiaries of the widened accessibility of higher education which occurred after the War. He had graduated from high school in 1930 just as the Great Depression was stunting the aspirations of an entire generation of Americans. Despite having been the valedictorian of his high school class, he could not afford college and went to work in a dairy. Thirty years later, at the age of 48 with a wife and three teenage sons, my father quit his job in a small factory in Grand Rapids, mortgaged the house, and enrolled at Western Michigan University where the tuition was low. Three years later, he graduated and began a twenty-year career as a high school teacher.

To say that I admired what my father did would be an understatement. I once asked him how he had the nerve to give up a secure, if unchallenging job, and change the course of his life so dramatically. His answer was succinct: "Your mother gave me the courage to break out. She persuaded me I had to do it. Not just to learn how to be a teacher. Most importantly, I had to learn how to live. Fortunately, we have a system in which it was possible." ✝

Eileen Moran Brown

President, Cambridge College

Academic institutions have always stood at the gate between the past and the future, usually preparing the next generation of leaders for a world that will be new culturally and technologically. American institutions of higher learning today, however, are among the more conservative forces in our society, continuing to educate in a hierarchical, individualistic, and passive manner out of tune with our society's growing need to create learning communities in every area of business, government, and social services. To contribute to the resurgence of the American economy and society colleges and universities must change *how* they teach, not just *what* they teach, because social innovation is likely to be at least as important in the next twenty-five years as technological advancement.

Society needs higher education to take the responsibility and provide the leadership to begin to create institutions which are true learning communities. These institutions, set in motion with a moral compass and a social mission, must reflect the strengths and meet the needs of all our citizens. Only educational institutions which themselves incorporate the dynamics of the larger society can aspire to contribute to the recasting of that society. Therefore, higher education must send the same structural message as its rhetorical message. It must reflect through its personnel and its practices its commitment to diversity. It must honor through its faculty and its curriculum the notion that each of us has things to teach and things to learn and none of us knows what all of us know. It must reflect through its infrastructure and its culture that the ways in which we are the same are so much more powerful than the ways in which we are different and that the only true aristocracy is that of the human spirit.

In order to be the true learning communities that the post-industrial age requires, institutions of higher education will have to learn how to become self-reflective and self-renewing. While we will always need centers of advanced scholarship, professional schools of distinction, and even elite, academically superior environments for gifted or lucky young adults, shaping an entire system around these models is the height of economic inefficiency and social irrelevance.

Changing our higher education system will require a reexamination of its central tenets and most sacred cows. It will require a rethinking of basic ideas, such as:

- The idea that it takes a certain number of credits to qualify for a degree.
- The idea that everyone learns the same way and that the best way of learning disciplined thinking is the academic approach.
- The idea that most academic subject matter can only or best be learned in a classroom.
- The idea that faculty know and teach while students learn.
- The idea that how an institution of higher learning structures itself, runs its classes, operates its dormitories, promotes its faculty, relates to its community, selects its students, and allocates its resources has little to do with what its students learn.
- The idea that tests and papers assess what students know and what they are becoming.
- The idea that particular grade point averages and degrees are fairly precise measures of an institution's output.
- The idea that intellectual competition and the structured search for truth are sufficient dynamics for change within academic institutions to keep them securely ahead of the rest of society.

In order to bring our colleges and universities into the twenty-first century and to once again put them in a position of leadership in our society, it will be important to:

- Add to the mix of undergraduates many more people who have life and work experience. Provide incentives for young people to delay going to college, coming later with a deeper sense of themselves and what they want to learn. Recruit more adults to enroll for undergraduate degrees.

- Recognize that people learn in different ways and make that clear to all students from the beginning of their time in college. Help students to discover their own learning patterns and how they can use the resources of the college to their own best advantage. Show how people can learn from and teach each other, in the classroom and outside. Create a variety of learning situations that modify the lecture hall and seminar formats to support better those learning styles that do not thrive in the traditional academic setting. Create forums (courses) where students can consciously help and encourage each other in learning how to learn and how to integrate what they know.

- Value the fact that everyone comes to college knowing more (and less) than their high school diplomas or test scores indicate. Find ways to determine this knowledge and give credit for it toward the degree. Enable each student to measure and track their progress along these multiple dimensions, making it possible for the student to accelerate, deepen, redirect and integrate their own learning in a more conscious, self-directed way than they can in college now.

- Accept the fact that the pace at which new knowledge is being created means that the model of mastering a field is outdated and that the metacognitive skills of a few fields are the essential knowledge one must have. Find new ways to teach and evaluate progress in learning those skills. Recognize, too, that for most adults the integration of knowledge, communication across fields of expertise, and accelerated learning of new, unfamiliar material are daily necessities, not more and more knowledge of a particular specialty. Create more cross-disciplinary courses and majors; prize the faculty members who work together across these barriers and those faculty who are open to fields outside their own and are able to draw them into their courses.

- Rethink the cost structure of undergraduate or graduate education from the perspective of outputs (students with certain metacognitive capabilities and sets of knowledge) rather than inputs (disciplines, specialized faculty, and particular areas of knowledge). Rethink the amount of time faculty actually spend teaching and working with students, the number of credits it takes to graduate, what one must know to receive the degree, the amount of administration needed, the possibility of combining many departmental fiefdoms into a few to reduce redundancy and inefficiency and of expanding the ways in which students can teach each other with faculty guidance and structuring.

- Operate on the understanding that content and process are equally important parts of the learning experience. Recognize that the academic model of largely individualized pure learning has little utility in today's society and economy. Students should be able to experience and reflect upon a variety of learning processes, working to understand the values of each and the ways in which each can be made most effective. The importance of diversity in learning groups, the ways in which a class or group becomes a learning community, the proper balance between unstructure and structure, the essential ingredient in learning from experience, how each learner can be affirmed, valued, and enabled to make unique contributions to the group's learning, and how the group can take responsibility for the learning of its members.

Restructuring colleges in the ways suggested above will profoundly unsettle faculty and academic departments. New incentives will be needed to facilitate and encourage these changes and to sustain the more open-ended, dynamic learning process that will be created. Faculty will have little conscious idea of how to teach/function in this environment and will need to be encouraged and helped to learn what it means and how to do it. Making it possible for faculty members to have non-academic working and learning experiences during sabbaticals will give them a better understanding of what their students need and will help faculty to become better learners and ultimately better teachers.

Underlying these suggestions is the notion that every institution in our society must become a true learning community, and colleges and universities are no exception. In fact, the great irony today may be that precisely the institution whose mission is learning may be less of a learning community in twenty-first century terms than many other institutions, including many of our corporations, service agencies, and cultural enterprises. Colleges must scramble to catch up. This is not something that can be accomplished superficially through an extra course or tutorial. It will require a profound reexamination of the historical evaluation of higher education in America, of the components of the basic mission of our colleges, of the most fundamental structural assumptions which shape curricular, assessment, and degree-granting, and of the function and role of faculty.

There is a deep issue of social values here, not just questions of the efficiency and pragmatic effectiveness requirements of our post-industrial, now global economy. We know that every institution teaches what it is, what it values, what its processes are as well as the specific contexts it intends to teach and to produce.

Thus to become once again the true leaders for growth and change they were originally intended to be, colleges will have to look like America in all its diversity and to function as an institution more in accord with the minds of ordinary people and groups in all their differences of intelligence and spirit. In short, colleges must strive to become once again true learning communities.

America's future will be shaped by those who are today learning how to create self-directed teams, how to make partnerships, how to work through the mis-communications and the conflicts that arise from diversity, and how to fashion a love for excellence and lifelong learning. Entrepreneurial groups within more traditional enterprises, collaborative task forces across departments, companies, industries, and even countries are all signs of the times that are coming. What they have in common is the need for people who know how to form, participate in, and lead learning communities. Colleges cannot hope to produce such people with the level of consistency and excellence they profess in every other area of their mission unless they themselves restructure. This is the task of our generation. ⋏

Paula P. Brownlee
President, Association of American Colleges

The public has been calling for organizations in every sector of civil life to become ones in which it has confidence and in which it can take rightful pride. Public opinion polls show that those surveyed are losing confidence (to varying degrees) in, for example, our criminal justice system, our business organizations, the press, the medical establishment and our nation's schools. Whether this increasing concern is rooted in a sense of the organizations' current inadequacies or in anticipation of their inability to meet future needs, the public's "voice" merits very serious attention. Until recently, higher education was remarkably free from public criticism—but concern is rising. The means must be found by which higher education, as a community, can be seen to be responsive and be known to be pro-active.

The public expects to see higher education represented by leaders engaged in the finest endeavors of the human mind and spirit. Our nation wants to be able to be proud of the real performance of higher education—*both* in its collectivity as a major national force for progress *and* for the good it effects in the lives of college and university students. We engage our diverse students in advanced education for their leadership tomorrow. Higher education in the United States is not a "system" as it is in most countries, and its strength lies in the distinctive character of individual institutions. Artists, teachers and architects, astronauts and politicians, nurses and philosophers, all receive the foundations of their professional and creative learning within particular academic communities. Their responsibilities as U.S. citizens, their humane understandings and willingness to take thoughtful action are shaped for a lifetime by their collegiate community and its values.

Colleges and universities should concentrate on what they are best equipped to do, namely: (1) to engage students in higher learning, (2) to provide research or artistic opportunities for professors, and (3) to link the two together. The knowledge gained from such activities should be disseminated in clearly understandable ways to various publics and needs to be applied, wherever appropriate, to the public good.

What then is higher education already carrying out well? Where are major improvements needed? How should society be helped to keep abreast of the advanced discoveries and other activities of academia?

It has been estimated recently that 95 percent of all undergraduates are required to take courses in *both* a major disciplinary concentration *and* across a number of disciplines. The requirements are, of course, intended to offer some exposure to the content of a liberal education. The intent is excellent: to develop liberally educated students who will be prepared not only for entry into first-level career openings or graduate study but also to take responsibility in several arenas in the adult world. Faculty members aim to have their students develop aptitudes and skills that they can apply with enthusiasm and intelligence to their first job and that will spur their continuing personal growth over a lifetime. They know that in a world where job opportunities shift from field to field, there are no assured places for narrowly trained students; and corporate leaders increasingly say, "Give us graduates who can reason well, who can speak and write articulately, and who have broad-based knowledge."

The goals of liberal education are long range—to instill in all students genuine eagerness to learn, competence across fields, and love for their chosen lives. The results should manifest themselves in adult lives of continual growth and development. Never has our country needed these qualities more in its shared leadership than now.

The recent presidential campaign and election gave citizens the chance to think hard about the extraordinary challenges our times are presenting. Never before have I personally heard so many remarks to this effect: "How can any one person have the capacity to tackle the immense problems of this country and in relation to such a shrinking world?" Citizens are deeply aware of the magnitude of the demands to be placed on the president—*and* on us, the people. They turn to education at all levels to meet the needs. They turn to higher education to educate well a wide range of problem solvers—for example, truly creative scientists and technologists, international strategists and the special people who can resolve the hostilities and conflicts among groups in our society. Furthermore, in a nation of individualists, how can we inspire the kind of cumulative actions that are clearly essential if we are to make progress on intractable societal problems?

In academic institutions across the states, some of the best minds are attending to many of society's challenges. Professors and presidents advise policy makers; partnerships abound between state universities and local governments for economic development; chemists assist in pollution control and industrial safety issues; linguists help develop computer-aided language training in rare languages; and deans of education work directly with public schools on the improvement of teacher training.

Despite probably hundreds of thousands of such public service partnerships, society at large is unaware of the collective weight of these efforts across our nation. While I may read in my newspaper that local community college students are tutoring elementary school students 300 hours per week, I have no means of knowing of the cumulative effort students are contributing in all states. Thus society receives little information on the extent (and limitations) of higher education's collective contributions.

On the other hand, higher education could multiply its effectiveness manyfold if it would but discern ways to extend pilot projects (such as the small example given above) to perfuse and renew an entire system. Our current slowness in extending successful new teaching practices or curricular reforms within an institution, or among similar institutions, does make higher education appear to be resistant to needed change. Associations such as AAC do intentionally link universities and colleges and their deans and faculties to disseminate good educational developments and practices widely; AAC is already planning to make such activities known far more broadly.

Change may be the imperative of this decade. In some respects, universities and colleges have been on the forefront of dealing with certain elements of it; in other respects there is still very much yet to be done. The university represents, in microcosm, a cross section of the emerging nation in which we live. On most campuses now, administrators have been successful in attracting and retaining very diverse student bodies. Men and women, young and old, come from very different family, educational, ethnic, and racial backgrounds. The institution, through its espousal of certain important educational values and practices, fosters the development of a living, learning community. Education is paramount, but a great array of other activities are encouraged or tolerated. People do not understand each other always, fears are generated, and some times—even here—ugliness and anger erupt. But most of these wonderful colleges and universities are "laboratories" in which diverse communities develop. There is almost always space to debate, to dispute, to "have it out." Everyone learns, and respect for difference grows often. Important learning is taking place in such an academic community, and its lessons will carry forward into the graduates' futures and so into our larger society.

As noted earlier, higher education's *intent* to produce well-educated students to meet contemporary challenges fits with a major societal expectation. The *results* among the millions of college attenders are variable and, in any case, difficult to discern since there is no means of quantitative "outcomes assessment" for comparability. We do know, however, that although many institutions are applying recent learning about the ways in which men and women of very different backgrounds learn well, that institutions are reforming and renewing graduate and undergraduate curricula, *most* students experience curricula and pedagogies that are similar, by and large, to those of thirty years ago.

One area in which great strides are being made is in the application of information technologies to the storing, retrieving and sending of information among the academic community. There is great confidence that this will aid learning markedly. Less clear, however, is how these technologies improve memory and increase understanding. It is important to distinguish the difference between the well-informed and the well-educated graduate!

Earlier, I alluded to the colleges and universities themselves as laboratories, places for experimenting. The ways that students choose to learn can best be studied right there. For example, some years ago, it was noticed that students in all-women's colleges formed their own informal "study groups" and profited from that interactive learning. Since then, we have learned much more about the efficacy of collaborative, active learning. Students who are *engaged* in their own learning are motivated to work hard. (We still have much to learn about how to engage the disinterested students.) Adult students, particularly, value strategies that connect their own life experiences to the new knowledge presented. All students need help to link knowledge across discipline boundaries, and numbers of institutions are developing general education "core curricula" to replace distribution courses (which are usually unconnected intellectually).

At AAC, a series of projects has taken on "the challenge of connecting learning"— to deal with the issue of redesigning the undergraduate arts and sciences major to be intrinsic to the liberal learning experience of the students. Our monograph of that same title speaks to several sorts of connected learning and goes on to sum up:

> In the final analysis, the challenge of college, for students and
> faculty alike, is empowering individuals to know that the world is far
> more complex than it at first appears, and that they must make inter-
> pretive arguments and decisions—judgments that entail real consequences
> for which they must take responsibility and from which they may not flee
> by disclaiming expertise.

Herein lies the heart of my response to the pressing question: "What does society need from higher education?" For within our higher education institutions reside the needed resources of intellectual capital and the deep commitment to educate well— and the will to meet the challenge. **⊀**

Russell Edgerton
President, American Association for Higher Education

It is important to understand not only what higher education needs from society but also the extent to which these expectations have changed. Higher education today is being criticized for doing what, a generation ago, the public asked it to do. Thus, in developing my answer, I begin with the "golden age" of expanding enrollments and rising political favor in the 1950s and 1960s.

The 50s and 60s

In the 1950s and 1960s, public expectations for higher education were shaped by three extraordinary events. The first was the launching of Sputnik in 1957, which both symbolized and spurred on the spectacular scientific and technological race with the USSR. America's political, military, economic, and cultural influence spread throughout the "free world." As training grounds for the "best and brightest," higher education soared to new levels of public esteem.

The second event was the civil rights movement. The GI Bill had demonstrated that helping "average" Americans go to college was a good investment, both for the individuals and for the larger society. In the early 1960s, this lesson of the GI Bill was joined to our rising concern for social justice into a powerful political rationale—"equality of opportunity"—for extending college opportunities to groups excluded from the mainstream of American life.

The third event was the baby boom. In 1964, the extraordinary cohort that began nine months after VJ Day and lasted 14 years hit college age. At the beginning of the 1960s, America's youth cohort aged 14 to 24 (the cultural "invaders") were outnumbered by older people (the cultural "defenders") three to one. By the end of the decade, the invading army had shifted the balance to two to one.

Each of these events was extraordinary. The convergence of all three created an unprecedented set of circumstances for higher education. All energies were focussed on the overriding concern for access and growth: how to build the buildings and recruit the faculty fast enough to keep pace with the surging demand for enrollment. What did the American public seem to need from higher education at the time? Rapid expansion in opportunities for access, with few questions asked about the kind or quality of education that was being provided. Rapid expansion of our scientific research and training capability, with few questions asked about what particular kinds of research and training related to what particular public needs.

Within this context, colleges and universities were relatively free to follow their own stars, to pursue *their own* visions of what kind of higher education society should have. As we now know, many institutions set a compass course on the *same star,* the model of faculty careers and institutional excellence set by the most prestigious research universities.

It's interesting to look back on what the influential sources of thought about higher education were saying at the time about what the important issues were. Research on society's need for higher education was largely dominated by economists of the "human capital" school, who bolstered the public's common sense with complex arguments about the returns to be gained from investing in higher education. It's instructive to note that all these analyses simply assumed that college was a common good, a single "it" to be accessed and graduated from. What went on inside the black box called "college" was not in question.

For over a decade, the analysis of public policy issues facing higher education was dominated by the Carnegie Commission and its successor, the Carnegie Policy Council, chaired by Clark Kerr. Here too, the focus of the Commission/Council was overwhelmingly on issues of access, public finance, and governance of "the industry." Little attention was given to what was going on inside the particular "firms" within the industry.

The 1990s

A generation later, America is a very different place. And public expectations for higher education's role in society have shifted remarkably.

Our preeminent national challenge is no longer winning the Cold War, but figuring out how to earn a decent national living in a competitive global economy. The commitment to social equity remains a powerful force in American life but for complicated reasons, some of the steam has gone out of this commitment and the advocates of compensatory strategies such as affirmative action are on the defensive. The baby boom cohort has passed on; their children are not due to knock on college doors until the late 1990s.

And the robust economy of the 50s has given way to the problematic economy of the 1990s. To understand higher education's new position, it is extraordinarily important to realize that the American middle class has been downwardly mobile since 1974. During the 1980s, with spouses entering the workforce and an Administration deluded by supply side economics, this decline was masked. Now it has hit home and industries like health and higher education, where price increases have far exceeded the rate of inflation, are confronting an explosive public reaction.

According to Daniel Yankelovich, 88 percent of the public feels that a high school diploma is no longer enough to qualify for a well-paying job in the United States. In other words, they believe that a college education is even more essential in the economy we have. Eighty-seven percent feel that college costs are rising at a rate that will put college out of reach for most people. In other words, college is becoming less affordable that ever before.

So what does the public *now* need from higher education? The things that were ignored in the boom years of the 1950s and 1960s. Not just research, but the kind of research, training, and professional outreach that contributes to solving America's present national challenges. Not just access to more of the same but access to a kind and quality of education that prepares one for the twenty-first century. Not just an enterprise adept at acquiring resources but an enterprise that can attend to the way resources are being used. Let me elaborate on these points.

Contributing to Competitiveness

To be sure, university-based basic research is a factor in competitiveness. But, as Derek Bok has argued, utilitarian arguments about the importance of basic research to competitiveness have been overblown in recent years. *The* most critical ingredient in the competitiveness challenge is the quality of the American workforce. *If* colleges and universities are to be major players in responding to the challenge of competitiveness, it will be through their contributions to a higher quality workforce.

Colleges and universities have the capacity, through *applied* research, training, and professional outreach, to address many of the social problems that currently undermine the development of our human talent. But no single discipline, especially through a research strategy alone, is up to this task. So the rub is, to meet this challenge, colleges and universities would have to internally reorganize to mobilize the resources of many disciplines, and develop multiple modes of involvement more common to the behavior of "professions" than to that of "disciplines," if they are to be effective players in these arenas.

Or, take the closer-to-home matter of *educating* the future workforce. The first and primary responsibility for this lies with our K-12 system. So, if colleges and universities really wanted to contribute to the public agenda, the question to be asked is: how can higher education help improve the nation's schools?

The answer is there are many ways, from developing admissions policies that encourage high school students to study what's most essential, to doing research that really matters to educational practitioners. But by far the most critical role is in recruiting and preparing the future teaching profession, and maintaining an academic connection with these graduates into teaching throughout their careers.

The rub is, colleges and universities cannot meet this need by simply up-grading their schools and departments of education. Unlike its role in preparing all other professionals, colleges and universities themselves model the profession that their graduates of teacher preparation programs will practice. Undergraduates going into teaching learn how to teach, not only from their formal studies but more importantly from how they themselves are taught—in chemistry, history, and so on. To meet the challenge of preparing world class twenty-first century teachers, colleges and universities must themselves engage in world class teaching!

Contributing to Nation-Building

Our economic future cannot be separated from our political and cultural health. Though public attention is focussed largely on the economy, the challenges we face in the civic arena are even more severe. If we had measures of the civic non-participation rate, indicators of gridlock, etc., equivalent to our economic measures, all thoughtful people would be alarmed. One way of characterizing the challenge is to think (like we do of underdeveloped countries) in terms of nation-building.

As in the case of competitiveness, colleges and universities have complex contributions to make through their functions of research, teaching, and service. But the principal challenge, it seems to me, is to colleges and universities as *communities,* and the educational outcomes they aim to achieve.

I see a broad shift in the educational/socialization tasks that American institutions perform. The decline of families and neighborhood communities and the rise of a powerful, advertising-based mass media, means that Americans, especially young people, are no longer acquiring many of the values and virtues (self-discipline, responsibility, etc.) that are crucial to our democracy. At the same time, technologies like television, public polling, etc., are giving the mass public, as distinguished from what political scientists call "the attentive public," newly influential roles in the working of our democracy. As George Kennan points out in his latest book, our founding fathers created a representative democracy, but in many ways we have become a direct democracy—and it isn't working very well.

Colleges and universities *could* function as a *counterweight* to the rootless, commercialized culture we have now. But to be effective counterweights, they would have to engage their students in much more intense, effective learning communities, and shift the emphasis from passive and "received" to active and "constructivist" approaches to knowledge and learning. I might add that with increasing competition from non-degreed, technology-based information services, colleges and universities that simply provide information-transmission versions of education don't have a very bright future in the long run.

Doing More with Less

The expectation to use resources more effectively is so obvious that I won't dwell on it here. Issues about what educational work should be done in high school and what work should be done in college, articulation and time to degree, what college students are really getting out of college, how hard faculty work and what faculty should work *at,* are already upon us. The question is whether the academic disciplines and professions, and our institutions, will take responsibility for addressing these issues, or whether external authorities (as in health care) will move in.

In Sum: the Challenge to Higher Education

The present generation of faculty and administrators who lead our higher education enterprise started their professional careers in the golden age of expanding enrollments and rising political favor. For my first job in 1965, I joined a political science department at the University of Wisconsin-Madison which hired five new professors a year for four straight years, doubling from 20 to 40 professors, while the university grew from 20,000 to 40,000 students. And I viewed this as normal! I had little awareness that my professional career and aspirations rode on a crest of public support that was based on historically unprecedented, abnormal conditions.

So one of our challenges is the challenge of change. As to the direction of change, let me end with a brief summary comment about each of the classic functions—teaching, research, and service.

In our educational, teaching function, higher education needs to move from instructing students about things (covering subjects) to helping students learn how to do things (complex abilities) and the deeper levels of knowledge we call understanding and judgement. Educating for abilities and judgement (which entails weighing values) requires very different methods than educating *about* things. Students learn about things by listening. They learn how to do things by *doing* them. They learn understanding and judgement through immersion and intense encounters, being in the play rather than just reading it.

Basic research, of course, remains important. But the academic enterprise is caught up in epistemologies that degrade the equally important tasks of analyzing and writing for audiences beyond one's peers. The fields that are *most* related to the competitiveness challenge (teaching, nursing, social work, etc.) are precisely those fields that are looked down upon by those who are caught up in the present hierarchical value system of scientific objectivism.

Third, higher education needs to renew its outreach to K-12 and other constituencies in the larger community. In the original land grant idea, the entire faculty were considered to be in the nation's service. Then universities evolved professional schools and other discrete units that performed the outreach function, leaving the arts and sciences faculty to live in a world of their own. We need to return to the original land grant idea.

Finally, higher education needs to all this at less cost. A tall order indeed. ⍅

David L. Featherman
President, Social Science Research Council

I received the invitation to address the question, "What does society need from higher education?," as I was finishing Paul Kennedy's newest book, *Preparing for the Twenty-First Century*.

Kennedy documents his understanding of massive transformations underway in international relations and speculates about their implications for global security and for the human and economic welfare of the developed and the developing world regions. The theme running through Kennedy's analysis is that a complex skein of interrelated transnational influences—namely, changes in population dynamics, in biotechnology of food production, in robotics and cybernetic manufacturing technologies, and in world trade—are rapidly reshaping the scheme of international affairs. According to Kennedy, these transnational forces were at work well before the end of the Cold War, but their implications for international and human relations assume the foreground in the post-Cold War era.

The world Kennedy portrays is a transnational one in which the sovereignty of nation states—even the United States—is challenged if not undermined, and where the driving forces of change for any nation often lie well outside its own borders. Nations appear to possess diminished powers to guarantee the welfare and security of their citizens. Multinational corporations, fundamentalist religious movements and diasporas, non-governmental interest groups, as well as national governments, each contribute to defining the focus and issues of global and national affairs. The unfolding post-Cold War world possesses extraordinary, subtle, and perhaps even volatile interdependencies of new forms, beyond those related to nuclear disarmament and deterrence over the past half century—e.g., interdependencies between humankind and its environment, between the developed North and the developing South. Consequently, Kennedy's twenty-first century would seem to defy a planful course of progress without costly unintended consequences. For example, population pressures on global land resources and uneven benefits of new agricultural biotechnologies—often developed in American university laboratories—potentially open wider cleavages between South and North. Adopting new technologies into developing nations of Africa, for instance, could actually accelerate the out-migration of displaced agriculturalists and other manual laborers into the lands of the "rich," even as food production capacity is rising in the "poor" regions. And the resolution of such complex dilemmas of human existence in these regions seems feasible only by the most creative approach to collective, cooperative problem solving on a global scale.

In such a vision of the twenty-first century, it seems to me that we cannot presume that progress is an inevitable handmaiden of more education, per se. I began to put the question about higher education—which I have assumed to refer principally to American higher education—into the context of America's place in an increasingly transnational world. While not necessarily subscribing to Kennedy's full analysis, I do believe his essential conclusion about rising transnational forces across the globe is close to the mark.

I therefore would answer the question about American higher education as follows: Our colleges and universities must prepare us—as a nation and as individuals—for a new form of international citizenship in which neither progress nor our own national leadership is guaranteed. They must prepare us for a transnational world. This is a challenge that our nation's universities, as they are now structured and proceed to educate through advanced research and teaching, may be hard pressed to realize.

Why? One reason is that we may already ask our universities and colleges to do too much; we have come to expect too much from them. Historically, the founding of American higher education drew its justification from two objectives: to offer liberal education to generations of future leaders of a democratic nation, and somewhat later, to offer a pathway of upward social mobility to intellectually talented and motivated sons (and even later, daughters) from humble estate. If public education was the cornerstone of this bold experiment in nation-building, then higher education was the keystone of our national progress—it was a bridge to individual advancement, and it buttressed the nation economically and politically through pathsetting scholarship and technical and scientific innovation.

These goals are no less compelling or worthy for the twenty-first century than in the eighteenth century. But the capacity of colleges and universities to attain these goals may have gotten worse. At least their current performance is far from laudable, judging from appearances. With regard to the liberal education of future leaders, one is shocked and baffled by all too common incidents of racial and ethnic intolerance— even violence—on even the most "liberal" and prestigious of our campuses. And while matriculation into some form of higher education is typical for most high school graduates, rates of matriculation for youth from less economically and culturally advantaged backgrounds are not relatively better—indeed in some cases, even worse—than a decade or more ago. Educators and employers alike are appalled by what students—even baccalaureates in the Ivy League—do not know. And students and parents alike are astonished by the rising costs of higher education and agonized by the declining guarantee of full employment and premium wages that once came with the diploma.

But are colleges and universities to blame? Of course they must stand accountable for that over which they can exercise some control. And therein lies the rub. To exercise control one must have both understanding of cause and possess agency to alter the status quo. The fact is, higher education lacks both in many instances where it is held to account. Take racial violence and insulting verbal abuse; is this a failing of higher education to develop capacities for deeper moral or ethical self-insight as a basis of community and the toleration of differences? Or, is it a consequence of more pervasive anxieties—in the wider society—about racial and ethnic competition, inequities, or even alleged unworthiness? Or, is the basis in still other factors? If any social scientist or educator ventured forward to offer the definitive explanation for these incivilities, that person would be stepping well beyond available research and data.

And suppose we had more data, and I surely trust that we shall—indeed, we must. Would college and university administrators and faculty possess agency to change? Probably in some cases, but in many, not. Sociologists and economists have studied enrollment and graduation statistics for decades, despite the limitations of these data. Only a few studies and federal data series are based on large enough samples to characterize the educational opportunities of "minority" youth or to assess the degree of limitation of opportunity by economic background, race, gender, and region. Indeed, and as a very slight digression, this nation should be ashamed at the insufficiency of its federally- and state-provided data on educational matriculation—for longitudinal cohorts—from primary into higher education; other nations do much better than we. Notwithstanding these limitations, however, the social science about attendance, matriculation and the contributing influences of social, economic, and cultural factors is substantial. But what agency is available to higher education per se to stem the high drop-outs from secondary schools, indeed, the often tragic loss of youthful talent into lives of crime or drugs? And what can or should universities and colleges do to overcome the disequilibria of supply and demand for college graduates, even Ph.D.s, that have driven down their relative wages and employment prospects? Can, or should, they limit their enrollment levels—or the ratio of "foreign" to "native" students in high enrollment fields—and thereby restrict supply? Can they influence the marketplace for their graduates, even in this country, as some industries and firms recruit from an international labor pool?

Perhaps we do expect too much from our colleges and universities. And perhaps, as well, American higher education—and its counterpart institutions of higher education throughout the world—may be less well positioned to be the engines of individual and national progress in the twenty-first century than up to the recent past. If Paul Kennedy is right in concluding that nations are less sovereign today than in mid-century and that the twenty-first century will see even further erosion in nations' capacities to guarantee the security and the economic and social welfare of their peoples, does it not follow that national institutions like systems of higher education might also be affected by globalization, by various transnational influences, and by the weakened sovereignty of the surrounding nation state? Could it not be that some of what we hold our colleges and universities now to account—and find them failing—are signs of that loss of effective agency—not just of the universities but also of America as a nation state?

Possibly, and one would need to consider the evidence very carefully—certainly more than I have or could in this brief essay. But let me address, in conclusion, a final question that follows from my prescription for the future of higher education, namely, if our colleges and universities are to prepare us and our children for a transnational world of the twenty-first century, what would they do differently? Here, too, my thoughts are quite preliminary, but I see four topics that should be considered.

First, we must reexamine the sufficiency of discipline-based training and the concept of disciplines as the basic building blocks of knowledge. In both the sciences and humanities—and even to considerable extent in the arts—we continue to rely upon "disciplines" to repose our fundamental knowledge, a practice well established by the seventeenth century. But at an earlier time, knowledge about human, social, and natural phenomena was less divided and was integrated under the general rubric of philosophy. We can expect no less specialization of narrowly focused expertise in the twenty-first century than now, as the existing disciplines further subdivide and, in some instances, recombine at their boundaries with second disciplines into third-order hybrids. (A good example of this structural recombination and hyper-specialization are the subfields of biology, which over the past decade have vastly reconfigured what once was a unified field in most research universities. The shifts are so profound that a current study of changes in the quality and output of graduate research programs in the U.S. since the early 1980s—carried out by the Conference Board of Advanced Research Centers—may not be able to include the fields of biology, owing to the lack of comparable departmental entities in the 1990s.) And yet, intensification of discipline-based specialization leads to a balkanization of knowledge and to great difficulties of communication, even in some cases between specialists in subfields of their own nominal discipline.

While no sensible scholar would recommend a reunification of all of today's or tommorrow's knowledge under a single rubric, we academics and academic administrators need to address the great and many divides in our expert knowledge systems that far exceed the "two cultures" of C.P. Snow's concern. And in doing so, we may want to examine the knowledge systems of other cultures. David Easton and Corinne

Schelling, in reporting on a series of exchanges between the American Academy of Arts and Sciences and the Chinese Academy of Science, describe a certain bemusement of the Chinese with our Western penchant for atomized specializations. Easton quotes one Chinese scientist as suggesting we are "looking at the sky from the bottom of the well" (Easton and Schelling, *Divided Knowledge: Across Disciplines, Across Cultures,* 1991). How do we both take advantage of our capacity for specialized knowledge and still possess expertise for reassembling the pieces into wholes? Our current institutional practices at the most prolific research universities mitigate against cross-departmental, cross-discipline, cross-college synthesis.

At a moment when many of the most pressing problems of our transnational era call for a "sky-down" view and comprehension, how will our universities prepare us to ascend from the "bottoms of our wells?" I have no simple answer to this question, but I do know that the answer must entail some rethinking about the structure of universities and of academic research careers as we prepare for the twenty-first century.

Second, we must develop—as early in the educational careers of students as feasible—an appreciation for multi- and interdisciplinary analysis and skills that enable them to engage in it. One promising strategy for combining specialized expertise with capacity for synthesis is the interdisciplinary approach. For the past 70 years, the Social Science Research Council has promoted interdisciplinary research among the social sciences and between them and the humanities and natural sciences. Each year we award hundreds of predoctoral, doctoral, and post-doctoral fellowships and seed grants for projects that address topics from a multi- and interdisciplinary vantage. We organize workshops and conferences on thematic topics—e.g. the human dimensions of global environmental change—and on methodological approaches that expand the technical repertoire and conceptual boundaries of economists, political scientists, geographers, and others. Some see this work as subversive, as undermining the integrity of the standing disciplines; we are held to account—as the Council always should be—for enticing the next generation of scholars to practice a craft for which there may not be jobs in the current scheme of tenure-track discipline-centered assistant professorships.

We at the Social Science Research Council—indeed all of us in higher education—face a fundamental dilemma. How do we instill the capacity, within the next generation of our intellectual leaders, researchers and teachers, to analyze and to recommend tractable solutions for the complex, multidimensional, and transnational problems of Kennedy's twenty-first century if the most important step is problem finding? A study some years ago, reported in *Science* magazine, concluded that the most intellectually pathbreaking and practically useful researches were most frequently those based on a pooling of disciplinary knowledge. They more typically rejected the tendencies of individual disciplines to define solutions for a problem in terms of extant disciplinary paradigms—i.e., conventional theoretical and methodological frames of reference. Instead, the pooling of disciplines permitted—indeed, required—a first step of "finding the problem," an iterative phase of problem redefinition from a variety of perspectives, that set the tone for a series of broadly conceived solutions.

How do we make it possible, within our discipline-based departments and laboratories, for our graduate students—even our postdoctoral fellows and scientists—to learn this rather novel approach to problem finding and problem solving? How should we design our universities and our curricula in higher education in order that the skills of analysis, problem finding and problem solving among our humanistic scholars, our scientists and engineers, and our applied and clinical researchers are more in alignment with the problems and solution strategies that will be encountered and required in an increasingly transnational world?

Third, we should expand the opportunities for collaborative analysis and the recognition of team-conducted research. One possible new approach to scholarship—ever more common in several of the sciences—is team research. In keeping with my view that problem finding and solving capacities—as much in basic as in applied or mission-motivated research—should align optimally with the presumed nature of a phenomena's complexity, I suggest that these teams should be multidisciplinary and intensely collaborative. Our universities still celebrate the model of the individual scholar pursuing his or her curiosities; a peer-review process regulates and sanctions the quality and direction of individuals' work. There is nothing inherently wrong or unproductive about that model, but when it excludes or diminishes the flourishing of other approaches to organizing inquiry, we need to ask if we are getting the most from it.

In a transnational world, it is unlikely that any discipline, any one university, or the scholars from any single nation will be able to make great headway against the problems of the twenty-first century by "going it alone." We need to ask if, as a first step, we might need to rethink the training of our graduate students in skills of research collaboration, team organization, and cross-disciplinary cooperation. Perhaps another model of research that should be explored—in addition to the current individual Ph.D. dissertations that "test" for individual research capacity within a "peer" (doctoral faculty) system of review—is one that embeds individual scholars within a team with some cross-disciplinary diversity.

Fourth, and perhaps most important, we should facilitate and encourage wider cross-cultural training, research, and team-based international collaboration in testing our collective academic knowledge against the practical realities, challenges and dilemmas of a transnational world. Knowledge and communication increasingly are globalized. But as with many features of a transnational world—from the beneficial impacts of multi-national corporations on rates of economic activity to the limiting effects of rapid population growth on human flourishing—the depths of knowledge and the flows of information are unevenly distributed. Scientific knowledge and scholarship in the twentieth century has been globalized, but the domination of the West is clear. English, for example, is the international language of science, accounting for about 80 percent of all citations in electronic retrieval systems (Kotkin, *Chronicle of Higher Education,* February 24, 1993). And in a field I know well—the social sciences—some have estimated that at least two-thirds of published research originates in the West. In the social sciences and humanities—as well as the natural sciences—America, especially, has exported the major theoretical frameworks, methods of research design and analysis, and with them, our disciplinary form of codifying and organizing scientific knowledge systems. Global diffusion of intellectual and scientific information from the West also has put forward the view that "it is both natural and desirable for knowledge to accumulate, as it were, into one international (dominated by Western/American) pool of ideas and methods that is freely accessible to all" (Easton and Schelling, Ibid., p.25; insert is mine).

America's universities and research centers should be rightly proud of their role in fostering this globalization of advanced and technical knowledge. By the end of the eighteenth century, migration of European scientists and intellectuals to the United States established the human foundations for unparalleled technological leadership and accomplishments. Higher educational institutions in America still receive some of the best and most productive of the graduate students from abroad. By the late 1980s, Asian-born students—mainly from China, Taiwan, Japan, India and Korea—comprised about half of all foreign students, and contributed even larger fractions in doctoral programs in natural science and engineering. Many of these foreign students—more than five out of every ten—choose to remain in the U.S. and contribute productively to our economic competitiveness worldwide (Kotkin, Ibid.). Those who return to their homelands, of course, also accelerate the global diffusion of U.S. scientific and intellectual knowledge.

Higher education and advanced knowledge may be one of our best export products in the global economy into the twenty-first century. And without gainsaying that possibility, I suggest that as we approach the next century we should ask our universities to heed the possible unintended negative impacts of the globalization of American scientific and technical knowledge. In a transnational world, these undesirable outcomes are as likely to constitute a problem for us as for others abroad as we grapple with the complex problems of mismatch between the loci of population growth and technological competence and of ensuing threats to international peace and security as well as to human welfare within nation states.

One potential downside of Western and especially American domination is that our ways of knowing, learning, analyzing, and of storing and organizing knowledge (e.g., conceptually, into disciplines; and institutionally, into their corresponding university units) are likely to reflect considerable cultural "bias." This possibility is very likely in the social sciences and humanities—fields from which we and our colleagues abroad must draw, in addition to the natural sciences and engineering, if we are to understand and meliorate twenty-first century problems in the environment, in population control, in international peacekeeping and security, and so on that have—at their very foundations—ineluctable human behavioral, cultural, and institutional features.

Easton and Schelling, for example, conclude from their American Academy workshops with the Chinese that non-Western cultures have not been unexceptionably well served by the globalization of intellectual knowledge systems arising from the West. Non-Western scholars have not been prompted to develop their own conceptual and philosophical foundations for cultural, historical and societal analysis and interpretation—for seeing themselves through their own eyes, rather than through lenses provided by Western epistemology, as it were. And we in the West, in turn, have constructed various formulations of "the Other," (e.g., as critiqued in Edward Said's "Orientalism") that have not benefitted from indigenous descriptions and inputs from colleagues of the region in question. Comparing the long history of Confucian-inspired scholarship in China—with its emphasis on a more holistic construction of knowledge systems—with the Cartesian, atomistic approaches in the West, Easton and Schelling ask whether the globalization and dominance of Western intellectual epistemology fosters considerable historical and cultural blindness worldwide:

> ...it poses the question as to whether our conceptions of method and of the resulting knowledge itself, as they have evolved over the last two thousand years in the West, are not, after all, just that, namely, products of a unique historical experience. In the extreme view, may they not be the singular outcome of one kind of cultural sequence? Why should we believe, except out of some cultural pride, blindness, or hubris, that our experience in the West leads to universal criteria for the production of reliable knowledge but that the divergent experiences of other cultures fall short of offering the same? May not this simply be what it is often seen to be outside the West, an arrogance or imperialism of the idea that has taken the place of (or, in the past, has accomplished) an imperialism of power? (Easton and Schelling, Ibid., p.27)

Another negative consequence is associated with the domination of English as the language of science and international scholarship. This fact is not likely to motivate American teachers or their students to learn foreign languages. Currently, about 15 percent of our high school students learn a foreign language and only 2 percent pursue it for more than two years (Kozol, *Illiterate America,* p. 212; cited in Kennedy). And by imposing English language facility as a "threshold" for the participation of foreign scientists and scholars in the flows and exchanges of ideas worldwide is, on its face, a very limiting condition.

One conclusion I draw from these observations is that knowledge systems have deep historical, cultural and institutional roots. That is an asset in a transnational world. Ironically, we must have detailed and nuanced localized knowledge if we are to gain way with the complexities of a transnational world. In his concluding chapter, Paul Kennedy calls for a radical "reeducation of humankind." When he elaborates on that educational regimen, he notes in preamble that each nation's dilemmas are unique and will require a different set of strategies in adapting to and coping with a new world order. Moreover, each nation must develop considerable empathy and understanding with the dilemmas of other nations. As to reeducation, in these circumstances, Kennedy suggests:

> (E)ducation in the larger sense means more than technical "retooling" of the work force, or the emergence of professional classes, or even the encouragement of a manufacturing culture in the schools and colleges in order to preserve a productive base. It also implies a deep under-standing of why our world is changing, of how other people and cultures feel about those changes, of what we all have in common—as well as what divides cultures, classes, and nations...Because we are all members of a world citizenry, we also need to equip ourselves with a system of ethics, a sense of fairness, and a sense of proportion as we consider the various ways in which, collectively or individually, we can better prepare for the twenty-first century. (Kennedy, Ibid., p. 341).

We should ask our universities and colleges to take up Kennedy's challenge for radical reeducation. But in doing so, I point out, we shall have to ask them to over-come some of the downside of their considerable successes in globalizing advanced scientific and intellectual knowledge. I have no foolproof prescription, but I would only mention in conclusion several opportunities that could be explored.

First, we need to make more effective use of the large and intellectually rich influx of talented graduate students and research scholars to our universities and research laboratories. They are more than simply a reserve of technical labor to fill the gaps and deficiencies in our own national labor pool. They bring insights and novel constructions about their worlds—and importantly, about our own—that too infrequently are solicited for the enrichment of our students and ourselves.

Second, we should foster even greater international exchanges of scholars and more truly collaborative educational and training projects with counterpart foreign institutions. The emphasis in the past has presumed that the "other" has more to learn and gain than us. But if Kennedy is right, then we need to refocus our appreciation on what we can learn from them—and, on how we can promote the development of strong indigenous scholarship as a counterpart or counterpoint to that which we can offer in exchange.

Finally, we should find effective means of building international networks or teams of interdisciplinary scientists and scholars who can tackle the major problems of this and the coming century. No single nation possesses all of the world's most active and productive scholars and scientists in every field or on every topic. But the global scope, local complexity, and regional interdependencies of the problems we face are of such vital importance to our common welfare that we can no longer pretend that American science and technology—or for that matter, the expertise resident in any nation—will prevail. Again, problem finding is an important first step in problem solving, and that step in itself requires active engagement across national, regional and cultural settings to "see" the problem in its various manifestations and representations. America's universities, together with research institutions with international reach— such as the Social Science Research Council, the American Association for the Advancement of Science, and the National Academy of Science—must take leadership in promoting a more truly collaborative, co-constructed science than we have achieved hitherto. The attendant tasks are not easy, and they will run counter to our well-honed tendencies to export our own institutional and national expertise and to act on behalf of our own best interests. We shall have to overcome considerable cultural and intellectual "hubris," as David Easton puts it, if we are to rise to Kennedy's challenge for a radical reeducation of ourselves, our students and future leaders, and of higher education in preparation for the twenty-first century.✦

John Gallagher
Journalist

The most remarkable, and certainly the saddest, characteristic of the debate about higher education today is what is not being discussed: What is the purpose of higher education in society?

For 45 years, that question has not been debated. There have been countless arguments about core curricula and multiculturalism, the social responsibilities of research, access by minority students to colleges, the spiralling costs of education. The chasms on campus have been the subject of a seemingly endless stream of books and articles. At times it seems that there is hardly a question that has not been asked and answered at least a thousand times.

Except the most fundamental one of all: the question of a university's ultimate purpose. Does college exist to be an agent of social change? Is specialized research a reasonable extension of the belief that knowledge for its own sake ultimately, if indirectly, benefits society? How close a partnership should colleges have with government or with corporations?

Those questions could be answered more satisfactorily, if not more easily, if we knew what higher education was meant to do in society. But while society has changed, and the campus with it, the idea of higher education has not since the end of World War II when colleges, with the help of a Presidential commission, reinvented higher education to absorb unprecedented numbers of students for what the commission called "the self-protection of our democracy."

Since then, higher education has been rocked by enormous crises: the McCarthy era, the youth movement and Vietnam; the growing tension between teaching and research, unparalleled attacks from critics within the institutions themselves, the erosion of civilized discourse. Any one of these problems—let alone the combination of them—would have been sufficient to prompt a sweeping reevaluation of the academy's role in society. But none of them did.

Of course, educational leaders and professors have written copiously about the aims of higher education in the past four decades. However, and with virtually no exceptions, they have concentrated on a description of what they have found higher education already is. Sometimes the description is largely congratulatory, such as Clark Kerr's; at other times, the report sounds more like a jeremiad, such as the one delivered by Allan Bloom.

In these writings, so much time is spent delineating the present role of higher education in society that the more important matter—what is the proper role—is given short shrift. As each new book or article appears, it becomes increasingly clear that higher education has fallen short of its ideal.

But what is that ideal? By focusing on the condition of or abuses in higher education, the writers miss the larger point. "Abuses are always of minor importance," said Jose Ortega y Gassett about Spanish colleges in the 1930s. "For either they are abuses in the most natural sense of the word, namely, isolated, infrequent cases of departure from usage; or else they are so frequent and customary, so persistent and so generally tolerated, that they are no longer to be called abuses...It is something in the usage, the policy, and not the breach of it, which needs our attention."

We have had our attention called before to the problem of defining higher education's purpose. "[W]e found in our study great difficulty, sometimes to the point of paralysis, in defining essential purposes and goals," Ernest Boyer, president of the Carnegie Foundation for the Advancement of Teaching, said in *College: The*

Undergraduate Experience in America. Boyer's experience visiting a range of colleges led him to conclude that there was an urgent need for a constructive debate about the meaning of the undergraduate college.

There have been other invitations for debate, on all levels of higher education, to end the paralysis Boyer described. Howard Bowen called for "a larger vision of where higher education could and should be headed in the twenty-first century" so that educators could make decisions from a sound philosophical basis. Sadly, Bowen noted, "this part of the discourse on the place of higher education in American society is strangely and tragically missing."

Yet another call to debate met with no greater success, even though it came from one of higher education's most visible leaders, the late Yale President A. Bartlett Giamatti. In two speeches in 1987, Giamatti tried to rouse interest in the issue by candidly tracing the public's disillusionment with higher education to the academy's inability to define its purpose.

Said Giamatti: "We hear of the tactics and strategy for this institution or that, but rarely if ever of the nature and purpose of a college: What is it for? How is an academic institution different from a government or a for-profit corporation? Why is it important that a college or university be different? What is the price paid when those differences disappear? The most pressing need in higher education in the next ten years is not for management strategies. It is for debate on each campus, led by its leaders, as to what the purposes and goals of each campus are..." Six years later, the debate is even more overdue.

Higher education is lost in a dark wood. If it is ever to leave it, it will have to stop concentrating on how dark the wood is and consider instead what path it wishes to be on. It is only when it knows where it wants to go that it will finally be able to leave the wood behind.

Should Education Be Practical?

One of the longest-standing complaints about higher study is that the end product is too pedantic for society. As long ago as the Renaissance, Francis Bacon was condemning some education as "a kind of adoration of the mind...by means whereof men have withdrawn themselves too much from the contemplation of nature, and the observations of experience, and have tumbled up and down in their own reason and conceits." Knowledge, he continued, should "not be as a courtesan, for pleasure and vanity only, or as a bond-woman, to acquire and gain to her masters' use; but as a spouse, for generation, fruit and comfort."

While Bacon's imagery would hardly be used today, his sentiment is still current, prefiguring as it does the dismissive phrase "the ivory tower." Bacon raises the perpetual question: How practical should an education be?

That question is one of the fault lines running beneath higher education, with two great traditions pushing up against each other. One tradition argues that the pursuit of knowledge for its own sake creates fully-rounded men and women with sharp enough minds to succeed at anything they attempt. The other tradition contends that pursuit of practical knowledge, particularly the scientific, sharpens minds as effectively as the study of Greek and Latin, and addresses the broad needs of the people.

The earliest education leaders in this country were clear in their preference. Colleges were meant to be schools for the highest vocation. Cotton Mather said that the pious founders of Harvard foresaw that without "a nursery" for ministers, "darkness must have soon covered the land and gross darkness the people." William and Mary's Charter (1693) noted the need for the Church to "be furnished with a Seminary of Ministers of the Gospel" who would in turn educate American Indians "to the Glory of Almighty God." Yale's charter (1745) expanded the vocation somewhat to include "the service of God in the state as well as in church."

The founding of a Republic which separated Church and State did not lessen the practical considerations of higher education. In a report to the Commissioners for the University of Virginia, Thomas Jefferson listed first among the goals of the new institution the formation of "the statesmen, legislators and judges, on whom public prosperity and individual happiness are so much to depend." The university students are also expected "to harmonize and promote the interests of agriculture, manufactures and commerce."

Ironically, it took a cleric to offer a scathing dismissal of usefulness as a goal of higher education. "The Philosophy of Utility, you will say, Gentlemen, has at least done its work," said Cardinal John Newman in a lecture in 1852. "And I grant it— it aimed low, and it fulfilled its aim."

Newman proposed in its place an almost monastic ideal of the college, "a pure and clear atmosphere of thought." There the student would pursue a "Liberal Education," which would lead to "the true and adequate end of intellectual training," "Thought or Reason exercised upon Knowledge."

In other words: knowledge as its own end. For Newman, research was the work of other institutions, not the college. "If its object were scientific and philosophical discovery, I do not see why a University should have any students," he told his audience in Dublin. Instead, the university was to sharpen the minds of young men (the advancement of women not being among the ideas that Newman himself had cultivated). The goal was nothing less than understanding our intellectual tradition and the principles upon which it rested.

But there would be a practical benefit to such a process, Newman admitted: the training of good members of society. A university training, said Newman,

> ...aims at raising the intellectual tone of society, at cultivating the public mind, at purifying the national taste, at supplying true principles to popular enthusiasm and aims to popular aspiration, at giving enlargement and sobriety to the ideas of the age, at facilitating the exercise of political power, and refining the intercourse of private life. It is the education which gives a man a clear conscious view of his own opinions and judgments, a truth in developing them, an eloquence in expressing them, and a force in urging them. It teaches him to see things as they are, to go right to the point, to disentangle a skein of thought, to detect what is sophistical, and to discard what is irrelevant. It prepares him to fill any post with credit, and to master any subject with facility.

All this, because an educated man has acquired the highest skill of all. He can think clearly.

We are still grappling with Newman's exacting standards, or to put it more fancifully, we are haunted by Newman's ghost. Every discussion about the role of higher education has his spirit hovering in the background. From Robert Hutchins to Clark Kerr and Derek Bok, Newman's presence can be felt in the discussion of the aims of higher education. His forceful apologia for the intellectual life may embarrass us a little now because of its Victorian certainty but its appeal to our nobility still leaves us awestruck.

American academics in the early nineteenth century had set forth many of the principles that we now associate with Newman. In 1828, a committee of Yale faculty members produced a report in response to complaints from critics that its classical curriculum was impractical. It was nothing of the sort, the faculty argued. The purpose of the college was "to lay the foundation of a superior education," not to train someone for a career.

"'Everything throws light upon everything,'" the Yale report said. "The great object of a collegiate education, preparatory to the study of a profession, is to give that expansion and balance of the mental powers, those liberal and comprehensive views, and those fine proportions of character, which are not to be found in him whose ideas are always confined to one particular channel."

But even as the Yale Report and Newman were defending liberal education, the example of the German University was leading other scholars to propose a different purpose for higher education, one in which research, particularly scientific, was uppermost. Francis Wayland of Brown University told the University Corporation in 1850 that "Civilization is advancing, and it can only advance in the line of the useful arts." Andrew White, the first president of Cornell, organized that university around the advancement, not merely the conservation, of knowledge. In his inaugural address as president of Harvard, Charles Eliot, the first scientist to hold the position, called for more science and an elective system for courses.

Years after he helped shape the idea of the modern university, Daniel Coit Gilman, the first president of Johns Hopkins, which was itself the first great graduate school in the U.S., reflected on the state of higher education in the 1870s. "When this university began, it was a common complaint, still uttered in many places, that the ablest teachers were absorbed in routine and were forced to spend their strength in the discipline of tyros, so that they had no time for carrying forward their studies or for adding to human knowledge," he recalled.

As the first great graduate school in the U.S., Johns Hopkins set a new level for academic standards, investing not in magnificent buildings but in magnificent faculty. (Early Baltimoreans sometimes confused the university buildings with a local piano factory, according to John Brubacher and Willis Rudy.) The faculty had complete freedom to pursue whatever research they chose to, and Gilman often took a personal interest in their projects. Along with this "Lehrfreiheit," as the Germans called it, students were given a corresponding "Lernfreiheit" to choose what they wanted to study.

Within 30 years, the innovations forged at Johns Hopkins were considered the standard for the modern university. In the process, universities shifted their loyalty to research, while trying to maintain their respect for liberal education. The reorganization was not without pain. The animosity between the two branches was so great that, for example, at Yale scientific students were segregated from their classmates in chapel. So unlikely was the combination on campuses, said Christopher Jencks and David Riesman, that why it was even attempted is "one of the more puzzling questions about the evolution of higher education in this era."

In part, at least, the question was not voluntarily raised. The Morrill Act, passed by Congress in 1862, was a tremendous advance for applied science on the campus. The bill resulted in the creation of more than three dozen colleges devoted to agriculture and the mechanical arts, a practical application of proposed theory.

Since then, higher education has been caught in continuing debate about how it best serves society: through practical education or liberal education. Throughout the end of the nineteenth and beginning of the twentieth centuries, supporters of liberal education found themselves on the defensive, pointing out the dangers of practical education while watching their own influence wane.

There were, however, some attempts to unite the two ideas together in a single vision, most notably by Alfred North Whitehead. Unlike Newman, Whitehead readily conceded the importance of the "usefulness" in higher education. "Pedants sneer at an education which is useful," said Whitehead. "But if education is not useful, what is it? Is it a talent, to be hidden away in a napkin?"

Whitehead wanted to merge the research and teaching visions of the university and proposed a simple solution. "Do you want your teachers to be imaginative? Then encourage them to research. Do you want your researchers to be imaginative? Then bring them into intellectual sympathy with the young at the most eager, imaginative period of life, when intellects are just entering upon their mature discipline."

Yet, in key ways, Whitehead echoed Newman. "What education has to impart is an intimate sense for the power of ideas, for the beauty of ideas, and for the structure of ideas, together with a particular body of knowledge which has peculiar reference to the life of the being possessing it," said Whitehead some 70 years after Newman delivered his lectures.

Whitehead's sense of utility bore more than a passing resemblance to Newman's sense of liberal education. "Of course, education should be useful, whatever your aim in life," said Whitehead. "It is useful, because understanding is useful."

It is that understanding which is the goal of higher education. "The really useful training yields a comprehension of a few general principles with a thorough grounding in the way they apply to a variety of concrete details," said Whitehead. The student's ability to comprehend something other than facts, to be able to glimpse the sweep of ideas, matters more to Whitehead than anything else.

What the university is meant to do, said Whitehead, is cultivate a mental habit, "a principle that has thoroughly soaked into you." Whitehead suggested that it is almost a Pavlovian response; a mind that has been properly trained will respond with vigor and clarity when it is prodded into activity. (This is not sharpening the mind, as Newman might have argued, since Whitehead believes the mind is always active in any event.)

The mind reaches that state of fitness by understanding how ideas are all linked. Whitehead decried the fragmentation that classes often unwittingly create. Instead, he stressed the need to throw ideas into fresh context with one another, so that they can be seen in different ways and be tested.

But Whitehead did not automatically confine the cultivation of mental habits to the liberal arts. Speaking at a time when Harvard was preparing to open a Business School "on a scale amounting to magnificence," he justified the new enterprise as springing from a long-standing tradition.

"At no time have universities been restricted to pure abstract learning," Whitehead noted. But he also stressed that universities have an obligation to do more than just present facts. Indeed, that is their purpose in society.

"The justification for a university is that it preserves the connection between knowledge and the zest of life, by uniting the young and the old in the imaginative consideration of learning," said Whitehead. "The university imparts information, but it imparts it imaginatively. At least, this is the function which it should perform for society. A university which fails in this respect has no reason for existence." Thus, a business school could—indeed, should—tackle such diverse topics as geography, psychology and government, in order to bring together as originally as possible the practical matters with which a business executive might deal. (One wonders what Whitehead's response might be to the modern MBA program.)

Others were less impressed with the idea of professional education. "[T]here has also come an increasingly habitual inclination of the same uncritical character among academic men to value all academic work in terms of livelihood or earning capacity," Thorstein Veblen wrote in 1918. In 1930 Abraham Flexner, director of the Carnegie

Foundation, similarly blasted higher education for its high regard of usefulness. "Why do certain American universities feel themselves under pressure to develop their 'service' functions, even to call themselves 'public service' institutions?" Flexner asked. He concluded that it was because they need to feel useful, "And when I say useful, I mean directly, immediately useful, for Americans like to see results."

Inevitably, the rising tide of professionalism on campuses led to a crusade for correction. The crusade found its leader in Robert Hutchins, the president of the University of Chicago.

"Every group in the community wants the university to spare it the necessity of training its own recruits," he warned in 1936. "They want to get from the university a product as nearly finished as possible, which can make as large and as inexpensive a contribution as possible from the moment of graduation. This is a pardonable, perhaps even a laudable desire. But the effect of it on universities will be that soon everybody in a university will be there for the purpose of being trained for something."

Hutchins proposed a bold reorganization along the lines of the liberal tradition, so that students "will learn what has been done in the past, and what the greatest men have thought," a common knowledge that will unite them. The professional schools themselves would concentrate on theoretical concerns, a proposal also put forth by Flexner. (Veblen was more of a purist; he wanted to ban professional schools from the campus, in order to preserve the research integrity of graduate programs.) The practice for Hutchins' doctrine was to be found in the study of great books, books that are "contemporary in every age," the repository of rational wisdom. The point of the great books was not to stimulate mental exercise, such as Newman suggested. Rather, Hutchins was promoting the life of the mind as the ideal life.

John Dewey immediately criticized Hutchins for authoritarianism, a serious charge at a time when the threat from fascism was growing. "Basically his idea as to the proper course to be taken is akin to the distrust of freedom and the consequent appeal to *some* fixed authority that is now overrunning the world," Dewey said. "...President Hutchins' policy of reform by withdrawal from everything that smacks of modernity and contemporaneousness is not after all the road to the kind of intellectuality that will remedy the evils he so vividly depicts."

Hutchins' proposals did find some takers, although his attempts at reform at his own university (e.g., eliminating football, recruiting high school sophomores, allowing students to graduate on the basis of comprehensive exams and not credit hours) generated so much controversy that they did not outlive his tenure. But Hutchins, and his colleague Mortimer Adler, did generate a debate about what higher education was meant to do for society.

The debate was interrupted by World War II, but resumed as the war came to a close. A committee appointed by Harvard President James Bryant Conant surveyed the problems of higher education in the U.S., and concluded that the lack of "common ground of training and outlook" on campuses was working "against the common good of society."

One point about education was clear, the Report stated: "[I]t depends in part on an inherited view of man and society which it is the function, though not the only function of education, to pass on." The committee summed up that view as "the dignity of man" and the individual's "recognition of his duty to his fellow man."

The committee also noted the perils of specialization, stating that "a society controlled wholly by specialists is not a wisely ordered society," while at the same time noting that specialization had become the means of advancement in society. The issue facing higher education was how to reconcile specialization with general education, "to adapt general education to the needs and intentions of different groups and, so far as possible, to carry its spirit into special education." (Brubacher and Rudy pointed out that the Report did not address just how that might be done.)

The tone of the Harvard Report perfectly matches its era. "The dignity of man" nicely describes the animating principles behind the allied efforts to free Europe and rebuild it. But if the war influenced the tone of the report, it also influenced the shape of higher education. With the passage of the GI Bill, colleges found themselves flooded with veterans, an influx of new students unmatched in American history.

Realizing that the veterans were reshaping the profile of higher education, President Truman appointed a commission to reexamine the objectives and methods of higher education in the U.S. The resulting six-volume report, issued in 1947 and 1948, provided a new rationale for admissions, urging the removal of any barriers that restricted access to a college education, whether it be race, economic background or even academic past. Any qualified individual should have the opportunity to go to college. To accommodate the new students, more faculty and more colleges would be in order.

But just as importantly, the Commission provided a clear statement of higher education's role in society. "The social role of education in a democratic society is at once to insure equal liberty and equal opportunity to differing individuals and groups, and to enable the citizens to understand, appraise, and redirect forces, men, and events as they tend to strengthen or to weaken their liberties," the Commission stated. The group assigned higher education three explicit goals: "education for a fuller realization of democracy in every phase of living," "education directly and explicitly for international understanding and cooperation," and "the application of creative imagination and trained intelligence to the solution of social problems and to the administration of public affairs."

Moreover, the Commission underscored the need for General Education. "The failure to provide any core of unity in the essential diversity of higher education is a cause for grave concern," the Commission noted. "A society whose numbers lack a body of common experience and common knowledge is a society without a fundamental culture; it tends to disintegrate into a mere aggregation of individuals." A core of common learning would give a student "the values, attitudes, knowledge, and skills that will equip him to live rightly and well in a free society."

The 28-member commission, headed by George Zook, president of the American Council on Education, was criticized for advocating the decline of academic standards to allow for more college students. Hutchins, who said the report "reads like a Fourth-of-July oration in Pedaguese," denounced its faith in improving the American populace by opening higher education to more students, since he believed the educational system offered no real direction to the students it already had.

Criticisms aside, the Commission's findings, coupled with the Harvard Report, sparked extensive debate in the higher education community, since they both were proposing nothing less than the reorganization of the principles upon which higher education rested. The Commission report, in particular, gave individuals a chance to examine specific goals in society for higher education and consider whether or not they were fitting. It was virtually the last time the debate focused on what higher education should do instead of how bad things are.

The Present Confusion

In 1964, Clark Kerr, Chancellor of the University of California, Berkeley, published a series of lectures delivered the year before on the state of the university or, as Kerr preferred to term it, the multiversity. His book, *The Uses of the University,* is a remarkable work, for while it is often a celebration of the condition of higher education, it became the target of severe criticism for its parade of overconfident, unstated and even offensive assumptions, often about the relationship between the university and current government policies.

To be fair to Kerr, he had ample precedent for his beliefs. In a speech titled "Princeton in the Nation's Service," Woodrow Wilson, then a professor of jurisprudence and political economy, said that ultimately "it is not learning but the spirit of service that will give a college a place in the public annals of the nation." Wilson emphasized that he did not mean party politics but instead "the air of the world's transactions, the consciousness of the solidarity of the race, the sense of duty of man toward man, of the presence of men in every problem," which require that "the school must be of the nation." (In fact, the first six American presidents believed in a national university and had urged its creation.)

Moreover, Kerr was writing at the peak of American certainty in the nation's goodness, when unimpeded progress stretched itself out on a limitless horizon. It was not a notable time for qualms. Doubt would follow later.

Kerr reflected that serene self-assurance. The university, he believed, could tackle any problem. "So many of the hopes and fears of the American people are now related to our educational system and particularly to our universities—the hope for longer life, for getting into outer space, for a higher standard of living; our fears of Russian and Chinese supremacy, of the bomb and annihilation, of individual loss of purpose in the changing world," he wrote. "For all these reasons and others, the university has become a prime instrument of national purpose."

It was not an especially unified instrument. Kerr acknowledged the pull of conflicting interests, kept in check by a wise administrator. "A university anywhere can aim no higher than to be as British as possible for the sake of the undergraduates, as German as possible for the sake of the graduates and the research personnel, as American as possible for the sake of the public at large—and as confused as possible for the sake of the preservation of the whole uneasy balance," he remarked.

Kerr presented knowledge as a kind of universal commodity, with the university as prime purveyor. Knowledge "is wanted, even demanded by more people and more institutions than ever before," Kerr boasted. "The university as producer, wholesaler and retailer of knowledge cannot escape service. Knowledge, today, is for everybody's sake."

But most of all, it was for the sake of the nation, "a component part of the 'military-industrial complex.'" The federal government's commitment to higher education, through the funding of key research projects, has already contributed much to knowledge, and will only contribute more.

Kerr may seem like a federal apologist, but he was noteworthy more for his optimism than for his point of view. The university in the nation's employ has been a theme of more than one scholar in the past four decades. Bowen lists ten economic, political, and social problems facing the nation, ranging from unemployment to pressure-group democracy, and stresses the necessity of higher education to address them.

But the most prominent proponent of the university in national service is former Harvard President, Derek Bok. Almost 30 years after Kerr wrote, Bok matter-of-factly accepted the close relationship between government and university although, like Kerr, he has serious reservations about the federal influence on universities. In general, Bok was firmer than Kerr about the need for academic independence. But about the basic requirements of higher education in society, Bok was in no doubt.

"Serving society is only one of higher education's functions, but it is surely among the most important," noted Bok. "At a time when the nation has its full share of difficulties, therefore, the question is not whether universities need to concern themselves with society's problems but whether they are discharging this responsibility as well as they should."

Some of that responsibility is in making sure that the country is getting something for all of its money. Professors receive over $6 billion annually in research and development funds, said Bok, to say nothing of state funding. "How could faculties possibly expect to go on receiving such support from the nation's taxpayers without making efforts to respond to society's needs?" he wondered.

If anything, Bok suggested, universities aren't doing enough for society. "Again and again, universities have put a low priority on the very programs and initiatives that are needed most to increase productivity and competitiveness, improve the quality of government, and overcome the problems of illiteracy, miseducation, and unemployment," he wrote.

Hutchins despised the point of view that Kerr and Bok embraced." [T]he American university is supposed to assist in the solution of any current practical problem that anybody has," Hutchins lamented. "And when there is money in it, and good public relations in it, the fact that the project runs counter to the purpose of the university, which is to pursue knowledge for its own sake, does not make the lure of such work any easier to resist. The purpose of the university has long since been changed; it is now regarded as a service station for the community."

Robert Paul Wolf, a philosophy professor at Columbia, was hardly more charitable when he criticized the philosophy in 1969. "When Kerr speaks repeatedly of the multiversity's responsiveness to national needs, he is describing nothing more than its tendency to adjust itself to effective demand in the form of government grants, scholarship programs, corporate or alumni underwriting, and so forth," Wolf charged. "But his language encourages the reader to suppose that the demands to which the multiversity responds are expressions of genuine human and social needs, needs which make a moral claim upon the effort and attention of the academy." In fact, said Wolf, there is a significant difference between the real needs of society and the market demands of the nation.

More recently, Page Smith has said that by allying with the military-industrial complex, the universities "sold their souls." The latest wrinkle in that Faustian bargain, the university-corporate contract for research, led Smith to write that what higher education is pursuing "with far more dedication than the truth is big bucks."

Bok fell into the same trap as Kerr, failing to make the distinction between society and the nation while extolling worthy goals. Is the nation the government? The public? Some combination of the two? Is society different from both of them? Exactly whose interests the university is supposed to represent is never entirely clear.

Others have been more cautious. "We need concerned people who are participants in inquiry, who know how to ask the right questions, who understand the process by which public policy is shaped, and are prepared to make informed, discriminating judgments on questions that affect the future," said Boyer. "To fulfill this urgent obligation, the perspective needed is not only national, but global."

Newman offered a similarly broad view. "There is a duty we owe to human society as such, to the state to which we belong, to the sphere in which we move, to the individuals towards whom we are variously related, and whom we successively encounter in life," he said.

The practical application of research had its philosophical complement in the professional schools, where students could be trained to meet the specific needs of the marketplace, and whose very presence served as an irritant to those who saw higher education as the center of knowledge, not vocationalism.

It was a long-standing complaint. "Some great men...insist that Education should be confined to some particular and narrow end, and should issue in some definite work, which can be weighed and measured," Newman said. "There is a conflict between one aim of the university, the pursuit of truth for its own sake, and another which it professes too, the preparation of men and women for their life and work," Hutchins said. Barzun ridiculed the idea that there could be such an animal as a professor of "effective living."

But Riesman and Jencks provided an important caveat. "In almost any discussion of higher education, whether with professors, students or the general public, somebody is likely to put forward the idea that the nation's colleges have been corrupted by vocationalism," they wrote. "In the good old days, it will be argued, colleges were pure and undefiled seats of learning...Like other pastoral idylls, this myth serves all sorts of polemical purposes, good and bad. But it is a myth nonetheless."

Student activists in the 1960s took the idea of vocationalism one step further, describing universities as factories producing Establishment men. "The customers for this product are the corporations, government agencies, foundations, military services, and universities whose destructive, repressive, antisocial activities demand an ever-larger supply of loyal and unquestioning workers," Wolf said in summarizing the activists' argument.

Wolf himself believed that any institution tied too closely to the government loses its ability to criticize the government when it is wrong. That is an argument often also used by the student activists of the 1960s against higher education. Pointing to colleges' connections to a government waging a war they believed was unjust, the activists accused higher education of being an active part of the military machine. (Kerr's ebullient recognition of the bond between campus and government did not serve him well in this regard at Berkeley.)

Implicit in the students' fiery accusations was another kind of societal role for higher education: reformer of a society gone bad. Jencks and Riesman, and Brubacher and Rudy, insisted that at least the early student protests were not aimed at the academic profession, but were directed at society at large.

"What students are saying, in their somewhat incoherent way, is that they no longer have any confidence in government, politics, business, industry, labor, the church, for all of these are hopelessly corrupt," said Henry Steele Commager. "Only the university is left. Clearly it is corrupt, too, but not hopelessly; it can still be saved and if it is saved, it can be made into an instrument to reform the whole society."

In an odd way, the students seemed to believe in the university as a pure and clear atmosphere, much as Newman had hoped it would be, free from the exigencies of the outside world. But, at the same time, the students seemed to have as great a faith in the power of the university to improve society as Kerr did. It was the definition of "improve" that differed. Whereas Kerr saw the university as an agent for national progress, protesters saw it as an agent for social change. Unfortunately, the formulation of higher education philosophy, including a considered appraisal of past traditions, was never really a goal of protesters. To the extent that they relied on a philosophy at all, they usually turned to Marxist principles, a revolutionary approach out of character with higher education's distinctly evolutionary nature.

Not everyone believed that the changes that the students sought were for the better. Bloom, for one, said flatly that nothing good came from the sixties. For him it was a time when civilized discourse, respect for the law and academic standards all fled the campus because of the capitulation of milquetoast professors and administrators. Wolf, a self-described leftist, foresaw in the use of higher education for political ends the demise of the academic enterprise.

The two men were not alone in their views. Commager described the student protests as "the most reckless attack upon academic freedom in our history." Sidney Hook warned that the student ideal of higher education as societal reformer would only imperil the independence of institutions and lead to "retaliatory curbs and controls."

But Hook, along with Jacques Barzun, was not a defender of the multiversity. Any attempt to turn higher education into a social service organization filled them with dread; in many ways they were harsher in their criticism of higher education than the students they attacked.

"Let us recall the provinces from which [the university] has abdicated," said Barzun. "The unity of knowledge; the desire and power to teach; the authority and skill to pass judgment on what claims to be knowledge, to be a universalist, to be a scholar, to be a basic scientist; finally, the consciousness of what is properly academic—a consciousness which implies the right to decline alike: commercial opportunity, service assignments for industry, the administering of social welfare, and the bribes, flattery, or dictation of any self-seeking group."

In fact, Hook in particular was a long-time critic of higher education's "deficiencies as an instrument of liberal education," echoing Newman and Hutchins, although giving liberal education Dewey's twist of pragmatism.

Liberal education's emphasis on the great texts of the past, even given a contemporary gloss, did not sit well with students demanding relevance, the students' own version of practicality. But their objections did not deter Bowen, who explicitly linked liberal education to practical needs. "A revival of liberal learning for both young people and adults may be an effective means of reorienting the values that propel our economy and our government," he said. "It is only as we improve our people that we can hope to improve our society."

By the time Bowen made his argument in 1980, the skirmishes over the issue had died down for a while, but they emerged with fresh vehemence in the mid-1980s in the debate over the core curriculum, particularly as it reflected Western Civilization. The core had staunch defenders, who relied on arguments set out by Hutchins, Hook, the Harvard Report—all the way back to Newman, though without Newman's emphasis on mental exercise.

"It might seem obvious that all students should be knowledgeable about texts that have formed the foundations of the society in which they live," said Lynne Cheney, director of the National Endowment for the Humanities. "But opponents argue that those works, mostly written by a privileged group of white males, are elitist, racist, and sexist."

In fact, says Page Smith, they are probably right, and the insistence on Western Civilization courses is only hypocritical. The university doesn't have "the human resources to do a decent job (a fact now proved over almost a century)," he claimed. "It can never be done properly, and thus shouldn't be done at all until the university has had a change of heart and becomes, in fact as well as name, a universe-ity, a genuine universe of learning."

There is a sense in which the core curriculum is the antithesis of social activism, harkening back to the debate over knowledge for its own sake rather than the efficacy of applied (now social) research.

"American colleges and universities are quick to proclaim their duty to address all sorts of things that are wrong in the world, to speak truth to power, to discourse on the most complex social and moral issues beyond their walls, and to instruct political and business and religious leaders on the proper path to follow," argued William Bennett while he was Secretary of Education. "But they have a prior duty, which is to see to the education of the young people in their charge."

Cheney made the point more explicitly. "Teaching becomes a form of political activism, with texts used to encourage students, in the words of one professor, to 'work against the political horrors of one's time,'" she said.

In fact, teaching as a form of activism is probably the most widely, if not most accurately, documented aspect of the current debate in higher education. The most compelling—to say nothing of lurid—of the reports, by Dinesh D'Souza, went so far as to state that the courses consciously promote a negative image of anyone who is white, heterosexual, and male, resulting in an education "in closed-mindedness and intolerance."

D'Souza, Bennett, and Cheney all pointed to the study of the classics as a way of promoting common understanding. Bloom went so far as to call for the return of Hutchins' Great Books scheme, although he clearly does not expect to see anyone follow his suggestion. Others, such as E.D. Hirsch, argued that not only will the classics help students formulate their own values, they will provide a grounding in facts and beliefs that every educated person should know.

Whitehead, however, was wary of the need for lists. "Whatever be the detail with which you cram your student, the chance of his meeting in after-life exactly that detail is almost infinitesimal; and if he does meet it, he will probably have forgotten what you taught him about it," he said. Better for the student to have acquired a spirited mind than a list of facts. More in keeping with Whitehead's belief in the need to link information imaginatively is Boyer's proposal for an "integrated" core, seven themes that cut across the curriculum.

But Boyer's proposal faced an enormous hurdle: the increased specialization in higher education. The freedom under Gilman's standard to pursue research freely has become, by all admissions, a cross of gold upon which faculty are crucified. Instead of a pleasure, research has become a duty. And the research must be original. "We built our universities on the Germanic model with our own particularly nasty twist, the added insistence that universities be judged in terms of their productive output," said George Douglas.

Thus, Gilman's goal of advancing society's knowledge has, in Barzun's word, been "preposterized." "Since the Second World War, as everybody knows, the mania has become endemic: everybody shall produce written research in order to live, and it shall be decreed a knowledge explosion," Barzun wrote. "An explosion it may be, of print and paper pulp, but the knowledge is extensively imaginary."

Cheney found that the explosion is made up of increasingly narrow pieces of research, with no professional incentive to break away. "There is still little vocational encouragement for a scholar to undertake the general investigations that can give pattern and purpose to specialized studies," she said. Indeed, there is substantial reason not to undertake such an investigation. Julius Getman detailed several cases in which tenure was denied to professors whose work was deemed too broad or popular to be "academic."

In fact, the descriptions seem to harken back to the confusion that Kerr described. But now the balance seems to be more lacking than ever. "There is an extraordinary gap between the rhetoric and the reality of American higher education," said Bennett. "The gap is so wide, in fact, that we face the real possibility—not today, perhaps not tomorrow, but someday—of an erosion of public support for the enterprise." It follows that if the gap is so great, then perhaps the rhetoric, and the principles upon which it rest, need to be reevaluated. "From time to time, it's not a bad idea to look at what's really going on, and to ask some hard questions," said Bennett. Unfortunately, the combative tone of some of his questions made them sound more like declarations of war than an attempt to address the philosophical issues.

Fragments Against the Ruins

In the past 25 years, writers have spent a great deal of time surveying the ruins of higher education. As long ago as Kerr, the cracks were evident. The more thoughtful analysts, such as Boyer, have noted that there is still much to celebrate, especially the commitment of many professors to educating undergraduates. But the steady stream of books published in the last seven years that describe a riven, fragmented, politicized campus with few if any commonalities leaves no doubt as to the extent of the problems.

What those reports from the front (which is how Bloom characterized his book) do not do is address in a detailed, comprehensive and equitable way the fundamental question of the role higher education is meant to play in society. "Without a coherent notion of what a university is for—some idea of what it should be and do—we cannot possibly evaluate existing universities," said Wolff.

Wolff did make an effort to rethink the university's purpose in society. It was, he concluded, "a community of learning...a community of persons united by collective understandings, by common and communal goals, by bonds of reciprocal obligation, and by a flow of sentiment which makes the preservation of the community an object of desire, not merely a matter of product or a command of duty." It served society best as a center of free inquiry, where scholars could transmit their knowledge to students and further rational discourse.

Wolff's ideal led him to some debatable conclusions. He considered a Catholic university to be "a strict contradiction in terms" because its adherence to doctrine prevented free inquiry. He considered the presence of professional schools to be so inimical to the pursuit of knowledge that he would sever their connection to the university, a move that Flexner also considered. But, as impractical as some of his ideas may sound, Wolff addressed the problems directly and proposed systemic solutions based on a stated ideal of the university's role in society. It is a claim too few can make.

Bowen proposed some questions that higher education needs to ask: "What kind of people do we want our children and grandchildren to be? What kind of society do we want them to live in? How may higher education be guided and shaped to help nurture people of this kind and to help create this kind of society?" He noted that higher education has increasingly relied on "bread-and-butter" arguments to justify its role in society, while downplaying the long-term educational benefits to society.

The debate Bowen envisioned would require a unified effort on the part of the higher education community, something that higher education has never been good at, he admitted. "But the crisis is severe enough, and the basic principles of academic freedom and liberal learning are sufficiently threatened that joint action is surely called for," he said.

Bowen also provided an important corrective to many of the reports on the problems of higher education, from Wolff on. He made efforts to include the range of institutions. By contrast, other reports are often skewed by their attention to the most visible institutions for examples of the problems. Those institutions are not representative of higher education as a whole, as indeed no small sampling would be. They are usually prestigious research universities. You are far more likely to read about Harvard than you are about San Jose State or the College of New Rochelle, to say nothing of any junior or community college.

Yet the students, faculty and administrators at those institutions are as much a part of higher education as their peers in the Ivy League. They bring an entirely different perspective to the debate, one that has, for the most part, been missing. Since many of those institutions were created as a result of the last great reorganization of higher education, their omission is especially glaring. While different institutions may ultimately arrive at different conclusions as to what role they should play in society, they all must engage in the same debate in order to establish their shared values and not merely the ones they do not share.

The debate clearly can no longer be delayed. The current stalemate has resulted in an educational system that is so divided in its aims and so confused in its direction that its benefits to society and to itself are dwindling. Giamatti put it eloquently:

American colleges and universities do not play the role in our society as centers for independent thought, for the open pursuit of truth, for the protection of minority or dissenting or critical views— they do not serve America—when they mimic governmental institutions or private businesses or allow themselves to be simply holding pens for competing dogmas. American colleges and universities serve neither themselves nor the country if they are unsure of their own principles and purposes or if they cannot convey them to the people at large. The deepest need is for the permanent parts of the place—the members of the faculty and the administration—to reforge common aims, to establish again a common set of goals and values, to lay aside the mistrust that corrodes the capacity to educate the young and to discover and share new knowledge, and to speak to the public of the nature and purpose of education.

Giamatti wanted to see the resurrection of higher education as "free and ordered spaces, for those who live there, for the country at large." His ideal is one that few would disagree with. If it is ever to be realized, we will have to reconsider the most fundamental principles. It is an examination with a single question, from which all others flow: what does society need from higher education? ⋏

Phillip A. Griffiths
Director, Institute for Advanced Study

In the decades following World War II, our universities became the envy of the world, the crown jewels of an educational system nurtured by a proud nation and a supportive government. Today, we see abundant evidence that this pride and this support are being sharply questioned. In the words of one leading educator, our universities are criticized for costing too much, spending carelessly, teaching poorly, planning myopically, and, when questioned, acting defensively.

It is difficult, and in some instances impossible, to refute these assertions, but that is not our task here. Instead, I would like to propose several concrete steps that the universities can—and, I think, must—take if they are to retain their primacy in the universe of education.

First, the research-intensive universities must refocus their mission on education. For four decades they have struggled to maintain a dual mission of education and research. In practice, however, education has faded to secondary status. The research grant is the badge of honor. The professor who devotes primary energy and creativity to teaching is de facto penalized, and often looked down upon by peers.

Society has accepted several justifications for this. One is the common belief that the fruits of research can only reach the marketplace by a linear progression from basic research to applied research to development to production. This places "pure" or basic research done on university campuses and supported by government money but free of government interference in an exalted position.

Today we know that this justification is a myth. The process of innovation is not linear but much more complex. It involves feedback loops, the integration of effort, and a balance of basic and applied research. We have also learned that while the best basic research usually turns out to be useful, so does the best applied research— whether performed under university, corporate, or government auspices. In the face of a skeptical Congress and public, it is hubris to argue that the university is the only seedbed for seminal ideas.

If universities focused on their mission of education, on the other hand, they could properly justify excellent research as both supporting that mission and creating new knowledge. For example, the need to expose young scientists and engineers to good research is obvious. Most of them will work in industry, where they must be equipped with state-of-the-art concepts and techniques.

Second, universities must streamline their operations. Our universities are overextended. Administrations are bloated, curricula have lost coherence, faculty are overburdened.

Streamlining must begin in the administration. It has been my observation that a president or provost is easily "captured" by staff and by competing constituencies, thus losing touch with the everyday life of the institution. The university president, in particular, is prey to a preposterous number of constituencies: faculty, students, trustees, federal and state governments, local communities, foundation officers, alumni and other potential donors, sports fans, parents. If the primary mission of the university is to educate, the president's true constituencies are two: faculty and students. No president can adequately serve these two while entertaining alumni, lobbying the statehouse, negotiating with unions, supporting athletic teams. All these functions must be done, but other people can do them.

A president's energy must be channeled toward articulating the institution's mission and leading the faculty in a discussion of how best to fulfill that mission. The faculty that has been invited into the resource allocation process, for example, is much more likely to see the necessity of reform and to initiate reforms themselves. A faculty invited into leadership is more willing to consider new ways, to think institutionally rather than departmentally, and to make a real commitment to undergraduate education.

I will offer one success story. The Stanford Faculty Senate Committee—not the administration—has written: "Stanford must become more agile in responding to new challenges and changing priorities. We must encourage and reward creative thinking, innovation, initiative, and responsible risk-taking."

Trustees, too, must push to streamline administration and define the parameters within which administration and faculty operate. Again, in my observation, trustees face an even greater risk than presidents and provosts of being captured and insulated by upper-level administration. They must press past this temptation and force the institution to define and carry out its mission.

Once streamlining has begun, administrators, faculty and trustees can begin to seek improvements in educational productivity. They can try to reconcile the best corporate management principles (efficiency, adaptability, customer orientation) with academic freedom and culture. Both the public and the Congress are clamoring for a better educational "product," and the universities must find ways to provide it—before "solutions" are imposed from without.

Third, the universities must differentiate the academic universe into the programs they deem most important. Traditionally, the largest universities compete with each other on every front, department by department, seeking priority in the decadal National Research Council's rankings of graduate departments. This has meant great duplication of effort for our educational system as a whole.

My own field of mathematics provides an illustration of how universities can better focus their efforts. At the turn of the century there were half a dozen research and Ph.D.-granting math departments; today there are well over 150, all competing for the same faculty stars and graduate students. A recent NRC study suggested a plan for differentiation. Some schools, said the study, can continue to train young mathematicians for pure research; others can train them to teach in four-year colleges; others can offer the engineering-oriented math required by industry; still others can focus on applications of mathematics to other sciences, offering joint degrees like Mathematics and Engineering. Such differentiation would help strengthen teaching, broaden the rewards system, and allow more effective use of constrained financial resources.

Fourth, universities must better adapt to current trends toward the integration of knowledge. The traditional academic disciplines have more in common with medieval guilds than modern task forces; they even reproduce themselves through the apprentice system of graduate students. The reward structure and loyalty of faculty are linked to the discipline rather than to the institution.

As one who spent many years in a traditional discipline, I appreciate its many positive benefits; the frontiers of disciplinary knowledge are being pushed far. But today we acknowledge that problems of the real world don't fit the boundaries of traditional disciplines. We need systematic, integrated approaches if we are to care for the environment, devise affordable and accessible health care, design competitive manufacturing. These challenges call for systematic solutions: synchronous combinations of specialties.

Already, government funding agencies have begun to favor a systems approach to society's problems. Interagency initiatives, featuring multi-disciplinary themes, are beginning to drive our research system—whether the universities are ready or not.

Finally, universities must seek ways to integrate the professional schools into other programs, especially the undergraduate colleges. Faculty in business, medical, law and divinity schools have much to offer undergraduates, and in my experience they welcome the opportunity. But internal financial structures create artificial barriers between the wealthier professional schools and the undergraduate colleges. Imaginative thinking can remove these barriers.

I hope that the universities can regain the trust of not only the public but also of their most important constituencies, the faculty and students of which they are composed. It behooves all of us with a stake in education to speak out during this period of evaluation and transition. The legislators who authorize funds and the industries who employ graduates are listening with the greatest interest.

I believe that the challenge before our universities is to emerge from this decade more focused on teaching, more socially relevant and able to focus efforts on selected areas of excellence. I also believe that if they fail to meet this challenge, they risk the continued erosion of support from the paying public and from the students who come to them for education. ⚲

Antonia Hernandez
President, Mexican American Legal Defense amd Education Fund

In these times of rapid, lasting change, what society needs most from higher education is for its leaders and institutions to change with the times. I will focus primarily on what has been my personal and professional mission for the past two decades—to expand the opportunities of Latinos to participate fully in American society and to make a positive contribution towards its well-being—and offer my insight on approaches higher education must consider as it strives to meet the needs of present day society.

The focus of this change in higher education must occur on two broad fronts. First, barriers that reduce Latino access to, and success in, postsecondary educational institutions must be removed. And second, the curriculum offered by colleges and universities must be one that ensures both academic success and placement in the workplace, while reflecting a multi-cultural, multi-ethnic America, offering an agenda that promotes and values diversity. At the same time it must promote those values that hold us together as a people.

Despite our steady rise in this nation's numbers, Latino participation in higher education remains comparatively, discouragingly low. While we are rapidly effecting the demographics of this country, thereby altering the face of America, higher education has not kept pace.

In contrast to the need for well-prepared Latino students is the actual representation of Latinos in higher education. As of 1991, 40 percent of Anglos who graduated from high school were enrolled in institutions of higher education, compared to only 31.4 percent of Latinos. Moreover, 36.8 percent of Anglos between the ages of 18 and 24 were enrolled, compared to only 17.8 percent of Latinos.

As of 1990, there were approximately 6,756,800 Anglo students enrolled in institutions of higher education, compared to 344,500 Latinos. As of 1989-90, only 32,686 Latinos were conferred bachelor's degrees compared to 882,996 Anglos.

The obvious would be to increase those numbers. Higher education, however, continues to place barriers that prevent many of our growing ethnic populations from taking full advantage of the services it has to offer. Those communities, and again I speak primarily of the Latino community, are striving to make the inroads needed to enter the ranks of higher education. There is a traditional value placed on education, both as a way of bettering one's economic well-being and as a way of giving back to the community. But increasingly, those opportunities—in the community college level, in state colleges and universities, and in private universities—are being placed out of reach.

Beginning at the elementary and secondary school levels, Latino students need to feel that access to higher education is within their grasp. Ask a kindergarten class to raise their hands if they intend to go to college and a roomful of children will reach for the sky. From that early age they recognize the importance of continuing their education to the ultimate. But as these same students progress in the public school system, many become discouraged due to the declining quality and quantity of resources available to them. They will either drop out or settle for less challenging career paths. Major state universities and other systems of higher learning must be encouraged to use their resources to work with school systems and individual students, to ensure that education received from kindergarten to the twelfth grade is of a quality that will lead to the increase of the pool of college-bound Latinos.

But even those students who strive to complete the requirements necessary to enter higher education face obstacles, as university systems effect major changes in admission requirements without any effort to ensure that students in poor and minority secondary schools be in a position to meet the elevated standards. Also, the increasing use of standardized tests affects the ability of students to enroll in institutions of higher learning and to continue in a particular major. Incidence of test abuse and misuses must be eliminated, especially if they prevent willing students from entering the higher educational system.

Rising costs, beginning at the community college level, are keeping higher education out of reach to all but the most financially fortunate. These increasing costs make it impossible for Latino families to send their children to school. Financial support and flexibility must occur. Higher education must understand that students need help to financially plan their education. While there continues to be a need in making financial aid—in the form of grants, scholarships and loans—more readily available, learning experiences must also be built into workstudy programs, to teach students responsibility and leadership skills.

At the present time, Latino taxpayers are subsidizing high quality graduate and professional programs that their own children do not participate in. Disparities in post-secondary systems exist where Latinos are concentrated. For many, the only higher education opportunities existing in their communities are those that are funded at minimal levels, with limited resources and narrow program choices. Also, those systems are often devoid of graduate and professional programs. To ensure equality and opportunity, per-pupil expenditures in higher education resources—between community colleges and universities and between diverse geographical areas and communities—must be reformed.

A related priority is the needed enhancement regarding the transfer of students from community colleges to four-year colleges and universities. With the vast majority of Latinos enrolled initially in community colleges (in California in excess of 85 percent) and with fewer than 600 Blacks and Latinos combined transferring from the community colleges to the University of California, transfer continues to present one of the most critical issues in higher education for Latinos. Strategies must be developed to ensure transferable curriculum, dissemination of information about transfer, transferability of financial aid, and maintenance of upper division places in universities for transfer students.

That brings to mind the issues and concerns I have regarding the curriculum offered and the support services available to students once they have achieved placement in institutions of higher learning. Getting into a college or university of one's choice is a great challenge. Staying and succeeding is an even bigger one.

What I see as necessary for higher education to meet the needs of society are: programs and services designed to help students develop habits and attitudes that lead to academic success; assistance for students in overcoming those barriers that are in the way of success; help for students to acquire learning that will meet the changing needs of employers; and full use of our rich cultural diversity as a catalyst for learning.

First of all, Latino students must receive assistance in achieving the competency that they need, not to be punished for not having it. Competencies in writing, reading, and mathematics, as well as study skills such as note-taking and the use of the library, must be enhanced. Those academic building blocks, which many Latino students lack, are the foundation for academic success.

Latino students also need to be assured that they are seen as individuals, not just bodies taking up space. Continual assessment of these students, with instructors, counselors, and peers tracking such items as class attendance, work habits, and comprehension of subject matter, needs to take place. Students need feedback and continued assessment of their response to the pressures of achieving higher education, to be aware of their progress so they can either stay on track or make the necessary adjustments.

The curriculum offered in institutions of higher learning need to reflect the changing needs of employers. As high technology continues to permeate all areas of the workplace, Latino students need to be made aware of the opportunities offered in the areas of science, mathematics, and engineering. Because of the continued increase in our numbers, Latinos will take on a larger, more vital position in the workplace to ensure the support of the infrastructure and to safeguard America's leadership in the global economy, Latinos must be trained and placed in positions of responsibility in high technology industries.

There is a need to interweave a foundation of multiculturality, an awareness that we live in a world of increasing ethnic and cultural diversity. Educators must be prepared to understand this multicultural society and speak to the needs of Latino students and those from other cultural and linguistic backgrounds. Courses need to be more reflective of multicultural concepts. One of the important issues is for students to see themselves in the courses they are studying, while encouraging students to learn from each other about their different cultures. There needs to be a proper balance between free speech and an environment free of radical and ethnic harassment.

Lastly, I sense that as in American society in general, the populations of our institutions of higher learning are becoming disconnected from each other, too separatist in their thinking and too parochial in their views. This kind of fragmentation harms efforts to meet the issues facing society as a whole. Our colleges and universities represent an opportunity to create an environment where the whole world is represented, where by virtue of the ethnic and racial diversity in the student population, it can be demonstrated that people can live, learn and work together in a demonstration of common values—to protect the individual freedoms we cherish, while giving great value to characteristics that enable individuals to show compassion and empathy, and to feel responsible for the condition of others.

While the issues I have raised are many, they are not beyond reach. The barriers mentioned that prevent the higher education needs of Latinos from being met are being addressed from without. I hope that the changes in the learning mechanisms are being addressed from within.

If colleges and universities do not meet those challenges, they will lose the public's trust. Society will not continue to support higher education if it feels that its benefits and services are available only to a select few.✦

Thomas R. Horton
University Advisor, Stetson University

Throughout its history, America has benefited from the contributions of its colleges and universities. Indeed, in many ways American society has been shaped by such contributions. The nation's work force has been constantly replenished, through new college graduates and opportunities for lifelong learning; scientific breakthroughs and important medical findings have flowed from university laboratories; new practitioners of the highest standards have streamed into the professions, many of whose practicing members have availed themselves of advanced training. Most important, much of the nation's intellectual leadership, and some of its moral leadership, have sprung from the academy. Against this background, perhaps the question is "What *else* does society need from higher education?" Still, there is an even more urgent question: How can society help higher education to maintain its capacity to provide such needs?

A quarter century has passed since the establishment in 1967 of the Carnegie Commission on Higher Education, and two decades have elapsed since the Commission sounded its alarms and made its recommendations. What has occurred during those years? Most important, what has happened to the relationship between American higher education and society? Although the "system" (or, more accurately, the amazingly diverse assortment of institutions) of higher education is today facing unprecedented challenges, it remains the envy of the world, a brilliant jewel in the American crown. Regrettably, this jewel appears to have lost some of its luster in the eyes of the public here at home. Do institutions of higher education still hold the special place in the hearts and minds of our citizenry that they once held? If so, does this preferred place still cause society's heartstrings to resonate sufficiently to affect its purse strings? The needs resulting from today's economic pressures on the academy spill over to a society sorely pressed by other needs. During the current and persistent period of economic doldrums, every kind of institution is engaged in downsizing and other drastic cost-cutting measures to assure their survival. Meanwhile, individual citizens try to stretch their paychecks to cover essential needs, including the inevitable and ever-rising medical insurance premium. If that citizen is a college student or a parent of one, he or she may be shocked by the realization that over the past few years college tuition costs have increased even more sharply than costs for health care. Is there then any question as to why the *value* of higher education is being challenged by today's consumers of educational services? It is relatively easy to calculate the cost of a bachelor's degree, but just what is its *worth* today? An academic dean of a leading university was recently quoted as describing a bachelor's degree as a "permanent incomplete." If this is true, or becoming true, then just what is the value of a graduate degree, given the fact that its total cost includes the cost of a prerequisite baccalaureate? What is the value of a professional degree? Is an MBA worth its cost in time, effort, and money? Or even worth the money alone? What is the cost/benefit ratio of a law degree, given the nature of our over-lawyered society? The fact that such questions are being asked in greater frequency seems to be evidence of a sea change in the public's perception of the worth of higher education. Ironically, the cost (or price) the student must pay to attain a college degree has continued to climb, even while its value has increasingly become subject to question. This is an enigma not just for the admissions office and college president, but for trustees at all institutions of higher education, and particularly so for those of the private sector.

Although these economic realities perhaps represent the single most important factor in the diminution of the special esteem in which higher education has been held by society, there are other causes. Throughout history, the subterranean stream of anti-intellectualism has remained closed to the surface of the American culture. Whenever a university or its faculty appears to hold itself above the rest of society, and whenever its solemn pronouncements wander far from the mainstream of American thought, academe risks a loss of public support. For example, the "political correctness" movement has had just this effect. Whenever a university's judicial ruling or administrative action on such issues as free speech or racial harassment or sexual conduct is inexplicable to the average citizen or is conveyed by circuitous or precious arguments, academe again drops a notch in the public's esteem. And whenever an academic institution appears to take a public position, any public position, acting as a political organization rather than as a scholarly institution committed to neutrality, public suspicions again are raised.

With the most noble of intentions, over the past two decades many institutions of higher education have launched initiatives aimed at helping to solve some of society's most intractable problems, such as racial injustice, inner-city poverty, and ineffective elementary and secondary education. To some, the failure of such institutions to "solve" these problems is, ironically, evidence both of higher education's incompetence and its arrogance for having tried, even though no other kind of institution has successfully yielded such solutions. All this has occurred at a time of desperate financial need on the part of many colleges and universities, and this coincidence has encouraged critics to disparage institutions of higher education for their failure to solve their own problems, while spreading themselves too thin by volunteering to solve larger, societal problems.

It is, then, both the economic reality and the clash in apparent values between academe and society that have tended to create what appears to be a diminution of public support for higher education. Yet although the support of society may have decreased, its need for the contributions of higher education has never been greater.

What *does* society need from higher education? First, as always, the transmission of knowledge from one generation to the next, through informed and challenging teaching. The need for the educated citizen who can think critically is a given in any democracy. Just as enduring is society's need for the creation of intellectual capital, for this represents the grist for economic growth. Quite apart from the economic benefits that may accrue from theoretical research is its inherent value. Still, as Kurt Lewin once observed, "There is nothing more practical than a good theory." Finally, there is a continuing need for the preparation of practitioners for the professions, as well as leaders for all walks of life.

There is a societal need, too, for an institutional model of integrity. In an age of repeated disclosures of corruption, conflicts of interest, and other ethical lapses that seem rampant in all sorts of other organizations, the higher education institution, given its intellectual resources and the very nature of its purpose, can serve as such a model. Yet before this can become a reality, colleges and universities must learn to govern and manage themselves with greater effectiveness than they appear to do today. This is imperative if society is to be persuaded to provide the public and private funds required for higher education to serve its needs. ⊀

Richard T. Ingram

President, Association of Governing Boards of Universities and Colleges

Society needs from higher education the same thing that higher education needs from society: a new social compact, a new covenant that binds one to the other in pursuit of solutions to enormous problems and opportunities brought on by a markedly changed social, demographic, economic, and political landscape.

Society urgently needs clear and compelling evidence from college and university leaders that they understand that they serve, and will serve, a very different society from the one they have served in the past. Higher education currently finds itself in the uncomfortable position of having to prove that it is, indeed, beginning to understand the society that supports it. And that it should meet more of society's needs as one important way to restore the public trust.

And as higher education seeks to work with society to shape this new covenant—to meet its new and redefined obligations—college and university leaders seek reassurance from society that it will hold its political leaders much more accountable for their actions affecting colleges and universities. The recent record of society's national and state political leaders is mixed at best; it shows little more than a superficial understanding of the academy and how it should best serve a free, complex, and dramatically changing society.

Society Needs at Least Four Commitments from Higher Education

(1.) Society needs colleges and universities to reassess their values, ethics, and mores, and to more vigorously and effectively regulate themselves. If society is to regain full confidence in their diverse system of higher education, it must be built on higher education's courageous determination to regulate itself. It must provide new incentives to reward undergraduate teaching, improve quality of academic programs, provide more effective public service, and instill more institutional loyalty in its faculty. The mistakes of a very few prominent institutions and academic leaders, caught in the web of shifting values of the 1970s and 1980s to those of the 1990s, have done much harm to the whole enterprise. Higher education may not be able to keep all of its leaders from sinning, but it surely can make it much more difficult for them to enjoy their sins (as should the corporation, the legislature, and religious communities with their own leaders).

Self-regulation should begin with restructuring "voluntary accreditation." The current system, like that of federal student aid programs, is in shambles. We must better define, raise, and enforce standards, and restore presidential and public control over accreditation processes now largely controlled by specialized and regional agencies—in part because presidents have been preoccupied with many other problems in recent years. What is being done in the National Collegiate Athletic Association to restore presidential control, enforce regulations, and contain costs, can be done in the business of accreditation which seems to have become, unfortunately, an industry unto itself.

(2.) Society needs higher education to be its equity engine, to enthusiastically educate the nation's future leaders from all parts of its multicultural fabric. The Higher Education Issues Panel of the Association of Governing Boards of Universities and Colleges, in its report entitled *Trustees & Troubled Times in Higher Education* (1992), concludes that higher education has fallen way short of the mark thus far. It should be noted, however, that precisely at a time when greater equity is needed, the crisis in the nation's economy has made it extremely difficult for colleges and universities to accelerate their progress.

(3.) Society needs higher education to be more relevant to finding solutions to poverty, racism, inadequate health care and coverage, infant mortality, crime, homelessness, and other social problems. These are not necessarily within the grasp of colleges and universities to help resolve, of course, but the best minds in the nation are on campuses and society expects them to be turned to the nation's difficulties.

(4.) Society needs higher education to be its economic engine. To do so, colleges and universities are expected to demonstrate their capacity to help meet the nation's aspirations for job creation and greater productivity in a global economy, but without sacrificing its many other purposes. Higher education must find a way to convince the public that it is making dramatic improvements in its own productivity.

These are but four expectations that can be reasonably held for higher education, an enterprise that continues to be the envy of the world even if our own citizens, and especially our elected political leaders, have large doubts about its purposes and effectiveness.

Any new covenant should start with the question of purposes; that is, what does society expect and need? There is hope that such a social contract will reflect society's understanding that colleges and universities need to retain the freedom necessary to meet the new expectations being held for them. There are many traditional purposes that must be respected by society if the academy is not to be transformed into solely an instrument for work force preparation.

Most importantly, the question of who should "control" higher education should be answered clearly. The fact that the question is ambiguously and variously answered today is symptomatic of the confusing relationship among society, its government, and higher education. State support of "public" colleges and universities has fallen and continues to fall below 30 percent of their revenue sources in most states. Yet, in state after state, legislators and governors continue to micromanage and second-guess the increasingly difficult judgments made by citizen governing boards—whose members political leaders themselves ultimately select.

Decide Who Should "Control" Higher Education

The new covenant should address whether society wishes higher education to be controlled directly by state government leaders and their agencies. There are many discouraging signs that this is already happening by default, even as state support declines. Notwithstanding that higher education has undoubtedly brought more governmental regulation and control on itself, is this the road that society really wants to take?

Earlier societies have reaffirmed that education at all levels needs to be part of a system of checks and balances—that education is too important to the development of the nation, and to the hopes and aspirations of its people, to be left entirely in the hands of educators *or* its elected representatives. Thus we have an enormous system of appointed and elected volunteer citizen boards, unlike most other industrialized nations whose education ministries call the shots (along with senior faculty).

It may be that this system of citizen governance is broken beyond repair at the K-12, higher education, or both levels. But it may also be that society's disappointment with the way public schools, colleges, and universities are governed is at least partly a result of how and why people are selected to serve on public education boards in the first place.

At the very least, society should expect its public colleges and universities to be: (1) supported adequately and consistently with tax revenues, and (2) governed effectively. It can direct its public policy makers to stop using higher education funds for their primary "reserve" fund to meet other pressing priorities. It can direct its state governors and legislators to provide for independent citizen panels to screen and recruit the best and brightest citizens to serve on governing boards. And it can tell its elected leaders that it should respect and support, rather than undermine, the functions and responsibilities of volunteer trustees and boards to get the job done with their academic leaders.

Many fewer than 10,000 people serve on the boards of public higher education (with 80 percent of the more than 14 million students on their campuses). More than 40,000 people serve on the governing boards of independent higher education. Trustee service is an enormous responsibility in these tumultuous times for the nation and for higher education. Society should decide if it should strengthen volunteer trusteeship by understanding it, raising expectations for it, and meeting some of its needs so it can function more effectively. Or it can replace trusteeship with strong state departments of higher education as we see in Europe, the Far East, and throughout the rest of the world.

Society needs more from higher education, and higher education needs more from the society that supports it. Let's begin with redefining their relationship and working toward a new social compact that the nation can respect and enthusiastically support.✦

Geneva B. Johnson
President, Family Service America, Inc.

> *If the object of education is the improvement of man, then any system of education that is without values is a contradiction in terms, a system that seeks bad values is bad. A system that denies the existence of values denies the possibility of education. Relativism, scientism, skepticism, and anti-intellectualism, the four horsemen of the philosophical apocalypse, have produced chaos in education which will end in the disintegration of the West.*

Robert Maynard Hutchins

Last summer, I participated in an exciting seminar called, "Teaching Ethics and Character." The seminar was sponsored by The Josephson Institute of Ethics. The experience of the seminar clearly identified for me the role of educational institutions in teaching ethics. At no other time has our society needed higher education to rethink the way ethics is being taught in all of its schools: law, medicine, business, and teacher education. There has been an overemphasis on social policy questions with little or no attention paid to private morality.

Recent events at the corporate level (Miliken, junk bonds, the S & L scandals), the government level (the House-Banking Committee, ethics scandals in the House and Senate), the non-profit (United Way, Covenant House), higher education (the research grants scandals at prestigious universities), and public schools (the repeated reports of students cheating, stealing, etc.) makes one wonder if higher education, in fact, has abandoned its main objective—the improvement of man.

We certainly know that education of our children tended to be "value-free". We do not educate our teachers. We train them with a smattering of "subjects" and institutional techniques. How—and what—are they to teach? Many cannot overcome the handicap their poor training imposes. And, their students, in turn, are even more handicapped when their generation enters the teaching profession.

Most Americans are concerned about the ethical health of our nation. What role does higher education play in assuming its role in preparing its students for life? An education system ought to aim at manhood rather than manpower. Training just for marketable skills is a limited partial education for a limited life.

Thomas Jefferson understood that the key to the values/ethics he espoused (honesty, fairness, equality, courage, loyalty, kindness, hard work, and respect), was education. Values are taught, learned, and practiced.

Lamar Alexander, former Secretary of Education, believes there is no such thing as a value-neutral education. Higher education must serve as a catalyst to bring us together to change our country. Secretary Alexander states "education should not be treated as another social issue. Education is the solution to a whole set of challenges we face, including the nation's ethical health."

> Education must continue to seek truth, but
> Education must also seek meaning in human life.
> It must seek justice in human affairs, and
> It must seek dignity in human aspirations.

No community can be a satisfactory homeland unless the systems through which it operates work for the people it serves and offers dignity for all. The quest for better communities should be a legitimate concern of every institution in society, including higher education.

Education is customarily defined as preparation for life; but what sort of preparation, and for what final purpose, makes all the difference. There are many diverse views of what the aim of education is, but I believe a shared view is to prepare one for the life of a whole person, in all things mental, physical, and spiritual. Such education is not "practical" in the sense of preparing one to earn a living; rather it seeks to make one ready to take advantage of the total potential of human life.

Education should be socially beneficial, a means of expanding knowledge and transmitting culture, values, and norms between generations.

Education is the preservation, refinement, and transmission of values from one generation to the next. Its tools include reason, tradition, moral concern, introspection, the examination from within of what can never be seen from without by scientific methods: ourselves.

Michael Josephson, founder and Executive Director of the Josephson Institute of Ethics states, "behavior-centered moral education should enhance ethical consciousness, strengthen ethical commitment, and increase the students' capacity to anticipate, avoid, and address moral challenges."

In summary, higher education must return to the inclusion of selected courses in the humanities and ethics for all students; it should enable students to think critically and recognize that values are taught and learned and basic ethics is something everyone needs. 𝍢

Stanley N. Katz
President, American Council of Learned Societies

The obvious answer to the question is: Everything. But of course in the United States the several systems of higher education are so complex that it is absurd to think of any single response that applies to all sectors of higher education. "Society" (itself a shorthand term for a diverse collectivity of social groupings) requires different things from different parts of the higher education system at different places in the country.

It is important to recognize that the totality of social demands on education comprehends needs that are contradictory. It would be easy to respond that society needs cheap, quick, effective programs to train Americans for the job market of the next century. Who could be against such a goal? But what knowledgeable person believes that "cheap," "quick," and "effective" have unitary definitions? Or that all Americans should receive (the same kind of) higher education?

The implication of the question "what does society need from higher education" is that twentieth-century American society needs something different than we currently derive from higher education. Most thoughtful people would agree. They would point, I think, to two elements necessitating change: demographic transformation of society and social transformation of the economy. As to demography, I suppose that four factors most clearly create new educational needs: increased ethnic and racial diversity; dramatic growth in the number of women's participation; rising Latino and Asian immigration; and the explosion in the number of senior citizens. As to the economy, the most obvious development is the decline in the industrial basis of the U.S. econ-omy and the emergence of a predominantly service economy, and in particular the decreased likelihood of lifelong employment in a single sector.

My expertise is in history, not social analysis, but I think it fair to remark that social futurologists have not been very successful in predicting long-term social change. My concern is simply that in defining educational needs for coming generations we avoid relying on dubious postulates. As Aristotle remarked, everything that is necessary is necessary upon some hypothesis. We had better be careful to base our predictions on defensible hypotheses.

Of the two predictive elements I have already noted, I think that the second, the future social organization of the economy, is very speculative and of dubious predictive value. The first element, demographic change, is however already a social fact, and one that higher education cannot escape. But the conclusions to be drawn from the demographic transformation are not so clear.

What do we make of the fact that, by 2010, four of our largest states (California, Florida, New York and Texas) will be home to nearly one-third of our country's young people, and that more than half of them will be "minorities"? Or that the current 30 million Americans over the age of 65 will rise to 65 million by 2020, so that many Americans will live as many years in retirement as at work? Or that the proportion of children under the age of 18 will have declined from 34 percent of the whole population in 1970 to 25 percent in 2000? Or that, if current trends continue, more than half of American children will be raised in single-parent families? The geography of demography is also changing significantly, with increasing concentrations of non-Europeans in certain parts of the country and in our cities and increasing concentrations of Europeans in the suburbs. We know that, in 2000, some 85 percent of entry-level workers will be combinations of immigrants, women and minorities. A recent Carnegie study argues that 70 percent of those jobs will not require a college degree. (These figures are drawn from Harold L. Hodgkinson's June, 1992 study, *A Demographic Look at Tomorrow*.)

What does society need from higher education, then, to cope with these dramatic changes in its structure? The answers will depend upon which sector of higher education is involved. If I were to make one sweeping criticism of U.S. higher education over the past couple of generations, it would be to second Ernest Boyer's complaint in *Scholarship Reconsidered* that colleges and general universities have modelled themselves upon research universities, subordinating the historic primacy of undergraduate teaching to a misplaced effort to support faculty research. Surely the first thing society requires of its educational institutions is that they continue to do what they do best—and to strive to improve their performance in so doing. A fault common to almost all types of institution is overexpansion—of purpose, plant, and personnel. The answers in each institutional class will be found in thoughtful specifications of purpose and reallocation of resources in terms of rigorous adherence to appropriate institutional goals.

I realize that conforming to traditional roles is not very dramatic, but it is what is most necessary. The fact of the matter is that the United States has the most highly articulated system of higher education in the world. We have institutions of every sort in both the private and public sectors which, taken together, provide all of the kinds of higher education the society requires: from trade schools to technical institutes, from community colleges to liberal arts colleges, from religious and ethnic institutions to comprehensive universities, and so on.

The necessary improvements must be designed within the traditional functions of each type of institution, especially in the light of the new population pressures. To use one of the most self-evident examples, how should institutions respond to the phenomenal growth in the number of retirees? There will be very different capacities and opportunities according to institutional categories, ranging from the enhancement of traditional continuing education programs and the development of new earned degrees to local, not-for-credit evening classes. The services a community college can provide to older citizens will be different from those available at a research university or a technical institute, but they will all respond to the same general social need. The same will be true of educational opportunities for minorities and recent immigrants, and for other specialized populations. We are capable now of giving society most of what it needs—if each type of school does what it can do best.

The danger of organizing one's thinking about higher education in terms of social needs is the danger of shortsightedness. For several years now, national discussions have focused on the need to make the country more "competitive," yet we know even less about the relationship of education to competitiveness than we do about its strictly economic components. Some would argue, for instance, that we should reorient our basic scientific research to emphasize short-term capacity for technological and industrial development. Yet it is not at all clear that such strategies will be best for either science or technology, much less the economy, in the long run. This is not an argument against the specification of social needs, but it is a plea for taking a reasonably long view of those needs.

In conclusion, however, I would like to make a case for traditionalism. What American society will need increasingly as we enter an era of enhanced social diversity (with the probability of enhanced social tension) is the intellectual common ground provided by liberal education. I do not mean to side with those who contend that the liberal "core" must be exposure to the classic works of the Euro-British tradition, but with those who (like Bliss Carnochan in his forthcoming book) believe that the genius of liberal education in the United States has been its capacity to adapt to changing social movements, student bodies, and national imperatives.

The liberal tradition teaches us to think critically and to question our intellectual, social, and political premises. Liberal education is carried on differently in liberal arts colleges and universities, and in other sorts of educational institutions, but one of the strengths of our education system has been its pervasive concern with liberal education. The abstract expressionist painter Robert Motherwell told a 1949 audience at the Museum of Modern Art how grateful he was to have been "armed" with the ability to speak and write, "the chief advantage of a liberal arts university education." (Hilton Kramer review of *The Collected Writings of Robert Motherwell,* NYT Book Review, February 28, 1993) In a democratic society, what is true for an artist is equally true for accountants, scientists, computer programmers, school teachers, and soldiers.

What society needs from those of us in higher education is rigorous self-scrutiny of our institutions to be sure that we are carrying out our traditional functions faithfully and efficiently. What society requires from us as a whole is our commitment to serving the long-term interests of an increasingly complex society. My own most profound belief is that a reconsideration of liberal education in the light of the social conditions of the next century is the most important challenge to our colleges and universities.✝

Donald Kennedy
President Emeritus and Bing Professor of Environmental Studies
Stanford University

The question is not as simple as it looks. Society's needs from higher education are increasingly multiple, and complicated; worse, they are frequently misunderstood both by those who run the institutions and by those, in government or in business, who are their most influential patrons. The issue is particularly challenging for the modern research university which, because of its functional diversity and its extraordinary capacity, finds itself at the vortex of an often opaque set of demands.

Nowhere is the confusion more evident than in that difficult domain where teaching and research vie for resources, time, and attention. The wise postwar decision to locate government-sponsored research in the places where the next generation of researchers is being trained has produced collateral costs along with its undeniable benefits. These costs include a contemporary conviction that the university is the answer to some fundamentally utilitarian questions—questions like "What institutions can society count on to restore international competitiveness?" or (most recently) "Where can we turn for the technology base to rebuild our regional economy?"

There may be answers to these questions, but I do not think "Aha! The university!" is among them. Stanford, because of its relationship to the genesis of Silicon Valley, is sometimes asked by business leaders in other regions how their institutions could create a Clone Canyon, or whatever. The answer is that, absent a special history and an unusual confluence of circumstances, it isn't very likely. And as to international competitiveness, the kind of research universities do has little to do with gaining advantage in high-technology markets. Other factors—cost of capital, industrial policies, product development cycles—have much more to say than the research base about how well a national economy can succeed.

Does this mean society doesn't want, or shouldn't want, research from its universities? Of course not. But we are mistaken to suppose that most people see us in terms as utilitarian as these; we need to examine carefully the content of the chorus of public criticism that has swept over our enterprise in recent years. Among its ingredients are first, a deep concern for the quality of teaching, especially of undergraduates and most especially for a perceived loss of care on the part of faculty for the personal development of their students; and second, a growing conviction that research commitments by faculty are partly responsible. (There are also complaints about price, but these mask a deeper set of misgivings about quality.)

What sense can we extract from this swirl of discontent? I think it reflects a public instinct that what higher education really ought to be about is students. Society wants people who can think well and act wisely. It still expects the colleges and universities to produce leaders; after all, we speak easily of *higher education*. It welcomes the fruits of faculty research but instinctively understands that even the heroes of academic science contribute more through their students than through their own work. Finally, it understands—perhaps more deeply than those in the academy—that a good liberal education enhances the skills and the values necessary for continued cultural growth.

So, despite all the attention that is given to the practical output of the university, I do not believe that we are looked to primarily as the means for economic improvement or technological gains, or indeed for any other utilitarian objective. Instead, society has recognized as central the mission we try to accomplish with its sons and daughters, and that in fact it expects not only that the university will train them to cope but that it will equip them to lead. That requires a kind of education much deeper than the kind of classroom encounters we ordinarily think of as "teaching". The best of our students gain something much more—sometimes from an especially inspiring personal model, sometimes from an episode of experiential education, sometimes from a challenging and successful piece of independent research. When asked later about their lives as students they nearly always tell us about one or a very few special teachers who made a difference in their intellectual and personal development. Experiences of this kind depend on close relationships between faculty members and their students—relationships that transcend traditional teaching roles.

Yet the faculties of our most distinguished research universities have moved away from, rather than toward, this kind of engagement. Many observers have mourned, along with Henry Rosovsky, the "secular decline of professorial civic virtue". Unless the leadership of universities reinstates the commitment to personal teaching as first among our labors, we will fail to meet society's highest expectations. That will be a difficult task of persuasion, for two reasons. First, those expectations have not been clearly articulated; there is no plainly written message. Second, deep-seated cultural change will be required; but that change must be undertaken gently, because it must not be seen as an effort to engage on one side of the ancient struggle between teaching and research. Instead it must seek a new convergence between these two, so that the latter creates and defines new opportunities for the former.

What our society really wants is for us to be the agents for generational improvement—custodians for the process by which we continuously reinvent our social order. To deliver, we simply have to put our young people first, at all times and in all ways.✝

James L. Koch
Dean, Leavey School of Business and Administration
Santa Clara University

To address the question of "what society needs from higher education," the starting place should be to ask how is society changing? In addition, one should ask what are the forces, both individual and in combination, that are reshaping society? Higher education is vital to the extent that it seeks to comprehend these underlying forces, to create informed discourse, and to shape the future through advances in knowledge that are relevant to salient issues of our time.

How Society is Changing

We are a global village—more richly connected in the flows of raw materials, information, technology, capital, products, services, and people than at any time in the history of man.

We are an information and knowledge based society—a phenomenon that has wide reaching implications for how we work. Distributed information technologies are fundamentally reshaping hierarchic organizations. "Learning to learn" is an overarching need for individuals, organizations, and sets of institutional relations (e.g., relations between business-government-labor and education). In our information age, there is real risk of widening socio-economic disparities and social disintegration among those who are left behind.

We are a society that is being redefined by accelerating technological change.

We are a society that is not only multi-ethnic, but multi-cultural.

We are a society with weakened integrative mechanisms in which the stabilizing presence of families, neighborhoods, communities, and organizations has been diminished.

We are a society in which human values and ethics have been subordinated to the pursuit of individual self-interests—as reflected, in the extreme, by such phenomena as the depletion of rain forests, financial scandal, greed, and growing violence. A restored balance is needed between the individualistic needs and the collective needs of society.

We are a society in which transnational organizations are redefining the psychological contract between employer and employee, and the compact between corporations and national interests, as companies develop global strategies to adjust to rapid change in markets and technologies.

What Society Needs From Higher Education

Our society needs graduates who understand the global context of public policy and how to develop new mechanisms for institutional survival and organizational growth in our "global village." We need—

Graduates who have "learned how to learn," who:

- Know how to utilize information; to develop useful information through access to on-line data bases; and, to utilize quantitative skills along with conceptual thinking and qualitative perspectives to understand complex phenomena.
- Know how to make decisions under conditions of complexity and uncertainty.
- Know how to formulate and test both scientific hypotheses and "hunches."

Graduates who understand science and technology, how they are changing, and how they can be a force to enhance the quality of life for a wider and wider spectrum of humanity.

Graduates who can relate across multi-ethnic, multi-cultural, and multi-functional "points of view" and who can collaborate in the pursuit of common goals. Increasingly, we succeed or fail in groups; and in cross-functional, cross-organizational, cross-sector, and cross-national relationships.

Graduates who know how to build community. In fact, the ability to "build community" may be more critical to our future than outmoded and individualist concepts of "leadership." Increasingly, the forces of community have supplanted those of family, school, or organizations as a stabilizing or destabilizing influence in our society.

Graduates who have strong human values and personal ethics as reflected in a readiness to perceive and value the "common good" and to exercise "principled leadership."

Graduates who will create organizations and institutions that meet the interests of multiple stakeholders (e.g., customers, shareholders, employees, and society).

What This Means for Faculty

Faculty must move from a focus that is parochially functional or narrowly discipline-based to one which is phenomena-based, and which seeks to comprehend *systems* (i.e., to understand social, scientific, economic, and other phenomena as systemic wholes).

Faculty must place a greater emphasis on *theory* and *application:* universities should seek to be "world class" in *both* (e.g., faculty should engage in more field research, bridge the classroom laboratory with practice, and focus on precompetitive science and technology).

Faculty should share accountability for the creation of environments that inspire a quest for learning, skills in collaboration, and a deep sense of responsibility to society. (Note: In addition, university faculty must do everything within their power to maintain access to higher education by controlling future costs.)

Finally, in the presence of hyperbole and "screaming headlines," faculty should be a voice of reason and compassion. ⭑

C. Peter Magrath

President, National Association of State Universities and Land-Grant Colleges

The short answer to the question is contained in two words: a lot. And, with the right leadership, the right spirit, and a positive attitude within the leadership of American higher education, a lot can be given by our colleges and universities to meet some of the most critical needs of the American society as it faces the twenty-first century. My answer is based on a stubborn faith born of my idealism and my practical experience that American higher education can both respond and help lead the drive toward needed social change.

I write from my personal experience "in the field" at a number of American universities, including service as president at three of them. I write also from a philosophical commitment to the land-grant principle that the purpose of public higher education is to serve the practical needs of the society, not only through quality teaching and research, but by reaching out and linking, when and where appropriate, with economic and social partners to further the public good.

It is my premise that, despite its flaws and failings, American higher education has served society well by developing superb research centers and graduate education programs that are literally the envy of the world; by providing access and opportunity to vast numbers of people who have in turn contributed massively to society's economic well being; and by meeting vital scientific and business interests of the American society through the education of men and women and the research and service that flow from its educational talents.

There are many measures of higher education's success. I cite but one: the fact that each year nearly 400,000 international students come to the United States to study in our colleges and universities, contributing, incidentally, about $3 billion of income to us, and making American higher education a great exporter on the positive side of our international balance of trade. These international students come to the United States purely for practical reasons, not out of sentiment.

But the world has changed and will continue to change. Many of the certitudes of the recent past—the comfortable framework of the Cold War and the implicit support it gave to science and research—are now history. So also has the context in which American higher education operates changed. In part it has suffered blows to its credibility because of a perceived lack of accountability, in many cases exaggerated, in some justified. Severe financial cutbacks in virtually all of the states, which are the major source for funding public higher education; rising tuition and concurrent questions about the quality and value of what is being done in our colleges and universities; charges, typically exaggerated, that research is somehow the enemy of quality undergraduate instruction; abuses in too many intercollegiate athletic programs; and occasional mistakes by higher education leaders and faculties in cases that raise conflict of interest questions, all have contributed to the fact that American higher education is no longer regarded as the bright, shining star that it was during the Cold War period.

But just as it is a mistake to underestimate problems and challenges, so too is it a mistake to overstate them. Much is still right about American higher education, despite severe fiscal challenges, a threatening erosion of scientific and research facilities, and the rising cost of attending universities due primarily to the severe economic pressures on our states. In this regard, our response to meeting society's needs will be enormously, indeed decisively, influenced by whether or not it is possible to keep open access for large numbers of men and women in our society, including the nation's minorities.

What the America of the twenty-first century needs from higher education flows directly from the philosophical spirit of the land-grant movement, which is by no means restricted to those universities technically labelled as land-grant universities. It is the spirit and application of "hands-on" engagement with society on matters that are essential to our society and that include the talents and skills that higher education can uniquely provide.

My list of what society needs from higher education—and that higher education can and must deliver—does, however, flow from one fundamental assumption: it is absolutely essential that the base financial support for higher education be adequate, so that research, both "pure" and mission-oriented, and quality teaching, are supported. There are no cheap, easy shortcuts to having a system of higher education meet the needs of society without an appropriate investment of resources to accomplish that mission. But by the same token, a willingness of American higher education to show that it is willing and eager to engage on critical issues of national need is also the best guarantor that the required investment of resources will be forthcoming. For example, in the Sputnik period of the 1960s, American higher education did not sit idly on its hands, complaining and being a reluctant dragon before engaging scientifically with the federal government to meet the challenges of Cold War competition. Quite the contrary, we were eager suitors and participants in meeting that challenge. And so it must be now on three issues that I propose as critical.

The first is that society needs, and American higher education must provide, a front and center engagement with the issues of elementary and secondary education—the issue of the public schools in our society. With some notable exceptions, the leaders and faculty of our colleges and universities have not made it a priority to engage themselves in a direct hands-on collaboration with business and industry and leaders in public elementary and secondary education to strengthen those many public schools that are in dreadful circumstances. This is not the place to sketch out the problem; it is well understood. But it is equally true that American higher education has not shown itself as engaged, both in deed and in perception, with movements to reform or improve our nation's schools. Society needs this commitment from higher education, and higher education has many of the talents appropriate to that task. Moreover, I believe that a genuine participation would be warmly welcomed by the leaders of our nation's public schools, its teachers, and the business community that understand so very well why a public school system that fails in too many places is absolutely disastrous to our society.

The second area of need that can be met by American higher education has to do with the core land-grant philosophy of extending the fruits of education in practical, direct ways to the needs of business and industry through outreach or extension programs appropriate to the twenty-first century. We have done this before in agriculture, with stunning success, and we have done it in more global ways by serving the interest of the federal government in defense and scientific research tied to the challenges of World War II and the Cold War. Again, as with the challenge of elementary and secondary education, there is no lack of models for successful collaboration, but there is too little extension and expansion of those models.

Put another way, our universities are absolutely capable of providing—in collaborative partnership efforts—trained agents and applied researchers who can link themselves through an industrial or business extension service to meet the needs of small and medium size businesses. This is the growth sector in our economy, the sector most in need of the kind of economic and informational skills that flow from universities. This endeavor must also involve vocational education and retraining, which can be done in collaboration with the nation's community colleges and vocational technical institutes. There is no reason why America's universities cannot link collaboratively with community colleges and vocational and technical institutes to provide the services needed and desired by small- and medium-size businesses in partnership arrangements brokered by local, state, and federal governments.

Universities alone cannot save or strengthen the nation's economy; but unless universities are in fact and in perception engaged in dealing with economic issues by contributing their talents directly and visibly, two things will happen: the nation's economy will not thrive and prosper as it should, and universities will not receive the support they deserve. Precisely the same principle applies to improving our system of elementary and secondary education.

The third need of our society may appear to be more abstract, perhaps even whimsical to some. It is the need for international education. Our society needs education and understanding about the world as never before because its complexities and interrelationships, economically, socially, and politically are even more dramatic and manifest than they were during the Cold War. American higher education has the unique talents and resources to fulfill a need that America has: educated men and women who understand the world of which we are inescapably a part, who can speak languages other than English, and who can function in complex cultural environments. Unless our colleges and universities are at the forefront of internationalizing their curricula, fostering relationships with people from other countries, and promoting study and research on international issues and interconnections, America will not be equipped to meet the challenges of the next century. And, once again, this engagement with international education applies as well to the need of elementary and secondary schools to be cognizant of the internationalization of our world and the need for business and industry to be able to function intelligently in our frustratingly complex world. All three of these "needs" of our society are ultimately interrelated.

These challenges can be met if properly understood and articulated with vision and verve. This requires leadership and support from all segments of American higher education based on the premise that its fundamental mission is to serve the needs of our society in interrelated ways. Ultimately, all of education must be seen as an interconnected, seamless, network that provides men and women with the thinking tools and the practical skills that society needs to progress. The one thing that the United States possesses, far more than its natural resources, is the ability to muster thinking men and women to identify challenges, develop ways to meet them, and strengthen the only resource base that is ultimately totally renewable and can, in fact, grow: education and the intelligent and imaginative uses of the mind. This kind of leadership can be mobilized because not only has the world changed, but because the circumstances affecting us have prompted and are prompting—as indeed this exercise illustrates—a fundamental reexamination of the role of American higher education and how it can meet the needs of its society in the challenging years before us.♱

Margaret E. Mahoney
President, The Commonwealth Fund

This is neither the worst of times nor the best of times, but it is certainly a time of change and the public is demanding it.

Across all sectors, the public is demanding well-managed institutions, cost efficient, productive entities, and universities are not exempt from meeting this challenge. Colleges and universities have to institute management practices that reflect a sense of accountability—to parents, students, faculty, boards of trustees, and funders. For some institutions, changes are required in such fundamental processes as accounting procedures.

But beyond the need for proven management capability, higher education leaders need to address their institution's central mission and to show how this mission translates into student ratios, into faculty, into curriculum—particularly into ethnic diversity in professional schools—and finally into cost and into budget. This is not a task for the administrator alone; it is a task to share with the governing board.

Precisely because colleges and universities are the strongholds for knowledge, they are also the potential site for helping to redirect society as it moves ahead.

What does society need from higher education? It needs assurance that higher education sees itself as serving the nation, and thus the purposes of a democracy—a point made 60 years ago by José Ortega y Gasset. It needs assurance that colleges and universities see their role as preparing students for the complex, global environment in which they will live and work.

To carry out this role, higher education needs:

- to present education on the continuum, making graduation and the commencement exercise only the beginning, not the end, of a lifelong learning process.
- to acknowledge that no body of knowledge is good for all time, and focus on developing the students' capacity for critical thinking, providing them the opportunity to examine not only the principles that undergird a body of knowledge but the framework and paradigms they need to understand the great movements in history as well as to grasp the meaning of the universe.
- to make liberal education a goal. As one critic recently said, "The failure to draw the young into a community of learning is a failure of what has been traditionally called a liberal education...elusive, as much a matter of style as of substance."
- to prepare students "to fill any post with credit" (John Henry Cardinal Newman) with an education that orients them to the world they live in; in short to prepare leaders for all levels of responsibility, forcing enquiry that includes their conduct.
- to acknowledge and deal with the inadequacies of high school education. Some of the brightest students with the highest SAT scores are coming to the undergraduate colleges inadequately prepared to do the work, for example in chemistry or math. A tutoring process to manage these inadequacies of intelligent students would reduce the number lost in the mainstream of higher education where they are caught up in a process of "get them through."
- to combat the growing stratification of American life that leads more people to associate within their own social, economic, and racial

groups, and to grow more removed from those outside them; help young people transcend their individual identity to assume a broader role, by providing opportunities for communal and community service.

- not just to recruit minority students but help advance their careers, beginning by offering opportunities at home within the institution itself. The sorry record in science and engineering is reflective of a massive failure throughout the university—medicine, as well as the learned professions—to nurture talent.[1]
- to encourage the integration of knowledge, bringing the disparate professional schools together in areas where cross disciplinary research and teaching could lead to new breakthroughs, for example, in environmental studies, educational policy, scientific work, and ethical engineering—a route proposed by Harvard's president to enhance Harvard's capacity to help advance inquiry while also, by inter-school collaboration, helping in the allocation of university resources and costs.
- to make partnerships with business, industry, and government that carry with them a strong commitment to discovering ways to improve the human condition—not only new insights that can lead to better health but also turning scientific discoveries into products that attract manufacturing interests, and thus create employment.

This agenda assumes a broad and active role of the university in society. Does the higher education leadership accept this role and will it lead in making it real?

The first and essential step is for higher education leaders to assert clearly the ideals to which their institutions aspire. The failure to articulate the role of the universities may account for the general public's failure today to actively support higher education, and focus instead on how much higher education costs. A. Bartlett Giamatti thought so, and wrote in 1988 that it was the universities' failure "to re-examine their norms, natures, and roles in a period of immense change" that led to their failure "to reeducate the public, whose goodwill and support are crucial to higher education's very existence, as to the nature of higher education—what it is for, where it fits the country's historical and current needs, what it alone cannot do... Of all the threats to the institution, the most dangerous come from within. Not the least among them is the smugness that believes the institution's value is so self-evident that it no longer needs explication, its mission so manifest that it no longer requires definition and articulation."

Now is the opportunity to clearly and openly respond to Giamatti's challenge. It is not too late, but it will be soon. ✝

---

1 Of the 366 U.S. doctorate-granting institutions, only 233 awarded at least one Ph.D. in science and engineering to a minority student in 1991; of the 149 that awarded Ph.D.'s to African-Americans, six granted 10 or more degrees; eight of the 151 awarding Ph.D.'s to Latinos granted 10 or more degrees—only 45 institutions awarded even one doctorate degree in these fields to a Native American. In contrast, Asian-Americans and foreign nationals together earned nearly 40% of the Ph.D.'s in science and engineering in 1990.

Wayne Meisel
Executive Director, The Corella and Bertram F. Bonner Foundation

College. Picture a bright crisp sunny Saturday in the fall. The campus is abuzz, with students going here and there, parents and alumni arriving for the day's activities. The visitors have arrived. The preparation has been great, the anticipation is high.

What does this sound like to you? Saturday football? Yes, but I have an image of a day when this is Service Saturday. On this day, like any other, the campus is busy with different service activities. The activities include tutoring, a camp for handicapped children, a basketball clinic, and a tour of the library. The parents are not the parents of college students but of local children. Adult literacy programs are offered through the Student Literacy Corps and personal finance classes are taught by the head of the business school. Alumni are there not to cheer but to participate in a seminar put on by students and faculty on educational reform. After a weekend seminar they will go back to their local communities and work with the school board to consider new model programs and suggestions on how to secure resources.

A new day. Possible? Yes. A reality? No.

This country needs higher education to define a new role for itself in society. Higher education must be a partner, a participant, and a member of the community, one that is connected at the local, county, state, and national levels.

Two clear examples exist of higher education responding and committing to a cause and an ideal that reaches beyond the campus.

During war time, colleges have made commitments to respond to society's needs, to rearrange schedules, to focus on the task at hand, to suspend restrictions and tradition, and to gear up for something that is not exclusively academic, but an area where academics and the development of young men and women is urgently called for.

But war is not the only time that the culture of campus has been changed because of social pressures. The revolution that has taken place in athletics and physical education demonstrates how colleges respond and are affected by the changing times and the pressures of the world. Athletics has altered and changed the way we think of higher education. It does not just affect what happens on the field, but the entire morale and image of the school.

Higher education needs to do for service what it has done and continues to do for athletics. It needs to understand the need and respond to the call to what President Clinton has dubbed the season of service.

These days call for it.

Colleges can no longer remain isolated from or be above the needs of society. Just as universities had to change during the Second World War so too do they need to respond to the raging wars that are going on, not in Germany or Japan but sometimes right across the street: the war on drugs, the struggle to provide health care, the battle of illiteracy, the arms conflict in our cities. These wars call on society to mobilize, sacrifice, and accommodate. They also call on us to focus, to rethink, and to renew our sense of citizenship and civic involvement. This call reaches out to every part of our society, including higher education, especially higher education.

Colleges identify promising young athletes, bring them to campus, support them financially, academically, and socially. We praise them. Their performance often determines what kind of year the school community has, not just in terms of sports but also the moral and the financial strength of the school. Athletics affect public image and support that in turn have a direct effect on the caliber of student a school recruits, services that it can deliver and faculty that it can support.

Young people are uniquely gifted in four areas. They make great soldiers. They are our best athletes. They created and lead the computer revolution. They are great community servants. The first three are admired and supported both throughout society and in higher education. The last, however, is left to club status or "extra-curricular" activity.

Higher education could change this. To do so it must alter its outlook, raise standards, not just a little but exponentially, focus its energies, rearrange its priorities, and make commitments and sacrifices for an idea that lies at the heart of every mission statement of every great institution of higher education.

I wince when I watch a school complete a newly renovated athletic facility for $25 million but cannot find the money to help transport students to their volunteer sites. Another school builds an Olympic pool, not because the old one doesn't work, but because some other school in the conference has one "so we need one too."

And who gives the money for these pools? Swimmers? Sometimes, but not necessarily. Individuals and foundations want to give. Why do they give to build pools? Because it is what the schools ask for, the president, the athletic department, the alumni, and society.

Many of these wealthy donors would be just as inclined to support the development of a community service center or scholarships for service internships, but it is not what we ask for, it is not what we "need". We have other priorities.

We do not have a vision of what higher education can do for our communities.

In recent years there has been a small but bright rebirth of service and activism on the part of students. The leadership for this activity has come from interesting places. Students and recent graduates through COOL and college presidents through Campus Compact have challenged their peers and built outreach programs.

But the culture of service that the times call for and that we are capable of has not been envisioned, let alone realized. The type of involvement and commitment required of higher education does not begin to exist even at the most involved and active schools. The standards we have set are too low, our expectation is unequal to our potential. We must be visionary, creative, and bold. Who better to be all these things than the higher education community? If higher education has one constant theme throughout history and across every institution, it is a commitment to excellence.

If you can not imagine it, you can not build it. Higher education must first be able to imagine a culture of service before it can develop one. We need to have standards, goals, targets, and something, some kind of passion mixed with competition that propels us to excellence and builds things we never thought possible. This new standard should be based on the principles that:

- every student should be challenged and supported to be involved in service activities.
- every organization, department, agency, and operation should develop a strategy and a program that involves service and ties it into the goals and operations of that entity.

Colleges and universities would then become centers of action, of community outreach, as armies of students reached out to the children and the seniors of the neighborhood every day. The brain power of the faculty and students would then be put to use to help build better schools, stronger local economies, and healthier communities.

The discussion of community service cannot be focused on one program here, or a few students there. It includes curriculum reform but is not limited to or entirely dependent upon it.

We can look to athletics again to gain an understanding of how to envision a culture of service. And while there are many who feel athletics is a poor example because it is a story of a good idea gone out of control, there are lessons to be learned.

For every piece of the infrastructure that supports athletics on a campus, I suggest a parallel position, program, or concept for public service. It should be noted that these comparisons do not call for equal budgets.

Athletics	Public Service
Athletic Director	Dean of Public Service
coaches	program staff & faculty advisors
weight training	leadership training
buses and vans	buses and vans
Sports Information	Public Service announcements
sports page	service page
Most Valuable Player	Most Valuable Public Servant
alumni boosters	alumni sponsored internships
pre-season camp	summer service fellowships
scholarships	scholarships
recruit athletes	recruit service leaders

To get an idea of how limited our support for service activities is, let's reverse the fortunes of athletics and public service. Imagine if athletics were organized and operated the way service organizations are forced to operate. Let's use the football team as an example.

Students arrive back at school. The captain elected last year is in charge of the entire program because there is no paid coach. A faculty advisor has been appointed but is on sabbatical. No one is sure who the new advisor is. After registration and rush week the captain puts posters up to have all those interested come to an organizational meeting. The room is packed. Interest is high.

They must hurry, though, because the team is supposed to have a game that weekend. The team sets its first practice three days before the first game. But practice is cut short. Money needs to be raised so that they can rent the vans to go to the away games. And the tickets, what about the tickets? At the first practice the captain learns that the head of tickets is on junior year abroad. No one followed up. The captain reminds the players on the way out of the bake sale planned for tomorrow, but no one knows who is baking what.

Amusing yes, but also the reality of the infrastructure that supports service on campus. Service on campus is at the intramural level. If we followed the scenario to game time, what would we see? The game might well be played and people would have fun. We would not have the level of play we have come to expect and demand.

Higher education trains young men and women to be world-class athletes and intellects. Why not the same type of commitment to train and develop world-class service leaders. We must think anew and commit ourselves to building and supporting a culture of service that we have yet to imagine and have not begun to realize.

Universities cannot do everything, but they can do a great deal. The hands, the feet, and the hearts of the students can bring about change. Their energy, creativity, idealism, passion, talent, ingenuity, and determination are great. They not only bring action and ideas but they also deliver inspiration and hope. For example, students majoring in political science with an interest in education should be encouraged and supported to both tutor in the schools and learn about public policy. Students can work in partnership with the school and community to develop something practical, applicable, and that can have real impact.

Institutions of higher learning may be tax-exempt, but they are not "responsibility-exempt." We are taught to love our neighbor and called on to be active citizens, to contribute to our community. In college a student can get an extension on a paper. There is no extension on responsibility.

With these goals and standards before us, we can move forward to design a structure, support leadership, and issue a challenge that can bring about a reform in higher education, a rebirth of freedom and citizenship in this country. We can provide local and world leadership through our commitments, acts of courage, and deeds of kindness. ✦

Alceste T. Pappas
President, Pappas Consulting Group, Inc., An Alliance Firm of KPMG Peat Marwick

The query "What Does Society Need from Higher Education?" is most profound as it seeks to begin to provide answers to global challenges and constraints from a systemic perspective.

Based on my own hands-on experience as a senior administrator at the University of California, Berkeley, as a trustee of numerous colleges, universities, non-profit organizations, and a regional accrediting association as well as a veteran of fourteen years of consulting to the higher education and non-profit marketplace, there are four things which I believe our society desperately needs. These are: (1) training for the moral act of leadership; (2) communication, analysis, and synthesis skills; (3) basic and applied research; and (4) global understanding.

Training for the Moral Act of Leadership

Much has been written in the last decade about leadership and continuous quality improvement initiatives. These have come about in large measure as the economic realities of a global society have forced directors and chief executive officers to rethink the ways in which their corporations do business and measure productivity and quality. Although I personally would like to believe that these motives have been truly customer-driven, I am pragmatic enough to know that the primary driver for these changes has been the bottom line. Although I can certainly sympathize with this motivation, I am concerned that the truly wonderful innovations which many corporate and governmental agencies have implemented will not realize their full potential until a new sense of moral leadership is instilled in women and men in their college and post-graduate experiences.

In order for colleges and universities to instill this sense of leadership as a moral act in their students and graduates, they first must change the way in which they as institutions work and communicate with their various constituencies. Robert Birnbaum, in his recent work, *How Academic Leadership Works*, puts it succinctly:

> Those in leadership roles can facilitate or hinder the effectiveness of follower initiative; they cannot demand it. Much of what happens in a college is due to the effectiveness of people in follower roles who, without title or authority, take initiative to do what they believe has to be done. As the number of such persons increases in a college, leadership becomes more dispersed. The college becomes a cauldron of ideas and interaction. Groups without "leaders" can be productive because their members themselves have the qualities of effective leadership. Followers share leadership tasks when they behave responsibly, respecting the institution's purposes. Good leaders empower followers to share the burdens of leadership, and in exchange good constituents produce good leaders.

What emerges is a shared or collaborative leadership model. Such a leadership style is the only way in which colleges and universities will be able to renew themselves and those who they are educating.

Strong leaders do not create institutional values; rather, they develop processes through which constituents can renew or redesign their institution's values—mission, vision, goals, and objectives. In my view, colleges and universities need to not only serve as paradigms of shared leadership, they must teach students how to design ways in which to redesign society's values to meet the highest standards of integrity and collaboration.

Communication, Analysis, and Synthesis Skills

In the last 25 years, corporate America has aptly criticized the academy's ability to produce graduates who can communicate orally and in writing. Although higher education can not be solely held accountable for this sorry state, it must make fundamental curricular reforms to address society's needs for a literate public.

As the world has shrunk and technology has enabled us to communicate in microseconds or less, the American public at large has lagged behind other nations in its ability to read, write, and communicate in its own language let alone multiple languages. The irony is that the diverse nature of the American society has not been reflected in our college and university curricula.

In addition to teaching fundamental writing, reading, technology, and language skills to our students through traditional day and non-traditional evening and weekend settings, colleges and universities must recognize that the rote learning that frequently typifies the American college experience in large lecture halls is antithetical to those analysis and synthesis skills required in a data intensive world. Clearly the proliferation of data has created a host of new challenges for our society and the world at large. The fundamental challenge in this regard is how to transform data to information, and, subsequently, how to transform information to knowledge.

It appears to me that what society needs of the academy is the teaching of processing skills—of analysis and synthesis. As much of the American professoriate is to retire in the balance of this decade and into the beginning of the next century, training and development programs for newly recruited as well as seasoned faculty must be put in place to ensure that students of all ages, abilities, as well as ethnic and racial backgrounds are grounded with the pragmatic analysis and synthesis skills required of this generation of the American workforce. It is this grounding that will enable the United States to compete globally in every sector. Failure to address the teaching of such fundamental skills will put the United States even farther behind than it already is in the global marketplace.

Basic and Applied Research

There is an insidiousness about performing basic and applied research in our academies these days, yet it is one of the most fundamental needs of our society within the global marketplace. What do I mean about insidiousness? There is an inextricable linkage between teaching, research, and public service in the annals of American higher education.

In essence, these are the three fundamental principles which undergird our institutions. However, we in higher education have been ineffective in our ability to balance the three. Fundamentally, our institutions are designed to teach women and men and rely on a professoriate which is both expected and rewarded to spend most of its time conducting basic and applied research. For those smaller liberal arts institutions which pride themselves in a teaching faculty, the demands on the faculty to conduct research are not typically as acute as they are in comprehensive institutions (both public and private) which often appear to be more concerned with their Carnegie classification, the number of members of the faculty listed among the ranks of the American Academy of Sciences, the number of star faculty or the number of Nobel Laureates rather than imparting wisdom.

Further, the way in which the Federal Government currently utilizes its indirect cost reimbursement policy has challenged the accounting and management creativity of some principal investigators and administrators to abuse the system and cast serious doubt on the academy's integrity to pursue research for research's sake rather than being motivated by the dollar for dollar's sake. In addition, the financial constraints facing institutions of higher learning have forced them to look at new opportunities for revenue generation. At a number of private and public institutions, there have been a number of attempts to develop research parks and incubators. This focus on applied research and technology transfer has for many institutions proven a boon financially. Concurrently, it has raised questions about the ability of institutions and principal investigators to maintain objectivity and distance from corporate influence.

Although I, too, have concerns about the growing fuzziness between basic and applied research and the ability of the academy to maintain an open research agenda with minimum influence from the corporate agenda, the truth is that the financial constraints of the day have seriously curtailed the ability of corporations to invest heavily in research and development. Clearly, institutions of higher learning will need to enhance their ability to conduct basic and applied research with a high return on investment while maintaining institutional and research integrity. It is further clear that society needs the academy to broaden its major focus of research from the hard and medical sciences to include the social and human sciences.

Global Understanding

It is my belief that most Americans are parochial by nature. Interestingly, only 10 percent of the American public carry valid American passports. Perhaps this helps to account, in some small measure, for the pervasive attitude that "America knows best."

Ironically, this so-called melting pot of humanity, while inclusive in terms of the multiplicity of cultures and races it represents, is far from accepting of its inclusivity. A look at the role of women and persons of color in corporate America, the world of government and the world of the non-profit and higher education reveals a very small number of directors and senior managers representing these cohorts despite the existence of a growing number of so-called minority majority states and environments (e.g., the undergraduate student body of the University of California, Berkeley).

American society desperately needs help from the academy to begin to understand more fully the challenges of co-existence in a growing diverse society where not only issues of race, culture, and gender abound, but challenges concerning aging and disabled populations seem to be proliferating. The academy, through its academic offerings and the presence of its health sciences centers, is in a position to help not only the United States deal with this host of vexing societal issues but indeed begin to address such issues on a world-wide basis.

There needs to be an intensive self-assessment at every institution of higher learning about its own ability to deal with diversity and inclusiveness. Interestingly, colleges and universities often lag behind their for-profit counterparts in the advancement of women and persons of color. Only until colleges and universities serve as role models of non-discriminatory behavior will society truly change its own behavior and broader attempts of human, global understanding be successful.

The four issues briefly enumerated in this paper are those which I believe are among the most pressing needs of society from higher education. Most of these issues require profound change in the way institutions of higher learning are structured and do business before society can truly experience systemic change.⚡

David R. Pierce
President, American Association of Community Colleges

Because "society" encompasses so many different groups, as well as every individual within "society," asking what society needs from higher education results in a multitude of answers. What business and industry need, society needs. What government needs, society needs. And most importantly, what individuals need, society needs. Each of the constituents of society is a constituency for higher education.

And yet, there is a remarkable amount of convergence between what is good for workers and what is good for business, between what is good for government and what is good for an individual: In our high-powered economy, workers need skills to get good jobs; businesses need highly skilled workers to maintain their market share. In a democracy, citizens need to be informed about their government, and government needs informed citizens. Much of what society needs is needed by more than one group.

Although higher education cannot solve all of society's problems, it can act as a resource. Higher education performs certain functions that cannot be done by any other segment of our society. It also supports other institutions, such as government, business, museums, etc. in vital ways.

Society requires the following from higher education:
- To train a skilled, intelligent, creative, and responsible workforce;
- To transmit, sustain, and extend the arts and humanities, the scientific tradition, the historical record, and other aspects of our living culture;
- To support a citizenry that participates responsibly in community affairs including public governance and cares about our country and the world;
- To provide a forum for integrating a multitude of peoples and synthesizing a wealth of ideologies;
- To be a resource for people searching for ideas and information on solving social, economic, political, and scientific problems;
- To give individuals access to lifelong learning in a changing world.

Training a skilled workforce. As society increases in complexity, its need for skilled, autonomous workers increases. The pace of change—social, technological, political, and economic—is accelerating, and with it the demand for highly skilled workers. As society moves from a manufacturing and industrial economy to a service and information economy, new skills are required. The information explosion has created a demand for people who have not only knowledge, but the resources to gather, analyze, and synthesize information. And technological advances require workers with advanced training in science, mathematics, engineering, technology, and other fields. Our economy will continue to evolve, and higher education must evolve with it, preparing workers for jobs that may not even exist yet. Society, workers, and businesses must be prepared for the unexpected—because that is what will face us in the future. Without workers who have the skills to adapt to new situations, businesses will fail. In addition, workers who lack skills for the future face a cycle of unemployment and despair. Society owes its members more, and it looks to higher education to provide citizens with the tools they require to improve their life situation.

Sustaining a living culture. Society does not live by bread alone—it also needs poetry. Preparing people for work gives them the means to live; the traditions and values of our culture give them a reason to live. The visual and performing arts, literature, philosophical and religious traditions, history, and the social, physical, and life sciences all have merit aside from their "usefulness" in providing people with work and solving concrete problems. Knowledge, ideas, and creativity are ends in themselves, and higher education must help strengthen them. There has been a storm of controversy surrounding this aspect of higher education; at times the battle over the curriculum threatens to turn into a bonfire of the humanities. Although higher education has often been criticized during these turbulent times, in a sense the controversy shows that colleges and universities are doing their job. Sustaining a living culture means preserving some old ideas while abandoning others, and selecting and incorporating some new ideas while rejecting others. This process can not and should not be easy, tidy, or painless. But it is necessary.

Supporting a participatory democracy. If we lived in an authoritarian nation ruled by a small group, society would have much less need for universal education. However, our society requires of citizens that they participate in their own governance. Under a democratic system, the government is only as good as the people who elect it—sometimes worse. If we want a government based upon intelligence, compassion, ethics, and excellence, we must inculcate those values in our future leaders and citizens. Citizens must be aware of the needs and problems of the community so that the political process will be energized to confront the problems. Community colleges can address these issues through programs to inform and educate the citizens, through activities that provide a forum and a voice for the diverse concerns and interests within a community, and through work with other institutions in the community to ensure the interests of all are represented and heard. As Thomas Jefferson said, "If a nation expects to be ignorant and free, in a state of civilization, it expects what never was and never will be."

Integrating diverse people and ideologies. As our nation becomes more diverse and our world becomes smaller, society has an ever-greater need to expose all of its members to other cultures and ideologies. To maintain a coherent and peaceful society—both national and global—requires that our people understand and accept one another—even if they do not always agree. The goal is not a homogeneous society, but a tolerant one.

Providing resources for solving problems. Like museums and libraries, which often maintain close ties to institutions of higher education, colleges and universities are a resource for businesses, government agencies, organizations, and individuals doing research into a wide variety of questions. While our society's technological and scientific progress boggles the mind, our intellectual and spiritual progress has not kept pace with the multitude of social problems that now plague us. Society is in desperate need of assistance in combating poverty, pollution, social unrest, racism, sexism, crime, and many other problems. Higher education, as other segments of society, must do whatever it can to help overcome the many obstacles we face. While higher education can not take sole responsibility for solving global problems, it can provide valuable resources—such as information, research, and facilities. Even more mundane, local problems faced by small businesses—such as how industrial processes work—and by individuals—such as one person's research into his or her own genealogy—may benefit from the resources available at the average institution of higher education.

Providing access to lifelong learning in a changing world. This would be a better society if everyone continued to learn. So goes the conventional wisdom. Simply encourage people who want to learn and the battle is nearly won. Well, that just isn't so. For one thing, it's a lot tougher to find access to learning than one might think. Barriers to access such as financial constraints, fear, complacency, age, sex or race discrimination are road blocks to learning. The open door of the community college is the access point to postsecondary education for all members of the community. This is often the most meaningful expression of equality in a community. This access must be supported by appropriate financial aid policies. It must be made real by the provision of remediation programs, occupational programs, and transfer programs. Ernest Boyer said that the purpose of education is to "empower individuals to live competently in their communities." That is an appropriate role for higher education; it is an appropriate role for the community college. ♁

Linda Ray Pratt
President, American Association of University Professors

John Henry Newman published his influential *The Idea of a University* in 1852 in England as a new literate middle class emerged in nineteenth century Europe and the United States. The liberally educated citizen would exercise wisely the power and wealth that empire and industrialization brought. Newman's now familiar definition of a liberal education in fact defined a new social ideal that an expanding university system was to bring into being. In the United States, there were as yet no major universities, and the discoveries that sparked the industrial revolution were not the product of educational institutions.

The essential but unspoken assumption behind Newman's ideal was the existence of a cohesive society in which the good citizens shared a common vision. "The public mind" and "the national taste" were concretely conceived, and the liberally educated man was "at home in any society" because he was at the center of world power. Many of Newman's justifications for a philosophical education that values knowledge for its own sake remain vital today, but the world that prompted those ideas of the university has altered dramatically.

The goals of higher education still reflect the belief that an educated citizenry is the foundation of a democratic society. Our traditional objectives of preparing a skilled work force, informed citizens, and a rich community life protect the stability of our society. Today's educated citizen also needs an awareness of cultural worlds outside the hegemony of the West, technological skills to access a computerized network of production and communication, research to keep a competitive edge in a global economy, and personal interests that enrich the cultural and intellectual resources of the self. This modern version of the liberally educated good citizen at home in the world may escape the cultural parochialism of the nineteenth century, but it fails to address the changed economic and social reality on which it was based.

The cultural consensus that structured European and American society until World War II has dissipated in its aftermath. What seemed the triumph of democracy and free markets against communism has vanished in the ensuing chaos and brutality that western democracies have not been able to control or alleviate. While the United States still struggles to attain the tolerance necessary for a successful multicultural state, other places have openly resorted to various versions of "ethnic cleansing" that border on genocide. Many underdeveloped nations are growing poorer and less able to enter a world market where advanced technology controls power and wealth. A few nations have apparently lost their footing in the modern world, their infrastructures so demolished by conflict that little remains of their society. The horror of poverty, ethnic conflict, and economic collapse we see in other societies is a nightmare vision of the possibilities within our own if education fails to play its role in finding new approaches and solutions.

The model of society as an organic whole under the cultural hegemony of a homogeneous group is no longer even a rhetorical possibility, but viable alternatives have not yet emerged. Society needs new models that both recognize heterogeneity and develop enough cultural consensus to preserve social cohesion. Although much of the multicultural study underway in institutions of higher education is unsophisticated and politicized, society is in desperate need of a new philosophy of social diversity that offers accommodation without requiring assimilation.

Definitions of higher education that think narrowly in terms of vocational skills and market economies, on the one hand, or abstractly of self-cultivation, on the other, limit the possibilities for society. Behind the approved functional roles of instruction and certification is the often disconcerting pursuit of new ideas. Society's greatest need from higher education is often the one it most resists: new ideas that recognize a radically altered set of assumptions about culture, science, and economics. But a society which attempts to control intellectual discourse or set the agenda for research in higher education has little safeguard against its own mistakes and few occasions to discover what it does not already want to know.

Higher education is increasingly subject to political pressures that could interfere with its meeting its proper responsibilities to society. When political agendas enter the university they often translate as the desire to control knowledge. But the changing nature of society requires a constant review of its past understandings. Instead of being only the repository of knowledge of the history and culture of a society, universities should debate differing visions of history and culture. Instead of serving mainly a middle class, our institutions must educate a wider public in order to ameliorate increasingly deep divisions between well paid educated citizens and poorly paid uneducated ones. Lacking the ideological and economic imperatives that shaped much of the twentieth century's political development, we must develop new policies for an unsettled world in which capitalism is not strong enough to support the undeveloped nations or sustain the former communist ones. Having invented technology to destroy the habitable earth, we must evolve an ecological ethic adequate to preserve it.

Our need for new knowledge, theories, strategies, and moral perspectives must not be subsumed in a short-sighted desire for a cheaper, more utilitarian education. Unfortunately, many recent trends are counter to the role higher education should play. Rising tuition costs and reduced funding are closing off higher education at the moment when successful employment increasingly requires advanced learning. Teaching becomes more difficult when the classroom is not unified by common objectives and abilities, yet the ratio of students to faculty grows. Many call for cutbacks in research at a time when society needs even more research in order to stay competitive in the global economy. The role of research in informed teaching is greater when the body of knowledge develops so rapidly.

Unless our society wants its scientific, technological, and industrial life closed within the narrow production interests of corporations—many of which are multinationals who have little loyalty to a nation's interest—it must call on higher education for more research, not less. To reduce the research role of higher education is to weaken our hand in the global economy and undermine our power as a nation.

Finally, a society confronted with almost unlimited technological possibilities, global designs on the planet's resources, and an increasingly rigid line of division between those who have and those who do not, must address the ethics of production and power. A highly technological society is especially vulnerable to questions of who will know, who will decide what we should know, and how we shall use what we know. Inevitably, those who control knowledge will be able to control both commerce and justice. We cannot look to government and industry for a searching ethical critique of their own self interest. With its traditions of academic freedom, disinterested criticism, and philosophical debate, higher education may best provide the forum in which a society in search of a new self definition can find a new moral vision. ✝

Gail B. Promboin
Assistant Vice President-National Issues, Corporate Public Involvement, Aetna

Something different from what it's been getting lately—otherwise, why would such an august group of foundations be asking the question? It can be argued that the university is the last medieval institution to have survived relatively intact into the twentieth century. Government, business, the family, public schools, the law, and other societal institutions have been transformed—radically, in some cases—but the tidal wave of change that swept over those institutions has affected higher education relatively little. There can be little argument, however, that higher education will look very different in the twenty-first century. The forces of change are growing stronger and more evident:

- Demographic Change: The age group that traditionally has populated higher education is shrinking as a share of the total; the older students who fill more of the seats have different goals and expectations than their younger colleagues. The student population is growing more diverse and, as it does, more likely to seek inclusiveness in the curriculum. And, according to a 1991 Harris poll, a large proportion of high school graduates fall short of colleges' expectations with respect to knowledge, skills, work habits and other measures of preparation for higher education. Thus, *higher education must serve new and different "customers" who have different expectations and different needs.*

- Economic Change: The economic value of a college education is growing, as the global market demands more knowledgeable workers and the income distribution becomes more bifurcated. That means more and more students' goals for higher education are based on expectations of economic reward. The investment required is growing faster than inflation and—more importantly—family income, resulting in a typical debt load of $20,000. The combined effect is that *students and their families are increasingly likely to assess the value of higher education in economic terms, to select majors and careers on the basis of compensation, and to question whether the pay-offs are worth the investment.*

- Financial Crisis: Higher education faces unprecedented financial challenges. Its costs have risen much faster than inflation, fewer can afford its services, public support has not kept pace with costs, and many institutions have a large backlog of capital investment needs. *If these trends continue unchecked, higher education risks financial crisis or dramatic erosion of the quality of its programs, or both.*

- Moral/Societal Conflict: Fairly or not, higher education's image as a societal asset has taken a beating of late. Whether it's a scandal over questionable overhead costs, falsified research results, incidents of racial or other intolerance, corruption in student athletics, violence and substance abuse on campus, *higher education risks being seen as irrelevant to addressing our most vexing social, political and economic challenges or even a major contributor to them.*

With that formidable yet incomplete catalogue of challenges, it's tempting, but too facile, to say that society needs higher education to simply "fix all of the above." Instead, three areas are suggested for attention that would, if pursued with great focus and energy, go a long way toward enabling higher education to prepare for the roles it should play in the twenty-first century:

1. Make teaching and learning central to all that higher education does.
2. Radically restructure the organization and operation of higher education to achieve large productivity gains.
3. Aspire to a leadership role in society.

These three tasks are interrelated and, together, begin to address most of the challenges elaborated above.

Make Teaching and Learning Central

Reflection on the term "teaching load" brings a recognition of how far higher education has strayed—the principal mission of the institution is seen as a burden to be borne (with gritted teeth, one imagines) so that the bearer can engage in higher order, and presumably more pleasurable, activities. Yet the general public, which pays most of the bills, sees teaching undergraduates as the primary mission of higher education, and perhaps the only important one. That perception, along with the appalling fact that nearly half those who enter college fail to graduate in *five* years— let alone four—leads to the inescapable conclusion that undergraduate teaching and learning simply must be accorded a higher priority. Consider, too, that minorities and low income students consistently have even lower graduation rates and it's clear that higher education's historical role as a stepping-stone to upward mobility has been eroded seriously.

In view of the changing demographics of the student body, the paramount importance of teaching and learning is even more apparent. The more diverse the student population, the more diversity there will be in their learning styles, in the knowledge and experience they bring to the process, and in what will best instill in them a taste for learning. This calls for even greater pedagogic skill than would have been required thirty years ago when the student body was more homogeneous. It also calls for a curriculum that is *inclusive*, that enables all learners to see something of themselves within it *and* to learn about the perspectives of other cultures. And it requires a curriculum that *engages* the critical challenges of today's global society.

Making teaching and learning central means focusing attention on what and how students actually learn. Higher education needs to engage in its own version of the wrenching struggle K-12 education is undergoing to define what its students ought to know and be able to do, how it should be measured, and how all those involved in achieving the outcomes will become accountable for their results. Parallels to business can be overdone, but there's truth in the saying that "what gets measured gets done" and it's not unreasonable to expect that a 50 percent-plus failure rate (i.e., drop-outs) should stimulate change. The outcomes of higher education should not be narrowly defined but, like similar efforts in K-12 education, should include the attitudes, attributes, and social skills needed to be a responsible adult in the twenty-first century.

To be fair, many higher education institutions have recognized the need to focus on teaching and learning, initiated programs that recognize outstanding teaching, and taken steps to make teaching a factor in tenure decisions. Many also have begun to make their curriculum more reflective of cultural diversity and global realities. On the whole, however, these have been token baby-steps, especially in light of the changes that are needed. It's obvious, for example, that until the academic reward structure gives teaching much more weight, faculty behavior is unlikely to change much.

Equally obvious, but less often recognized, is the absurdity of the implicit assumption that faculty were born knowing how to teach. If this were not assumed, wouldn't we see some kind of requirement that they demonstrate some know-how before they are dropped into the classroom? We criticize the preparation of K-12 teachers for emphasizing pedagogy over content; the reverse is true in higher education. There is a massive and growing body of knowledge about how people learn, but hardly anybody is using it. If they were, more students would be learning more, learning it better and, most likely, persisting to graduation in greater numbers. Maybe faculty would even come to find teaching more rewarding than other academic pursuits.

Making teaching and learning central to the enterprise will help to achieve other valued goals—restoring higher education as a means of upward mobility, raising the skill level of the future workforce, building the foundations of a multi-cultural society that sees its diversity more as a strength than a problem, and building the know-how to help address the social, economic, environmental and technological challenges facing the world today.

Achieve Dramatic Increases in Productivity

Society needs higher education to succeed at this task so that it will have a fighting chance for success in achieving the others that are of more direct value. Higher education simply cannot provide what society needs if the average family cannot afford to send its children to college, if research investments carry inflated overhead costs, and if dollars are not redirected from low-return investments to high-return investments. Again, although the application of business paradigms to other endeavors can be overdone, some of the principles of total quality management and reengineering should prove useful.

First and foremost, every higher education institution needs to reexamine and clarify its mission, if it hasn't already. Not every university should be a comprehensive research institution, offer graduate and professional programs in every field, or even offer graduate programs at all. Not every institution should continue to exist, and none can be all things to all people. There is an urgent need for consolidation, elimination of duplication, and reduction of excess capacity—especially at the graduate level and especially in programs requiring large investments in technology and facilities. While there are some benefits to overlap and duplication, we cannot afford them anymore.

When an institution is clear about its mission, it can stop doing things that don't advance it; the largest cost reductions will come from eliminating entire functions or programs that, while they may be beneficial to some, are not "mission-critical" to the institution as a whole. Conversely, the institution can identify gaps in its current program that need to be closed, and close them with redirected dollars rather than new ones.

Serious attention must be devoted to increasing productivity in administrative and support functions. Between 1975 and 1985, total higher education faculty increased 6 percent while administrative staff grew by 60 percent; no wonder costs increased at a rate of 30 percent above inflation. That has to change, by eliminating lower-priority tasks, reengineering processes, and making better use of technology. Faculty productivity is frequently criticized (often unfairly), but thoughtfully defined gains in facultyproductivity should be achievable as well.

Clearly, this will require a real culture change that engages academics and administrators alike. However, as urgently as society needs higher education to reduce its cost spiral and increase its productivity, this must be done in a way that doesn't detract from achieving large gains in student learning. Fortunately, just as many businesses have found that higher quality often costs less, higher education will probably find that it can do a much better job of teaching when it gets rid of all the distractions and clutter that impede the learning process. For that reason, the astute institution will link its work on increasing productivity with its efforts to focus on teaching and learning.

Aspire to Leadership

That higher education seems to have given up its moral high ground is, of course, a reflection of the larger society's loss of its moral compass, its confidence in the future, and its commitment to its core values. Though higher education didn't necessarily lead society to this point, it can and must play a key role in leading us out of it.

The solutions to so many of our social problems lie in every individual and organization taking responsibility for their own destiny and being accountable for the consequences of their actions on others (a theme worth an essay of its own, but stated as an axiom here). By taking responsibility for getting its own house in order—making student learning central and getting costs under control—higher education will set a valuable example for all other segments of society. It will also become the means whereby students *can* prepare to take control of their own futures.

Every facet of higher education life and every discipline reflects broader societal conflicts and challenges, yet each is also a potential tool for helping to resolve them. For instance, if higher education can change its curriculum to reflect our multi-cultural society, build the diversity of faculty and staff, and create a truly civil society on campus, then the rest of us can learn from it, and the next generation will have internalized the experience. If higher education makes it a priority to bring its intellectual resources to bear on our most pressing societal problems—school reform, health care reform, global competitiveness, environmental management, etc.—we will be that much closer to solving them and will be graduating students prepared to work on them. To do this means to emphasize the connectedness of higher education to the rest of the world rather than its separateness and to build durable links to other sectors of society.

The question of values and moral leadership is more difficult to discuss, but no less important. We tend to shy away from consideration of values because we fear they will divide us rather than unite us—and sometimes they do. Unfortunately, in the process of trying to avoid conflicts about values, we have detached our hearts and souls from our work and civic lives. Yet we cannot be effective without engaging our hearts and souls as well as our minds. How can higher education help us reconnect our humanity with our intellect? Clearly, one way is to deal forthrightly with the kinds of ethical breaches that have tarnished its image of late. Another is to build on the very promising growth of student community service programs, through which students (and sometimes faculty) gain a sense of community responsibility and learn how to use their knowledge and skills to fulfill it. Still other approaches will be needed, but these are a start.

Conclusion

This prescription for higher education is pretty much what is required for any other sector of society. Some are further along in the task than others, but we will not have addressed the challenges we face as boldly as we must if every sector of our society does not in some way respond to these three imperatives:

- Focus on a very few of the most important things.
- Do them very, very well.
- Bring your values to work.

Any person or institution or sector of society that consistently does all three cannot help but succeed. ✝

Robert M. Rosenzweig

Former President, Association of American Universities

By most conventional measures, the development of higher education since the end of World War II has been one of America's outstanding success stories. Its range, diversity, flexibility, and in many respects its quality are admired throughout the world. Paradoxically, however, the view from home has become a good deal more critical than the view from abroad. The last decade has witnessed a growing disenchantment with institutions of higher learning across a broad front of grievances. Why is it that an enterprise that so many would like to emulate has spawned a virtual industry of sharp and even bitter criticism?

There is no simple answer to the question, but a clue might be found by looking at two related but very different questions. The first is, "What does society need from higher education?" The second is, "What does society want from higher education?" There is an unavoidable tension between the approaches to the two. The question of needs can, in principle, be answered by comparing an assessment of social needs with a similar assessment of institutional capacities, and seeing where they fit and where they do not. It is, of course, not quite that easy, because setting a list of pressing social needs is as much an exercise in values as it is in analysis, but it is still a vastly different matter from establishing a list of wants. That is a question that can be answered by market research, because determining what people want, in commerce, politics or education, is the essence of a market system, and in this country we are pretty good at that. So good, in fact, that the pressures to provide what society wants, and the rewards for doing so, have turned attention away from what society needs, a condition that has produced a measure of disenchantment outside the academic gates and a measure of disquiet within.

This is by no means an easy dilemma to resolve, especially in America. American higher education, as Martin Trow has argued, grew up alongside a market-oriented economic system, a fact that distinguishes our educational system from all others in the world. A consequence of that fact is that American colleges and universities have always been highly responsive to what society wanted of them, and where market forces have clashed with what might be called the autonomous values of the academy, the former have almost always won out. The most dramatic instance in our history was the creation of the Land-Grant College system when the existing public universities failed to attend to the rising demands of a nascent industrial society with its attendant commercial and technical requirements for both industry and agriculture. Adherents of free markets will argue that meeting wants, at a price that people are willing to pay, is the best way of meeting needs. Maybe yes and maybe no; but what is unambiguously clear is that, in a market system, failure to supply what the public wants will foreclose the opportunity to supply what it may need, as failure of office-holders to win reelection will end their chances for further service to the public.

In the list of what society wants from higher education that follows here, no attempt is made to distinguish public from private, though a somewhat different list might be made for each. Nor is any serious attempt made to distinguish among different types of institutions. Much of what follows is applicable to universities; some, but not all of it, may be applicable as well to other types of institutions.

Society wants from higher education:

- Broad access to some kind of post-secondary education for any student who wishes to try.
- Some degree—here the expectations vary widely—of acculturation and preparation for citizenship.

- A credential that is useful for occupational purposes and the training that the credential implies. The former is sometimes more important than the latter, but the credential should be available for a large and ever-growing menu of occupations.
- New knowledge, especially in science and technology, with the expectation that some, though perhaps not all, will have useful economic or other social benefits.
- Advanced training for those professionals—doctors, lawyers, scholars, for example—whose services are essential and whose training had better be all that is implied by the license they receive.
- Service to the community through outreach programs that may take a variety of forms, such as continuing and post-professional education, agricultural extension and its contemporary cousin, technical extension.
- Mass entertainment on a large scale, primarily through programs of intercollegiate athletics, made available to the public not merely through the opportunity to buy a ticket and attend an event, but through the opportunity to stay home and watch the games on television for nothing.
- All of the above at a low price, whether measured in tuition charges or taxes.

Someone else's list might differ from this one, but most lists would include most of the elements in my list. The striking thing about the list is that for the most part American higher education has delivered, and it has been richly rewarded for doing so. It would be hard to find a period in the history of any nation in which institutions of higher learning have prospered as have America's in the last thirty-five years. In that time the system has expanded to accommodate enormous numbers of students, many of them from racial and ethnic groups that had previously been denied access to higher learning. Women have entered the mainstream of higher education as undergraduates, and increasingly as graduate and professional students and as faculty and administrators. The most creative and productive research enterprise in the world has grown up in universities providing benefits far in excess of society's investment in it. Occupational, pre-professional and professional curricula are thick on the ground and seem to grow with every expression of need. And, of course, few can complain about the quality or quantity of entertainment our universities provide for the public virtually year-round.

In the process, higher education has become a multi-billion-dollar industry; faculty have largely gained economic security; the industry's leaders are handsomely compensated; and national, state, and institutional bureaucracies have grown apace.

And yet, there is a sense that, notwithstanding the successful operation of the educational market, not all is right in higher education. Partly that is because the price has become higher than the public wants to pay; that is always a cause for unhappiness. But there is more to the current unease about higher education than price alone. The ground is slippery here, and hard evidence is scanty; but it is possible that what so many are sensing is a gap between what the public wants and what it needs. It is at least an hypothesis worth exploring. What, then, might be on the list of society's needs from higher education?

- Rigorous academic standards. There is no large constituency asking to be made to work harder and be judged more rigorously. Such a policy would be bound to produce more failures, at least in the short run, and run head-on into the demand for occupational credentials. Yet, in very many colleges and universities, the declining level of academic preparation exhibited by incoming students has led to much greater emphasis on remedial work and, arguably, a broad easing of expectations and standards of performance. No society, certainly none in the modern world, can prosper under a regime of flabby standards for the higher education of its youth. Greater rigor is an unpopular but necessary medicine.

- Engagement with the improvement of elementary and secondary education. Long-term improvement of academic standards in higher education can only occur if the erosion of the quality of the nation's lower schools is reversed. Many colleges and universities are working with schools in their areas, and some have mounted impressive efforts of broader scope. But the sum of it all adds up to considerably less than a response to an urgent need that is grounded in both self-interest and national interest.

- Open and honest address to the problems of racial and ethnic tension. This remains the American dilemma, and higher education, which has become a major gatekeeper to the good life in America, has been thrust into the center of it. As a consequence, a variety of natural experiments has been taking place on campuses in every part of the country. Some address the problem by some variation of separatism—separate dormitories and social and cultural centers are the most common manifestations. Others have taken a more rigorously integrationist position. In few if any cases, however, have these experiments been seen as experiments. Rather, they have grown out of doctrine or political combat and have operated with largely unexamined consequences. There is no simple answer to America's racial and ethnic problems, but surely their resolution would be advanced by honest evaluation of and open debate about the consequences of the various approaches taken on campus. To put it bluntly, nowhere else in the society will that evaluation and debate take place; it has not yet taken place in higher education and its absence has constituted a failure of higher education to provide for an urgent social need.

- Greater attention to issues of scale, mission, and priorities. At this moment in its history this nation needs successful examples of institutions that know how to subtract as well as add, divide, and multiply. Like the rest of the nation, colleges and universities have grown opportunistically, and like the rest of the nation, they now find themselves with commitments larger than the resources available to meet them. Bringing those two into balance will require hard, collective thinking about which programs and which processes are central to an institution's definition of what it means to be an institution of higher learning at the turn of the century. That is an exercise that, if undertaken with brutal honesty, will result in every institution doing less of some things it is now doing and perhaps doing what remains in some different ways. Not only will the result be healthy in itself, but the example can be valuable to a society that must do the same on an even larger scale.

- Avoid becoming institutionally partisan on divisive social and political issues. American society needs colleges and universities to be active exemplars of the values that they have always professed, values like civility of discourse, respect for evidence and proper inference from it, insistence that truth is the only antidote to error and that today's truth may turn out to be tomorrow's folly, that dissent from the conventional wisdom is an essential element in reaching the truth, and that dissenters are not only to be protected from punishment but listened to because truth is often found in unlikely and unlovely places. When institutions become partisans, none of those values is safe and the loss to society is incalculable, for what is striking in this list of academic values is that all of them are central to a properly functioning democracy and no other social institutions both profess and practice them. Colleges and universities are the natural teachers of democratic values because those values are in their genes. Indeed, they are the only natural teachers, and if they fail to give society what it needs in this respect, then all of their other contributions, no matter how richly rewarding they may be, will be debased.

In some particulars, what society wants and what it needs from higher education are in conflict. If, in 1993, America and American higher education have left the psychological '80s, and are moving to a greater willingness to confront hard questions and suffer some pain for their answers, then it may be possible to turn needs into wants with enormous benefits to all concerned. It is important that we test that proposition. †

John E. Roueche
Professor and Director, Sid W. Richardson Regents Chair
The University of Texas at Austin

The obvious intrinsic value of a college education for Americans is the basis for a tradition that had its beginning in the earliest days of our country. To millions of families across the nation, a college education represents the clearest and best-marked path to a better life, a more satisfying career, a brighter future. The depth of our collective faith in the power of postsecondary education can be measured by the enormous growth in the number of institutions that have arisen in a clear and expanding progression from the land-grant colleges created by the first Morrill Act in 1862 through the twentieth century proliferation of the modern community college. Higher education in America has evolved into a vast and complex system of public and private institutions that serve over 12 million students of every age and background each year. The system represents, in the words of Ernest L. Boyer, the realization of "one of the most enlightened visions any society has ever collectively endorsed...a remarkable achievement unmatched by any other nation." Together our nation's colleges and universities comprise an investment in our collective future on which we spend the astounding sum of more than $95 billion annually.

There are now over 3,300 degree-granting institutions of higher education in the United States. This incredibly diverse group—large research-oriented universities, comprehensive state universities, small liberal arts colleges, urban and rural community colleges—forms a rich tapestry in which each institution fills its own special niche in the fabric of higher education and brings its own unique history and traditions to the task. Yet, in spite of the diversity of our institutions, the system's internal hierarchy of values, measures of academic respectability, and faculty reward and incentive structures are, as Ernest A. Lynton and Sandra E. Elman have noted, "astonishingly uniform." While some 300 of our institutions carry the sobriquet "university," only 20 to 50 of these, all large research-oriented universities, are considered to be of the highest level, deserving of the title "world-class." Nonetheless, as Page Smith and others have noted, these elite universities set the standard of excellence for the entire system. The result is a monolithic status system that pervades all of higher education, a system which places an inappropriate value on so-called "pure" research and on the national reputation for the person and the institution that this research can bring.

Unfortunately, as we look to the societal demands that higher education will be asked to satisfy as we move into the next century, this narrowly defined value system appears woefully inadequate. Instead of accentuating the rich diversity of higher education by recognizing a broad range of valuable contributions, this model serves to homogenize and limit our institutions. The sad consequence is that institutions perhaps perfectly suited to satisfying new, yet vital needs of society may fail to achieve their potential because the internal system of values, priorities, and aspirations emphasizes and rewards only a tiny set of traditional scholarly activities and ignores a much larger set of potentially more valuable contributions.

The roots of this lopsided value system are deep and woven tightly within the history of higher education; nonetheless, its deleterious effects are clear and have been documented (and lamented) by some of our most noted educators. This compelling body of work, of which Allan Bloom's stinging criticism of the core curriculum in *The Closing of the American Mind,* Smith's detailed history of the decline of higher education in *Killing the Spirit,* Boyer's insightful analysis presented in *College: The Undergraduate Experience in America,* and Lynton and Elman's comprehensive *New Priorities for the University* are conspicuous examples, clearly evidences the need for higher education to refocus its efforts, to somehow "reinvent itself" into a more responsive and effective social entity. Of course, the question of *how* is left begging. José Ortega y Gasset, in his landmark essay entitled *The Mission of the University,* crystallized the issue almost 50 years ago: "Any alteration, or touching up, or adjustment about this house of ours, unless it starts by reviewing the problem of its mission—clearly, decisively, truthfully—will be love's labors lost." Ortega y Gasset's conceptualization of that mission has come to be the definitive expression of the post-war university's reason for being. As society's primary and most important repository of knowledge, the university was compelled to satisfy society's needs in three areas: the transmission of culture—i.e., the vital system of values and ideas attained through the totality of human experience; the teaching of the professions; and the search for new knowledge, a process which involved both scientific research and the training of new scientists. Assessing the success of the institution in accomplishing these purposes at that time, Ortega y Gasset concluded that two, the teaching of the professions and the search for new knowledge, were well-served; the third, the transmission of culture, was barely and haphazardly addressed.

If Ortega y Gasset's yardstick were to be applied to American higher education today, many of the same conclusions would be reached. Our graduate and professional schools are, by any measure, the best in the world, attracting the best and the brightest from every part of the globe. The United States has undisputed leadership in almost every scientific research field; our scientists have dominated Nobel Prize competitions for years. Most of the major innovations in technological fields such as electronics and biotechnology were discovered in American laboratories. Yet, as Bloom, Boyer, Smith, and others have detailed, we fall woefully short of success in transmitting our collective values, ideas, and culture. The similarity of these conclusions to Ortega y Gasset's original thoughts speaks as much to how little has changed in higher education over the last 50 years as it does to the enormity of the challenge.

And the challenge *is* enormous. While colleges and universities have not seen any significant change to their mission in the last 50 years, the world around them has changed dramatically. According to Bruce Merrifield, former assistant secretary of commerce for production, technology, and innovation, 90 percent of all scientific and technical knowledge has been generated within the last 30 years! By the end of the 1990s, the field of knowledge will have doubled again. Dale Parnell, in *Dateline 2000,* estimates the half-life of new knowledge at somewhere between five and 10 years. Improvements in areas such as robotics, production techniques, computers, and telecommunications have rendered countless processes and products obsolete, in some cases virtually overnight. Millions of jobs have been transformed or eliminated. New industries have appeared on the scene; the knowledge and skills necessary for their work forces to be competitive bear very little resemblance to what business and industry required of our educational system just a few years ago.

What higher education needs today is not just another academic reexamination of its mission, with a curricular adjustment made here or a new extension effort established there. Higher education's very stock in trade—knowledge—has fundamentally changed, and with it, society's needs and expectations for its colleges and universities also have changed. As the pace of discovery has accelerated, an increasing pressure has surfaced for new theories and findings to be swiftly incorporated into practical applications. While applied research lacks the cachet of "pure" research in terms of rewards and value structures, the volumes of new data and information resulting from pure research efforts must be aggregated, combined with other knowledge, and interpreted to maximize their utility.

Although our higher education system can proudly point to a long history of cooperation and exchanges with industry and government, the press of global competition will require that new knowledge be distributed much more quickly and pervasively than existing systems will support and reach beyond the university to far more sectors of the economy than existing links allow. While it should be noted, in all fairness, that our system of higher education is moving on many fronts to address these needs, the sheer speed of technological changes still represents an enormous challenge. Indeed, a General Motors executive, when asked why GM did not enter into more partnerships with colleges and universities, replied, "Their speed is deceptive...they are slower than they look."

A significant byproduct of the changing nature of knowledge is that the traditional recipients of postsecondary education have changed; the image of the young, well-prepared college student became a myth for most of the higher education system years ago. While our graduate and professional schools are doing an excellent job of preparing the best scientists, engineers, and other professionals in the world, these institutions are training only the top 20 percent of the population. To remain competitive in the global economy, economists and labor analysts generally agree that the remaining 80 percent of the population must be provided with the basic reading, writing, computational, information processing, teamwork, and learning skills that will allow them to continuously adapt to the press of new technology and knowledge. For our system of higher education, this task presents a difficult, yet absolutely critical challenge. Compounding the problem is that, as some have estimated, up to 75 percent of the *existing* work force will require significant retraining in the next decade and that up to 80 percent of the new jobs created during that time will require at least two years of postsecondary education. These estimates must be viewed in light of the fact that 85 percent of the work force in the year 2000 is already at work today. Traditional college offerings, bound by outdated concepts such as the 18-week semester and daytime-only classes, are geared toward an increasingly rare full-time student. Other than some notable exceptions, mostly within the system of community colleges, few of our postsecondary institutions have addressed the fact that most of the adults working today face an ongoing, lifelong need for education and skills training.

A New View of the Mission of American Higher Education

As we face the challenges posed by the press of technology, global economic demands, the changing nature of and need for knowledge, and the influx of non-traditional and returning students, it is quite clear that a serious refocusing of our purpose is needed, one that faithfully adheres to Ortega y Gasset's standards of clarity, decisiveness, and truthfulness. However, because the job is so large and the need so urgent, we cannot afford a wholesale restructuring of the system, even if that were possible. We must play to our strengths, channel our resources where they will do the most good, and recognize that while each institution can, indeed *must,* play a vital role, those roles will not be the same for every institution or class of institutions. Rather than a hierarchical system, with the great research universities placed reverently at the head, we must view higher education as a *system,* a *team* if you will, with each institution performing an important, yet distinct role. We must begin to visualize the overarching mission of higher education as, necessarily, the sum of those roles and work to restructure our internal value and reward systems accordingly.

What then should the mission of our system of higher education be? Using the past as prologue, we can use Ortega y Gasset's elegant triad of purposes as a model and combine it with a systems' perspective that incorporates the rich diversity of our institutions and the external pressures acting on the system. Viewed from this angle, the essential elements of the overarching mission of higher education quickly unfold. They represent the fundamental societal expectations for our colleges and universities, our collective higher education needs. These needs are fourfold.

The need for a well-informed citizenry. Perhaps the most difficult of society's needs to satisfy, it is nonetheless vital to the public good that we have citizens able to analyze and asses policies and actions on the basis of our common belief system. In a time of ever-increasing emphasis on diversity, we still must find a way to focus on, and convey, our common human and democratic values, and to validate their expression in a multi-cultural context. Traditionally this has been approached through the core undergraduate curriculum, an anachronism which has tried, as Bloom scathingly detailed, to be so many things to so many people that all the values have been boiled out.

Boyer, in the keynote remarks to the 1992 Leadership 2000 Conference, eloquently noted that, for all our differences, we have much more in common. Among these distinctly human commonalities are the experiences of life, birth, and death, the use of symbols to express feelings and ideas, the communicative power of the aesthetic, the capacity to recall the past and anticipate the future— Boyer argues that these and similarly universal experiences hold the essence of our most deeply held values and should form the basis of the core curriculum. Such a curriculum, at its best, would move students from competence to commitment, would make a real difference in the civic and social responsibilities they are willing to accept, and ultimately, affect their world view. Vachel Lindsay expressed the challenge: "How can we help students to understand that the tragedy of life is not death; the tragedy is to die with commitments undefined and convictions undeclared and service unfulfilled?"

The need for an adaptive, professional, world-class work force. As a society, this is without a doubt our most pressing need. The insidious combination of rapidly advancing technology, spurred on by the pressures of global competition, and the learning deficit spawned by a failed K-12 school system is producing a serious social dilemma—America is simultaneously creating more high-skill jobs and more low-skill workers. As Parnell observed, "Unless our nation resolves this problem we will create a de facto class segregation between the happy and productive citizen and the miserable and unemployed citizen." Changing demographics have shifted the immediate burden of this problem from the public school system to the higher education system. Fully 85 percent of the work force in the year 2000 is already at work today. From these already employed workers, a new group of unemployed is emerging—experienced workers displaced by technology and vigorous international competition. Indeed, community colleges report that up to 15 percent of their students already possess at least a bachelor's degree and are returning to college to upgrade their skills or train for new careers.

Community colleges are well-placed to meet much of the need for retraining, both on and off the job; a community college is located within commuting distance of 90 percent of the nation's populace. A national priority is emerging, one endorsed by the American Association of Community Colleges, to develop a first-class system of worker training and education that, like its sister system in the graduate and professional schools, will be the best in the world. Community colleges are uniquely suited to play a major role in such a system. Indeed, a recent survey by the League for Innovation in the Community College found that nearly all community colleges are already providing customized work force training to employees of business, government, and industry; most offer technical programs to prepare students for the world of work as well. The infrastructure of a nationwide worker training and education system is already in place at these institutions, but unfortunately, these efforts do not comprise a world-class system yet; many programs are hampered by inadequate resources and facilities. Without significant new funding, whether from traditional sources or from public-private partnerships, our current training system cannot be counted on to meet the projected need.

The need for new knowledge, new technologies, and new applications.
Scientists around the world generally agree that American research efforts continue to lead the world by a wide margin in all but a few fields. Nonetheless, there is a growing concern that the U.S. lead may be narrowing because of declining funding as well as a drop in the number of young scientists entering the research field. Of even greater concern is that American manufacturers have not been able to capitalize on the U.S. research lead and have lost important battles in the marketplace, especially in the area of consumer electronics. Some experts believe that America is losing its competitive edge, not because of a decline in new research and important discoveries, but because of an inadequate mechanism for quickly transferring the technology from the laboratory to the production line. Part of the problem lies in the implicit values and rewards of our higher education system; applied research does not attract the funding of its more prestigious cousin. The National Academy of Sciences has lamented that there are few publicly funded activities supporting the adaptation of new technologies in the U.S. and noted the sharp contrast between our country's attitude on this subject and the policies of some of our primary international competitors. Parnell observed that "relatively few American inventions or industrial improvement ideas make it from research organizations to the marketplace, or they are developed so slowly that aggressive international companies are allowed to capture that particular market niche."

Despite the long and successful history of technology transfer in the fields of agriculture and medicine, the challenge posed by the combination of intense global competition and the onslaught of rapid advances in fields such as electronics, biotechnology, computers, and telecommunications is immense. Complicating the issue is the fact that much of the activity in these fields occurs in small-to-medium-sized companies, while many of the most successful efforts to date have involved partnerships between the elite research universities and large corporations. In some cases such partnerships make considerable sense; the

Sematech consortium between The University of Texas, the federal government, and the large computer chip manufacturers is pursuing state-of-the-art lithography and chip manufacturing processes that are enormously expensive to explore. The financial clout these partners can bring to bear on the problem is a vital part of the solution.

Nonetheless, technology transfer is a large enough problem that all levels of institutions can play an important role. Ohio, facing a severe economic crisis in the early 1980s, formulated a multi-agency strategy called the Thomas Edison Program. With an original appropriation of $67 million, the program has stimulated working partnerships between business and academia and produced a host of new technologies, ideas, products, and companies. An essential part of the program was the establishment of extension agents at each of the state's community and technical colleges. The Edison program helped Ohio move from a dismal 49th place in job creation in 1982 to 3rd place in 1986.

Technology transfer, to be successful, must be viewed as a sort of communications network, with two-way knowledge transfer occurring not only between institutions and industry but also between and among levels of institutions. One such example is the Community College and the Computer project of the League for Innovation in the Community College. This partnership between the nation's leading computer manufacturers and key community colleges located strategically across the country was designed to develop computer applications that would improve teaching and learning in higher education. The result has been an ongoing series of projects that have resulted in direct investment of over $30 million in computer technology for community colleges. Through publications and conferences, the benefits of this project and the countless spin-offs it has spawned are shared with virtually every community college in North America.

The need for a community nexus and catalyst for change. The purposes outlined above are not independent—they are, rather, mutually reinforcing and complementary. In combination they represent a powerful force for societal change. This is the basis of the final and overarching purpose of our higher education system. Because of its involvement in communicating societal values, in preparing our citizens for the world of work, and in the discovery, adaptation, and dissemination of knowledge and technology, our higher education system is suited uniquely to the roles of convener, collaborator, partner, even catalyst for change in the community. As more and more partnerships are formed between colleges and universities, government, industry, and business, connections are being forged that establish these institutions as involved and able players in both the public and private arenas.

An example of the need for colleges and universities to seek this role and of the good which can spring from it can be found in the tremendous number of public-private partnerships which have been established across the country. The Super Conducting Super Collider Project, while politically controversial, already has advanced much more than the esoteric boundaries of quantum physics—in hundreds of business and industry links resulting from the effort, new jobs have been created, new manufacturing techniques and technologies developed, and professional collaborations established across a wide range of fields. The economic benefits of this collaboration between prestigious research universities such as The University of Texas, federal and state governments, and dozens of industries across the nation already measure in the billions of dollars.

In a notable example of social involvement, Miami-Dade Community College has enlisted the support, commitment, and resources of dozens of agencies and organizations in a real effort to revitalize and renew one of the poorest neighborhoods in the nation, the Overtown section of Miami. With the Medical Campus located squarely in the center of Overtown, Miami-Dade's interest in this project is as real as its partners, and significant changes are taking place. When Hurricane Andrew devastated south Florida, many residents assumed that plans for a new Miami-Dade campus in Homestead would be abandoned along with the hundreds of devastated homes and businesses, but the campus is being built and is serving as the catalyst for a revitalized reconstruction effort.

The message communicated by that decision is clear—far from an isolated and detached ivory tower, the modern college or university must be integrally and vitally connected with the community of citizens which supports and sustains it. In *Habits of the Heart,* Robert Bellah notes, "Perhaps the notion that public and private lives are at odds is incorrect. Perhaps they are so deeply involved with each other that the impoverishment of one entails the impoverishment of the other. Parker Palmer is probably right when he says "that in a healthy society, the private and the public are not mutually exclusive, not in competition with each other. They are, instead, two halves of a whole, two poles of a paradox. They work together dialectically, helping to create and to nurture one another."

The examples of Miami-Dade Community College, and other institutions like the Community College of Denver, which is supervising child care services for the entire metropolitan county in which it resides, and St. Petersburg Junior College, whose collaborations with its neighboring public schools are attracting considerable national interest, illustrate the broad and largely untapped potential of our country's community colleges. These institutions, more than any other segment of our higher education system, represent the greatest potential for expansion and growth, a tremendous resource of opportunity that is either unused or underutilized in much of the country. For 350 years, American higher education has continued to broaden its mission, to create new structures and organizational forms, to evolve in response to the needs of its society. Today, with a clear eye on our history, it is obvious that the need was never more pressing. The strength of the American system lies in its diversity—our colleges and universities can and will rise to meet the challenge. ✝

Terry Tinson Saario
President, Northwest Area Foundation

The pressures that will bear on American higher education in the decades to come will be more contradictory and immediate in nature than forces for change have been in the past. Until relatively recently, institutions of higher education have had the luxury of serving a clientele that essentially shared the same class, gender, and race perspectives. Moreover, the products produced by these institutions—well educated, white, middle to upper middle class, young males—were almost certainly guaranteed well-paying jobs and places in society.

That world is no longer. America, in the twenty-first century, will be fundamentally different. Demographically, white males will be in a minority in the decades to come. People of color, immigrants, first generation college-bound, women, and displaced workers will be more the norm for the average student. These individuals do not share the same world view, have very different interests and needs, and place widely varying demands on institutions of higher education. Certainly since the 1960s, institutions of higher education have been wrestling with the changing composition of their student bodies. These pressures will only be more exaggerated. Questions about the nature of a curriculum based on western thought and perspectives will only increase. Concerns about how to maintain standards and quality as a diverse student body advances into graduate schools will heighten. Pressures to change the composition of the faculty and administration to match the diversity of the student body will be greater. These are not new tensions for higher education. They will only increase in proportion, immediacy, and amplitude.

In some ways, though, these are not the gravest demands that higher education will face in the twenty-first century. Far more serious are pressures that may threaten the very existence of institutions of higher education. The U.S. now functions and must compete in a world economy that is dependent upon knowledge, information, high technology, international capital, and a well educated and culturally sophisticated citizenry. Upon casual glance, this seems to be the ideal environment for higher education. But is it?

Eighty-five percent of the U.S. workforce needed by the year 2010 is already on the job. The greatest job growth in the U.S. over the last decade was in the service sector, not manufacturing, where wages are higher and in some instances required skill levels are lower. R & D investments in the U.S. significantly lag behind those of Japan and Germany. Looming trade and budget deficits hamper government's ability to shift significant resources to address pressing societal problems. With poverty rates rising, and the differences between the "haves and have-nots" expanding, state and local governments are increasingly hard pressed to make rational decisions about the allocation of limited tax revenues between problems seen as urgent (health, welfare, K-12 education) versus those seen as discretionary. Higher education is being cast more and more into that discretionary category.

Moreover, the public's broad, and to some degree unquestioning, support and endorsement of the value of higher education is waning. The direct connection between a bachelor's degree and a good career has been broken in the labor market. "Real world" value to the research and teaching that takes place in most institutions of higher education is not clear to many observers. Key public policy makers see less and less relevance to much of the scholarly output that most faculty members produce. Other institutions, government and business for example, turn less often to academia for advice on how to solve the ever-pressing problems facing our society today. With the protection of tenure and the remote "ivory tower," accountability in higher education seems to be lacking.

So, what does society need from higher education? Structurally, it needs institutions that can renew themselves, that can truly reject the medieval trappings that have removed colleges and universities from relevancy to the rest of society. It needs institutions that can be on the cutting edge of research and development that will help keep this country economically competitive. It needs institutions that embrace many different ways of knowing, of the lore of other societies, and of diversity in all its forms. It needs institutions that can produce graduates who are flexible, forever questing, culturally tolerant, historically literate, technologically sophisticated, capable of analysis and prose, independent of thought, ethical, self-reliant and yet respectful of community. It needs institutions that embrace many different measures of accountability and recognize the many constituencies to which they must now be accessible and responsible.

Lastly, it needs institutions that can function in a global marketplace. Resources around the world are finite. Collaboration between sectors and across institutions to address common goals and objectives will have to be more of the norm. Society needs higher education to undergo a radical reformation, take on these multiple demands, and yet not deviate from a high quality product—the truly enlightened citizen of the world.

Society needs higher education to walk on water. ⋏

Peter W. Stanley
President, Pomona College

This is a question framed in terms of abstract collectivities: society and higher education. Yet one of the critical realities of our time is that collective units are becoming less meaningful in the lives of people and less relevant to policy makers than the components that make up the unit. In this respect, we may be experiencing one of the great sea changes of modern history. For hundreds of years, the most powerful social, political, and economic forces in the world have been integrative. This was the age that saw the development and consolidation of the nation-state, within which it seemed reasonable to speak of the goals and values of society. Today, however, whether one looks at the political and cultural divisions within countries such as India, Yugoslavia, Spain, and the United Kingdom, or the ethnic, gender, religious, and class divisions within our own country, it is arguable that *dis*-integrative forces carry the day. One exception may be the continuing economic integration of the world, but the larger impact of this is often to encourage division and fragmentation in other spheres of human activity by reducing the authority of nations and the individuality of regional cultures.

In the world that is emerging before our eyes, society continues to make claims upon individuals and institutions, but it does so only at very lofty levels. Operationally, the claims that dominate decision making are those made by society's constituent groups, many of which want things that are at odds with each other. What society needs from higher education may not be the sum of what its parts threaten, cajole, and reward higher education into providing.

If society is in some respects a problematic term, so is higher education. Higher education is a man-made category. It is higher in comparison to that which is lower: in a word, it is *postsecondary*. The category includes public, private, and sectarian universities, colleges, and community colleges, as well as professional and proprietary schools. At its best, each of these types of institution makes a contribution. If higher education is to be held accountable for meeting society's needs, however, this can occur only in the aggregate. It is senseless to ask community colleges and proprietary schools to advance knowledge, and it may be equally unrealistic to ask high-end research institutions to prepare disadvantaged and under-educated youth with the workplace skills necessary for employment. How then can society, in all its divisions, articulate what it needs from higher education in all *its* variety?

Let me attempt to answer this question for one small but important sector of higher education, the liberal arts college. The relationship between liberal arts colleges and the public interest is, to begin with, paradoxical. Liberal arts colleges do not claim to be (and are not *meant* to be) instruments for training people to fill the particular employment needs or solve the specific social and economic challenges of the moment. For the purposes of liberal education, any substantial field of study, any subject matter, any developed set of methodologies is as relevant and valid as any other, because the point is to train the mind in ways that are foundational in character. One indication that this works is that liberally educated people often end up working successfully in unexpected fields, fields apparently unrelated to their undergraduate major, and contributing to society in ways that could not have been foreseen when they were students. So, the argument goes, the role of such colleges is to take the long view: to help students develop the core skills of perception, analysis, and expression, and the qualities that make one productive, responsible, and intellectually resilient. Instead of focusing on specific problems or issues, such colleges aim to help people realize their potential and equip themselves to live and work not only in the environment we know today but also in the unexpected and perhaps even unimaginable circumstances we may encounter in the future.

On the other hand, an observer who followed the advice of political analysts and paid more attention to feet than to mouths, would probably conclude that liberal arts colleges are much more of this world than they sometimes claim to be. That they resist vocationalism is true, but they long ago surrendered any notion that liberal learning must be value-free or socially neutral, and have accepted (even embraced) the responsibility to help shape society through the young people they graduate.

To do this well, these colleges need to show discipline and intentionality. The typical liberal arts college in this country has about 150 faculty and somewhere between 1200 and 2000 students. Given its size, it cannot teach everything that is important, cannot prepare its graduates to meet all the particular needs society may have at any given moment. Nevertheless, these small institutions are enormously, disproportionately rich in their concentrations of intellectual power and human promise. For all sorts of reasons, good and bad, they are constantly tempted to overreach themselves and take on not only the agenda of a university many times their size but also an enormous range of social commitments that can make their communities better. The paradox is that by doing this they may sacrifice the opportunity to have an impact upon the world commensurate with their potential.

The disaggregation of society into constituent interest groups threatens to impose upon liberal arts colleges an instrumentalism that will ultimately prove counterproductive. It is in society's interest that liberal arts colleges avoid being pulled apart by the sometimes conflicting demands of those who wish to appropriate them to address particular problems. Instead, the colleges should concentrate on what they do best: educating their students for advanced study and equipping them to lead productive and intellectually resilient lives. Their alumni already play a disproportionately large role in setting standards of practice in education, business, the professions, public service, and the arts; and it is the colleges' responsibility to see to it that they do this with an eye not only to personal reward and to group advantage but also to the common good. If the colleges succeed in this and in their traditional role of helping students to discover and develop their potential and to equip themselves for lifelong growth and learning, they can contribute powerfully to the public interest.

To keep faith with such students and justify what some will see as society's indulgence, liberal arts colleges need to make sure that their faculty and curricula rise above the extreme forms of disciplinary specialization and involution that turn students' vision and concern away from the real world. One of the striking academic phenomena of our time is the meta-character of much advanced scholarship, its fascination with fine points of methodology, and its tendency to conceive inquiry along lines that are either too specialized or too abstract to address the normal range of questions on which a student or a citizen seeks illumination. For whatever reason, much of this scholarship appears deliberately to turn its back on life. I think, for example, of the very distinguished economist who brought to the Ford Foundation while I worked there a model he had created that was not, as he put it, "susceptible to empirical test." He wanted the Foundation's money so that he could teach graduate students how to do this sort of thing for themselves. We said that what he had done had not only the intellectual elegance but also the social relevance of a world-class chess game, and that we preferred instead to help teachers figure out how students could use the tools of the social sciences to inform their practice of citizenship.

Because they are at heart undergraduate teaching institutions, liberal arts colleges have the opportunity to conceive their intellectual life and their educational mission more generously. Their campuses can be—and actually *need* to be—settings where scholars are rewarded for teaching across disciplinary lines, and are encouraged to enlarge vistas and suggest the connectedness of things to students in order that they might escape intellectual narrowness and parochialism: in order that they might actually use their understanding to make the world a better place. The liberal arts college, because it integrates social context and serious scholarship with a primary focus upon very high quality teaching and learning, offers extraordinary opportunities to articulate the relationship between thought and action. To do this effectively is to equip graduates for citizenship and for lifelong learning. And this is a major contribution to the public interest in a country where employers spend an estimated $45 billion annually to add value to the education of people who already possess high school or college degrees.

Society also needs liberal arts colleges to help broaden the pool of talent and advance the cause of social equity by continuing to diversify their student bodies, faculty, and staff. If I am right about the value of liberal education, it is in the public interest that this education strengthen the democratic and meritocratic values of our society rather than reinforce its divisions and rigidify its inequalities. To be true to its own values, liberal education cannot be race-, gender-, class-, culture-, or caste-bound. A liberal arts education is a privilege, but it should not be confined to the privileged.

Qualitatively speaking, I doubt that there is a more powerful engine for social mobility and personal growth in modern American history than the liberal arts college. The number of students with whom the colleges deal are small, but the effects they have upon students' lives are immense. It is easy to miss the social significance of this fact. Because the most visible liberal arts colleges are among the most expensive undergraduate institutions in the country, people sometimes infer that they serve only the economic elite. But this is not so. In fact, one of the benefits of the relative affluence of many liberal arts colleges is their ability to provide enough financial assistance to make it possible for economically disadvantaged students to attend the college. As a result, the median family income of students at my own college, Pomona, is actually *below* that of students at the public campuses of the University of California; and students of color (many but not all of whom are economically disadvantaged) comprise 1/3 of the student body and 2/5 of the most recent entering class. As the costs and uncertainties of public higher education unfortunately grow, it will be particularly attractive to poor and first-generation college students to attend colleges that are not only good and financially accessible, but also graduate most of their entering students in four years. If it is in the public interest for liberal arts colleges to continue to broaden access—if society *needs* this from the liberal arts sector of higher education—then state and federal governments, in turn, need to reverse their recent abdication of responsibility for helping colleges to bring this about.

There is at least one other thing that society needs from liberal arts colleges, and this arises from their nature as residential communities. For the reasons I have just indicated, most liberal arts colleges are increasingly diverse places intellectually, socially, and culturally. If one conceives the community, as I think one should, to include not only students but also faculty and staff, it is a community richer than almost any other we know in American life, encompassing people who differ from each other in age, gender, race, class, style, religion, politics, geography, sexual orientation, and fields of work. Because the people who embody this diversity end up living and working together in remarkable intimacy on these small, intense campuses, what one has in the typical liberal arts college is a kind of social laboratory.

Most of the students and faculty at these colleges have never before experienced so diverse a community, and some of them frankly hope that they never will again. Some of them respond defensively or destructively to this challenge; but countless others—by far the majority—are trying very hard to figure out, and some time to write, the rules of a new social and cultural era. They are doing this moreover, in a time of economic constraint when it is often the case that one person's or group's gain leads directly to another's loss. The press and the true believers at the extremes of this set of encounters would have one believe that college communities are being rent in destructive and demeaning ways. The real story, however, is that in spite of substantial pain and bewilderment, and numerous mistakes, the experiment is beginning to work. People are finding ways to live together with respect and sometimes enjoyment of each other's differences, partly because they share the bond of having chosen to come to college in order to learn in each other's company, and partly because the alternative is too dismal and ultimately hopeless to be accepted. In this way, too, liberal arts colleges can meet society's needs.

In a world whose central feature is change, society needs its young people to enter upon their lives as workers and citizens well-grounded in the skills and habits of mind that make one intellectually resilient. Society needs institutions that equip people for more than the demands of the moment. And when it finds those institutions it should help them to aim high: to have the courage of their educational convictions, focus upon teaching and upon the relationship between thought and action, strengthen their diversity, and help to develop and model social units that balance commonalty and commitment with individuality and respect for difference.🏃

Donald M. Stewart
President, The College Board

As we near the end of the century, the question of what American society needs from higher education is a provocative one. The environment in which higher education finds itself is changing dramatically. There is a new cohort of students; new and amazing technologies for learning; a new generation of faculty that will replace those who supported the great expansion of higher education after World War II; and new economic pressures facing the academy. Yet perhaps the most interesting aspect of this question is that, in fact, society expects something of higher education. It *expects* higher education to respond to the profoundly changed environment beyond the ivied walls. And all of us involved must take this expectation seriously. We must respond.

Based on European models, higher education in America has essentially called its own tune throughout its 350 year history. Except for the rise of graduate education in the mid-ninteenth century, and most recently the expansion of the ranks of community colleges, the academy has remained essentially unchanged—first, as a small sector that served the sons of the elite before World War II, and then as a booming, democratized version of its former self, increasingly serving the daughters and sons of virtually all races and backgrounds after 1945. Apart from their willingness to open their gates to the meritorious of whatever background, the only outside force that really influenced traditional four-year colleges and universities in the past half century is the federal government, and somewhat more lately, major corporations. The voluminous appetite for research fueled tremendous growth, but also created what many feel is a serious distortion of balance in the academy's mission: research, teaching, and service. Rightly or wrongly, the perception is that today there is too much emphasis on research and not enough on teaching. This perception adds bite to questions that are painfully coming to the fore from state legislators confronted by fiscal constraints, and from parents and students trapped by sharply rising costs in an era of economic downturn: "What are you doing with our taxes and our tuition dollars?" "Are we getting educational value for all this money?"

These are not easy questions. After years of being the darling of the public and public policy, the acknowledged escalator of social standing, the pathway to the realization of the American dream for millions upon millions of Americans, this deep expression of public and political doubt, exacerbated by a decade of the fierce, and often unfair bully pulpit rhetoric during the Reagan years, is the cause for much defensiveness, perplexity, and ultimately soul-searching in the groves of academe.

What began as a rhetorical attack in the early 1980s, is anything but that now. What society needs from higher education is first and foremost, responsiveness. Not so much in essence, as the basic mission: teaching, research, and service remain as true as ever, but rather that these must be conducted, delivered, conceived of in a different key, in a different way, in a different context. This may require: streamlining the entire system and reducing the duplication of programs, instituting new forms of assessment that chart the progress of students and the effectiveness of teaching, using technology to structure classroom and individual learning in wholly new ways. From these possibilities, it is clear, therefore, that this call is not a philosophical or a partisan political demand. Rather, it grows out of the enormous changes in the world beyond the ivory tower, on which academia now depends.

Change is coming at us from many directions. First, demographically, the U.S. is a different country than it was even 20 years ago, especially among the young. At a recent academic conference, it was noted that in just two years, there will be no single majority group among college freshmen either in California or in Texas. Moreover, for the first time in America's history, the majority of young people do not come from European backgrounds.

Second, expectations have changed. Our goal is no longer to sort out the top 25-30 percent of students and prepare them for college. To compete successfully with our global economic partners as we enter the twenty-first century, we need a sophisticated, well-prepared work force able to think for itself. Therefore, all students need to be prepared at a pre-collegiate level, no matter when, whether, or how they eventually undertake postsecondary education. This realization has inspired the development of the College Board's new programs, Equity 2000 and Pacesetter. These two major initiatives for education reform represent a push-pull strategy. Equity 2000 helps middle and high schools "push" students into more demanding academic preparation by requiring them to take pre-algebra, algebra, and geometry. Pacesetter, a high school project, provides the "pull" toward a goal of high standards of achievement for all students before graduating from the twelfth grade. Pacesetter is an integrated program of standards and course syllabi, teaching, and assessment designed to raise expectations and improve the performance of high school students. There will be Pacesetter courses in English, world history, science, Spanish, and mathematics.

Third, college-going itself has changed. Fewer than 20 percent of college-going students are traditional-age students enrolled full-time in four-year programs. Traditional, four-year colleges in the 1990s will resemble community colleges of the 1970s. The similarities will be in: the average age of the cohort (now about 25), as well as the significant number of students who are attending part-time, working, and in need of developmental courses. One recent projection suggests that traditional college will be only for the very able and the financially comfortable. For most students, higher education will occur as part of, or mixed in with, work, and may take place in workplace settings and/or through electronic, distance modes of learning.

Finally, politics have changed. The federal and state governments have become major players in education at all levels. At the national level, one might even say that there is a drift toward the creation of some form of a ministry of education. And national standards and assessment are a high priority for the Clinton Administration whose goal is to prepare all students. This was an unthinkable idea even five years ago.

Whereas up till now the demands of the collegiate curriculum set the pace for education K-12, educational reform in the lower grades appears to be more in tune with the times. And if not in actuality, this is true at least in the widespread acceptance of the need to create new standards, new curricula, new assessments, new preparation of teachers, new understanding of students as active, engaged learners who must acquire the complex skills of thinking, analyzing, problem-solving, and communication. Stunning as it sounds to say it, higher education must catch up with these expectations. It must form creative collaborative partnerships with education K-12. It must redirect the energy of its schools of education to catch up with these new needs and expectations. It must reconceive its own pedagogic processes in tune with the media and computer sophistication of its own incoming students and younger faculty. A futurist has noted, for example, that the college professor can no longer be "the sage on the stage in front of the class," but rather "a guide by your side with an array of new high technology teaching materials." And anyone who has watched the explosive growth of technology at the leading edge of pedagogy and information resources intuitively understands how at risk the traditional classroom is. While the traditional socratic model of teacher and learners will no doubt survive to some degree, in many cases it is too expensive, inefficient, demeaning, and ultimately old-fashioned.

Along with these economically and technologically driven factors, is a social and philosophical one. Linked to the support for high academic standards and the development of high level reasoning skills both mathematical and verbal, there is also an equally important drive for academic equity. This is a very exciting, and important point. Until quite recently, the development of reasoning skills was viewed as an indirect by-product of schooling and other life experiences. Today, however, new cognitive theories show that these skills can and, I believe, must be formally taught. The development of problem-solving and critical reading skills in students need no longer be left to chance. It is now the specific responsibility of schools. At long last, these skills are no longer viewed as being attainable only by an elite group of college-bound or unusually gifted students. Rather they are fundamental educational competencies, competencies that can be attained by all students. Curiously, this is something that results on the SAT have borne out for decades, namely: the more high quality, academic courses students take, and the higher the grades and rank-in-class they achieve through their own hard work, the higher the average SAT scores turn out to be. Academic ability is not something randomly occurring and predetermined at birth; it can be produced through quality schooling, equity of opportunity, and hard work.

Ultimately, what society needs from higher education is that forward-looking leadership that it has so consistently provided to American society and American education. What society needs is for higher education to turn away from merely resting on its comfortable laurels (which, in any case, economic realities are pulling out from under it), and deal with the new worlds of demographics, workplace needs, technology, and democratic expectations that are already shaking the foundations of education K-12. Assuming it can and will respond to these challenges, then what society needs is exactly what higher education has the gift to give.⭐

Estelle N. Tanner

Trustee, Wellesley College

Higher education—before the feminist and the civil rights movements, the traumatic events of the late 1960's and early 1970's, before computers and word processors and E mail and fax machines and cellular phones, before awareness of the profound demographic changes and the resultant clash of visions and polarization—served a different purpose and faced different tasks.

A tour of college and university campuses today reveals the enormous changes that have taken place since the late 1960's. A more heterogeneous student population looks, dresses and speaks differently. Locks and increased security measures protect dormitory rooms, now repositories of complex and valuable technology. The volume of college life has been turned up, as students today act out social tensions and test beliefs and assumptions that Americans formerly took for granted.

Many alumnae/i, alarmed by what they regard as the politicization of the curriculum, urge a return to "the basics" and to a canon (most likely the curriculum *they* experienced) that they believe should continue to inculcate students with what they see as the fundamental values and traditions of American life.

Debating what, how, and why colleges teach is not new. Alfred North Whitehead, for example, wrote in the 1920's:

> "The universities are schools of education, and schools of research. But *the primary reason for their existence is not to be found either in the mere knowledge conveyed to the students or in the mere opportunities for research afforded to the members of the faculty.* Both these functions could be performed at a cheaper rate, apart from these very expensive institutions...*The justification for a university is that it preserves the connection between knowledge and the zest of life, by uniting the young and the old in the imaginative consideration of learning.* The university imparts information, but it imparts it imaginatively. At least, this is the function which it should perform for society. *A university which fails in this respect has no reason for existence.*" (Italics mine) (*The Aims of Education*, pp. 92-93)

Today's critics are more numerous and more direct about what they see as education's profound flaws and pitfalls. In his book, *The Unschooled Mind*, Howard Gardner, Professor at the Harvard Graduate School of Education and a MacArthur Fellow, states the concerns that many share:

> Not only have most schools experienced difficulties in achieving their avowed goals, but even those deemed a success yield students who, by and large, do not display deep understandings. The deficiencies with the schools reflect deficiencies in the wider society: in our grasp of learning and development and in ourselves—and our value systems—as teachers and citizens. (p. 249)

Pervasive criticism of America's educational system in books, articles, on television and radio, may account for the schizophrenia with which many Americans view colleges and universities. Pride is mixed with distrust. Parents decry what they see as "political correctness", accuse schools of greed and inefficiency, yet mortgage their houses to pay their child's way. These conflicting feelings reflect a national yearning, a recognition of our country's ongoing need not only for literate, numerate and responsible citizens, with the practical skills to be productive members of society, but also for men and women with open and flexible minds, who will be capable of identifying and ultimately rejecting dogma, orthodoxy, and conspiratorial formulations.

While in one sense this is a frustrating and difficult time for education, it is paradoxically, a promising time as well. Never before have so many educators, psychologists, feminist scholars, sociologists, and others, been actively engaged in the study of teaching and learning. Their work is offering, to anyone willing to pay attention, new insights into how people learn and under what conditions. Additionally, there is a growing appreciation of the exciting opportunities that technology might bring to the educational equation. The question is how colleges and universities can best use these opportunities to respond to the challenges society faces. While different people will offer different answers, those that follow are mine.

First, and most importantly, our schools must doff, perhaps forever, the image of the ivory tower. This country needs its schools to be partners in the social enterprise, and can no longer afford institutions that see themselves apart from the realities of the outside world.

Second, we need schools to approach their educational mission with humility, and a willingness to examine, continuously, their practices as well as the assumptions behind the practices. They must be willing to accept the challenges inherent in a changing population of students, and to recognize the extent to which our thinking is influenced by tradition and traditional approaches as well as the tenacity of long-lived habits of mind and patterns of behavior.

Third, we need colleges and universities to keep abreast of the cognitive research that is providing new insights into how people learn. They should welcome, into the academic circle, those educators, psychologists, feminist scholars, philosophers, and sociologists who are thinking and writing passionately on the subject of teaching and learning. What, for example, are the implications of Howard Gardner's argument that humans learn, remember, and understand in different ways and are capable of knowing the world not only through language, logical-mathematical analysis, and spatial representation, but also through musical thinking, the use of the body to solve problems or to make things, an understanding of other individuals, and an understanding of ourselves? The growing evidence of how people differ in the strength of these intelligences raises serious questions about an educational system that assumes that all students can learn and be tested on the same materials in the same way.

Another book with educational significance is *Women's Ways of Knowing*, in which co-authors Belenky, Clinchy, Goldberger and Tarule contrast two epistemological orientations—a "separate" epistemology favored by men, based upon reasoned discourse and impersonal procedures for establishing truth, and a "connected" epistemology which many women use to perceive the world, based on the conviction that the most trustworthy knowledge is contextual, and comes from personal experience rather than from authoritative pronouncements.

While books like *Women's Ways of Knowing*, Gardner's and others' suggest the importance of experimentation with different learning configurations, different kinds of engagement between teacher and student, and different kinds of academic dialogue, American classrooms, to date, remain remarkably immune to change. In most, the expert (usually male) stands as he has always stood, in front of the class, instructing. He has, as usual, on average, an hour to transfer a certain amount of information to the students, who are, as usual, sitting in rows, taking notes on the material presented. At some point during the semester the students will be, as they always have been, tested on the material. At some point after finishing the course, they will have forgotten much of its content, and by graduation much of that particular class experience will be a dim memory. Few would describe this process or environment as one that promotes either the "connection between knowledge and the zest of life" that

Whitehead argues for, or Gardner's "deep understandings." Clearly, it is time for higher education to question the assumptions behind this model and to be open to alternative ones.

Fourth, colleges and universities must be willing to experiment with the possibilities of interdisciplinary team teaching, apprenticeship programs, group exercises, and to make innovative use of the new technology. They must be willing to examine the relationship of a competitive, grade driven academic environment to a society that needs men and women who will be comfortable with collaborative and cooperative approaches to problem solving, that needs the creative thinking that comes from social and intellectual interaction.

Fifth, we need our schools to hold themselves accountable for the progress of their students, and to find ways to measure how successfully their students have been educated. This measurement process should include continuous discourse with all the constituencies involved—those who are paying for the education, those who are in the classroom, those who are employing the graduates, as well as anyone who is dependent upon an informed citizenry.

Sixth, we need our schools to provide, for everyone, an environment of trust and mutual respect, to offer opportunities for better communication and understanding through discussion and debate, in and outside the classroom, and to encourage all members of the academic community to think sympathetically about preconceived notions in themselves and in others.

Lastly, but far from least, society needs colleges and universities to serve as models for unity in diversity, to be living examples of the proposition that a heterogeneous community can be effective *only* within the context of mutual respect. Students and faculty must be encouraged to embrace, wholeheartedly, the *value* of community, to see themselves as privileged members of a community *to* which everyone belongs, and *for* which everyone is responsible. They must be helped to find common ground, a set of shared values by which each will be moved "out of his isolated class and into the one humanity." (Paul Goodman, *Compulsory Mis-education*)

Society needs graduates who appreciate the values of a free society, who recognize the innate tension between the ideals of personal liberty and a constitutional democracy, and who understand that, despite the profound changes our society has undergone, what Henry Rosovsky (formerly Harvard's dean of the Faculty of Arts and Sciences) calls the basic issues of human moral choice—justice, loyalty, personal responsibility—remain the same.✝

Robert E. Tranquada, M.D.

Professor of Medicine and Public Policy, University of Southern California, and Chairman, Board of Trustees, Pomona College

The wisdom of inquiring into society's *needs*, as opposed to *wants*, provides wonderful degrees of freedom for a response. This response is from one who teaches in a research university and participates in the governance of a small liberal arts college. Those two very different views of higher education should not, of course, affect the definition of society's true needs.

It seems possible to divide society's needs from higher education into two major categories: those relating to the production of educated graduates; and those related to the other functions of higher education which have evolved in modern times as important adjuncts and critical aspects of the production of graduates.

One would imagine that there should not be great controversy concerning society's needs for the basic product from higher education. That must be graduates who are prepared to function in modern society with the following capabilities:

- The ability to express themselves orally and in writing with clarity and precision;
- The ability to locate relevant information;
- The ability to understand human behavior;
- The ability to analyze information, using rational processes, and to interpret data with the competent use of basic mathematics and statistical elements;
- An appreciation of the development of ideas and a well honed sense of where we are in the history of humanity; and
- An informed appreciation of the capabilities and limitations of contemporary science.

All of the above are simply subdivisions of the two highest priority contributions of higher education to its graduates, which are:

- The empowerment to realize one's full potential and
- The maximum stimulation of intellectual curiosity.

In addition to those basic attributes of the graduates of higher education, of course, society needs graduates whose basic, or liberal education is variably enhanced with the skills, knowledge and attitudes necessary to assure the graduate's ability to contribute effectively in a needed occupational or professional role.

Society needs institutions of higher education who are independent enough to allow genuine academic freedom in both research and teaching. At the same time academic freedom must be coupled with enough involvement in and dependence on the real world to maintain a sense of belonging, responsibility and participation by academia without the presence of stultifying or distorting levels of conflict of interest.

Society needs institutions of higher education which are encouraged to be sites and sources of intellectual debate on any subject without fear of retribution or imposed compromise in the exercise of responsible academic freedom. The continuing health of society, the ability to predict the future with confidence and to adapt to change in the world are all very much dependent upon the dedicated maintenance of the capability for free debate within the academy.

Society needs institutions of higher education who are actively engaged in the creation of new knowledge and understanding through research in all intellectual fields and disciplines, and institutions who continue to furnish society with minds trained and skilled to carry on the critical tradition of free inquiry. Society should not depend solely on institutions of higher education as sources of research and inquiry. Since such activity is integral to the ability to provide the most stimulating environment for learning, it is critical to the higher education establishment, and society must give significant priority to maintaining such strong capability in higher education.

Society has the need for institutions of higher education who value faculty skills in enhancing learning (one element of which is teaching) equally with research productivity. There is a need to balance the rewards, in terms of promotion, tenure and pay, for both educational skills and scholarly activity in faculty. Society needs both and should be prepared to insist on both.

Society needs institutions of higher education who maintain a continuing lack of satisfaction with the product they produce (including graduates, new knowledge and service to their communities) and who therefore continue uninterrupted their efforts to improve in every respect. Self-satisfaction does not meet societies needs.

Society needs institutions of higher education, across the entire spectrum from research-intensive to teaching-intensive institutions, who are prepared for and are deeply involved in the challenge of preparing *all* segments of our society to realize their full potential. There remain significant failures in the educational pipeline leading to admission to higher education. While society cannot hold higher education solely responsible for these failures, it can be held responsible for making major contributions to their alleviation. These contributions can be both in the form of producing a better understanding of the causes of such failures, and direct action to influence improved results. But as we improve the flow of students from underrepresented segments of society, higher education must be prepared to adjust its educational processes to allow each of them to reach their full potential without regard to differences in prior life and cultural experiences or quality of prior education. As we move into our post modern society, or post-industrial, or whatever the current appellation may be, we cannot tolerate the existence of segments of our society who have not been empowered to reach their full potential.

As society experiences the ebb and flow that marks our geopolitical process, we must depend upon higher education to maintain the continuity of our historical, cultural, and philosophical underpinnings. While we recognize higher education as a major source of that cultural glue that contributes to the stability of society, we find ourselves needing simultaneous input from higher education both to the maintenance of our foundations and to the needed changes in our superstructure. That is a daunting challenge to the denizens of higher education. On the other hand, it is just that productive tension between the preservation of culture and exploration of change that should continue to invigorate our higher education establishment.

Finally, as society finds it necessary to discipline elements of higher education who may have lost sight of their obligations to society, or who may have become overly impressed with their importance or abilities, it must direct its discipline with rifle shots and not with shotgun blasts. Society cannot afford to cripple its institutions of higher education with broad-based higher education bashing. Pinpoint discipline for those transgressions will deliver the message to the higher education community just as well and will not threaten the overall delicate balance of trust which creates the climate in which higher education will function best. Society's dependency on higher education is too basic and far-reaching to risk serious damage to the whole enterprise.

Society needs a higher education establishment that is able to maintain a reasonable balance between properly earned self confidence and respect for its dependence on the world outside the academy. Such a balance is the critical prerequisite to the delivery of all of society's needs.✶

Malte von Matthiessen
Trustee, Antioch University

Background

I joined the Antioch University Board of Trustees in the summer of 1980; and since 1987 have served as Chairperson. This has been an unusual period of time in the history of Antioch and for higher education.

Antioch has always been important to higher education; among other things it has a distinctive role and rich history as an innovator. In many respects, Antioch has always been an experiment; one of the consequences being, it has never had a strong financial foundation. On the other hand, it is a value-driven place that focuses on the education of the whole person.

Antioch believes that education is more than classroom study; it should also include real life learning beyond academics. Finally, the notion of community and an interactive governance structure make up the third component of the Antioch education model.

Douglas McGregor, the President of Antioch College from 1948 to 1954 wrote "there is no educational institution in America more intimately interwoven with free enterprise ideals. Our work study plan is based on belief in our American economic system. Our College government is completely patterned on the American principles of representative government. The College has been a seedbed for many successful private enterprises."

He went on to write, "we value the individual at Antioch; we think that he (she) should have the freedom to grow intellectually according to his (her) own abilities."

All of this is still true today. Antioch is now more than a liberal arts college tucked away in the corn fields of Southwest Ohio. It also has adult campuses in Kenne, New Hampshire; Seattle, Washington; Southern California (Santa Barbara and Los Angeles); and Yellow Springs, Ohio. While maintaining an innovative liberal arts residency program at the College, that is still grounded in the principles of whole life learning, Antioch is pressing ahead with the education of adult learners.

I've taken the time to share all this because it helps put the issue— "what does society need from higher education"—into context. To summarize, I am a Trustee of a private sector institution—one that is value-driven, has a strong commitment for the tolerance of diversity and self-expression; an institution that recognizes education as a life long endeavor.

The Present

We live in an age of enormous change. Everyone talks about it, writes about it, analyzes the consequences—most institutions just try to keep up. Everywhere market forces are rapidly invading every sphere of our society. Here in America, we are witness to the erosion of trust in our institutions. For a long time, people in higher education thought they were exempt from the public's right to know and to question. No longer.

Whatever happened to civility? Has militancy replaced the open give-and-take forum that used to be found on college campuses, where views and ideas could be exchanged without having to posture or position oneself to be politically correct.

Which among us are willing to speak directly to the diverse fears we live with— HIV infection, domestic violence, crime, inner city decay, child abuse, gay rights, poverty, health care, literacy—and many others.

America is endowed with a resource second to none—a higher education delivery system. People from all over the world flock to this country to study and learn. Yet, these institutions are also competing for a shrinking slice of the pie. Therefore, it becomes even more important that we understand the changing nature of the market; the demographic forces shaping this country and the world. And consequently, focus! This will mean the tough choices will have to be made. Every institution will no longer be able to be everything to each representative community.

The Future

Once again, this brings us back to the issue— "what does society need from higher education?" Several things:

First, we need a comprehensive program that provides for the education (and retraining) of adult learners; the on-going need to re-educate and retrain the American worker so that we can ensure our country's ability to compete in the global economy. We must convince the citizens of this country that we need to make a significant investment in higher education for the remainder of this decade if we want to maintain this unique national resource.

Second, we have to face the issue of access, especially in the private sector. The risk is we end up becoming an elitist community that denies access to a whole section of society. Can we truly justify a system that will deliver a liberal arts undergraduate education for close to $20K a year?

Third, relevancy. The external environment is one of exploding choice and unpredictable change. So, education must be relevant—but relevant to what? Shouldn't education also concern itself with values, with trust, and integrity? Shouldn't we be concerned about helping folks learn how to adapt and adjust to change; with issues of process rather than procedures and form?

Fourth, the nature of work. Work fills many individual needs. It gives us money to support ourselves. It structures our time and establishes a routine. It lets us see ourselves positively as contributors, and if we are lucky, it gives us a sense of accomplishment, self-satisfaction, personal growth, and self worth.

Technology has created the real prospect that any routine a human can perform, a machine can do better and less expensively. How should we—as a society and a nation—feel about the prospect of technology producing a two-tiered society (a high standard of living for some and lower standard of living for everyone else)?

Certainly there is a need for these issues to be debated and discussed; and hopefully resolved. What better place than for higher education to take a leadership role on this front? It may be that the crucial dimension is knowledge; and the amount of value that knowledge brings to each and every job in the work place. And knowledge in the business of higher education.

Final Thoughts

One couldn't conclude without addressing the leadership question. Educational institutions must nurture a spirit of leadership among the young. We also need to encourage leadership among adult learners; to look in unlikely places and among people who, through their own examples, convey a spirit akin to the values we wish to propagate within our institutions.↑

Arnold R. Weber
President, Northwestern University

The question, "What does society need from higher education?" reflects the contemporary *angst* that has afflicted America's colleges and universities. In recent years, higher education has been rocked by scandals involving financial improprieties and scientific fraud, pummeled by economic adversity, riven by racial controversies and—the cruelest cut—has been accused of inattention to its core function of providing a quality education to the young people who grace its campuses.

These deficiencies have been enlarged by the media to the point of exaggeration, if not caricature. However, collectively these episodes indicate that if higher education has not lost its moorings, its self-assurance has been shaken and it must confront the erosion of public confidence in the institution's integrity and constancy of purpose. Spokespersons for higher education can no longer dissipate the public's concerns by reminding it that American universities are the best in the world. Thus, the query, "What does society need from higher education?" appears to combine elements of brooding introspection and market research by an industry that has too long taken its clientele for granted.

Before a sensible, albeit general, answer to the question can be offered, some operational definition of "higher education" must be provided. "Higher education" in the United States is a many-splendored thing ranging from community colleges to the most precious refinement of the "research" university. One of the problems of determining what society needs from higher education is the necessity of identifying which segment of higher education you have in mind. We may "need" graduates from community colleges with highly specific skills for immediate use in particular jobs and industries, but few research universities would embrace this goal. For purposes of this brief rumination, "higher education" is defined as the comprehensive university with real or illusory pretensions of being a "major research university."

The concept of "need" also requires some definition in framing the functional obligations of higher education to society. Certainly, "needs" should be distinguished from "wants." A major contributing factor to the current afflictions of higher education has been the confounding of "needs" with "wants." Over the last forty years, universities have been transformed from special purpose institutions to generalized engines for social change and amelioration. This transformation was signaled by Clark Kerr's characterization of the university as a "multiversity" with multiple goals and constituencies. The concept was accepted, tacitly or otherwise, by many institutions as giddy confirmation of their prowess, or to strengthen their claim on public resources.

In this manner, universities came to promise economic growth, solutions to vexing social problems, cures for disease, and other public boons. All of these are meritorious goals but their adoption as "needs" by higher education was unrestrained by any notions of functional competence or what economists call "comparative advantage" i.e., an appreciation of what universities can do best compared to the capacities of other institutions. The perceptible gap between what universities said they could do in satisfying society's "needs" and what they delivered is surely an important factor in the public's recent disenchantment with higher education. Any specification of what society "needs" from higher education should be disciplined by the concept of comparative advantage rather than feeding institutional ambitions. Undoubtedly, higher education can and does make significant contributions to economic growth and the solution of social problems; but these contributions are best viewed as a beneficial joint product of its primary mission and core competence.

159

This more modest definition of higher education's capabilities helps to simplify the designation of society's "needs" to which it may constructively respond. The overriding societal need which universities can best satisfy is for educated young men and women who have the basic knowledge, analytical skills, and understanding of institutional behavior in an historical framework which promote productive participation in economic activities and democratic processes. This assertion has something of an "emperor's clothes" quality and is perhaps symptomatic of the extent to which universities have diffused their sense of mission. Satisfying this need clearly implies a renewed emphasis on undergraduate education in order to achieve a better balance with the more monkish pursuits of graduate study and research. There is no consensus concerning the optimum undergraduate curriculum and pedagogy, but the widespread experimentation and argumentation on these issues is an encouraging sign that higher education is responding to the public's exasperated statements of need and expectation. The record indicates that the design of an ideal undergraduate program is intellectually more challenging than defining the requirements for a Ph.D. in say, Economics or Physics.

The reemphasis on high quality undergraduate education which creates the durable "human capital" for economic and social progress identifies another, derivative "need." That is, such education requires skilled, dedicated teachers. Obviously, there are many practicing academics who meet this standard. Their cultivation is almost a random process, however, reflecting a process of self-selection more than on explicit acceptance of this goal. Most university professors are the product of graduate (Ph.D.) programs and the stations of the cross that must be traversed to successfully complete the programs almost all have signage marked "research." The development of pedagogical competence is largely a matter of innate ability, individual interest, or a casual master-apprentice relationship between the doctoral candidate and his or her professor. Society needs talented, trained teachers who are willing to give primacy to the educational process. We must recalibrate our graduate programs to provide the direction and incentives to achieve this goal.

Reaffirmation of the educational mission of the university does not mean the denigration of research activities, but it does imply a reassessment of the role of research in the contemporary university. Achievement in research—or the appearance of achievement—is the *sine qua non* of individual and institutional distinction in the academic universe. We are all in thrall to the German concept of the university that was implanted in the United States about 125 years ago. This concept asserts the primacy of pure knowledge and therefore research, in defining the mission of the university. It is redundant to state that the achievements of the research university in expanding the base of knowledge have been prodigious and have enriched our lives and society in general. But this congratulatory observation does not mean that all research in all fields has equal merit and potential. Nor does it address the question of what is the optimal balance between teaching and research in terms of some generalized notion of academic productivity. Moreover, although universities may have been the principal source of new knowledge—particularly in the sciences— forty years ago, this is certainly not the case today given the proliferation of independent research enterprises, corporate R & D programs, and government laboratories. Research should continue to be an important activity of the modern university. It is problematic, however, that the nation "needs" another "major research university" as that term is used in the metric of academic prestige. What we need is a revised concept of how university-based research fits into the national research enterprise.

At this time, there are great pressures to move academic research closer to industrial (i.e. practical) applications. Because these pressures are emanating from the government funding agencies, academic constituencies are highly attentive. Nonetheless, it is arguable whether universities best exploit their comparative advantage by becoming extensions of, or substitutes for, corporate laboratories. Rather, the satisfaction of society's needs probably lies in making normative judgments of where academic research can make significant contributions and tilting the agenda to basic phenomena which are not likely to be pursued in a market context. Investors like to talk about "patient money": universities can be most supportive of society's needs endorsing "patient research" rather than instant applicability.

The emphasis on satisfying the need for quality education, exemplary teachers, and the generation of new knowledge does not mean that education should be aloof from current problems. The time has long passed when universities can be viewed as isolated enclaves of contemplation detached from worldly ills. Indeed, public universities have enjoyed widespread support because of the expectation that they will be instruments of economic and social advancement. Nonetheless, it is critical that we again appreciate the comparative advantage of higher education in defining its role as a service agency. Experience indicates that universities have no special competence in running programs aimed directly at the solution of economic and social problems. Indeed, the evidence is largely to the contrary. Universities have not ameliorated the deficiencies of urban school systems, harmonized race relations, mitigated the impact of unemployment, or protected the family farm from the erosion of market forces. To some extent, the loss of public confidence in universities is the consequence of unrealized expectations that they would do so. Where universities engage in service activities to the community at large, they generally should eschew direct operational responsibilities and instead adopt a more modest agenda. That is, they should be particularly concerned with the development of institutional mechanisms which facilitate the transfer of new knowledge to other, functional organizations in society and be a source of specialized expertise in addressing well-defined issues rather than generalized problems. Viewing universities as a knowledge-transfer agency and source of focused consulting services is less heroic a role than the public—and many administrators—may desire. But these functions reflect a realistic appraisal of higher education's special competence and lower the risk that service activities will undermine its core function of education and discovery.

Society's interest in higher education extends beyond external dimensions of performance. Taxpayers and parents also expect a sense of economy in the conduct of the universities' affairs. For many years, the idealized notion of the university transcended managerial considerations. As economic enterprises, they were viewed as an intermediate organizational form somewhere between a commune and a 7-11 store. This view, of course, had little relationship to the fiscal realities. Universities are large, complex organizations whose activities encompass a serious mass of resources. Public awareness of this reality has grown as a consequence of the outsized increases in tuition over the last fifteen years and the incessant demands of the institutions for expanded public funding. Consequently, society has demanded a new fiscal and managerial discipline from higher education before transferring more resources for its use. The failure to heed this public sensitivity to considerations of cost and efficiency has also contributed to the loss of grace that has so dismayed the academic community in recent years. As is the case with other institutions, higher education must respond to greater demands for accountability for what it does and how it carries out its charge.

As recent events demonstrate, universities play a complex, and even unique role in American society. On the one hand, they are relentless agents of change through the education of students and the creation of new knowledge. On the other hand, they are viewed as a source of continuity and stability in the volatile social environment they have helped to engender. This duality is often perplexing to the public at large and gives rise to an ambivalence in the public's regard for higher education. Within universities, the need to balance the imperatives of change with the obligations of continuity is often played out in political terms. Witness the current controversies over "political correctness" and "multi-culturalism" which have excited the public's interest, if not concern. Recognition of society's need for the conservation of values and democratic traditions has been diminished within universities as the velocity of change has increased. The balance between change and continuity will never be in a stable equilibrium, but universities should incorporate the need to strike such a balance in responding to societal expectations. Indeed, the continuance of "the permanent American revolution" requires the preservation of the central values of freedom of inquiry and speech upon which it was founded. ✝

Robert W. Woodson, Sr.
President, National Center for Neighborhood Enterprise

As this nation moves closer to the twenty-first century, America's institutions of higher education must become more responsive to a diverse array of social and economic needs among its citizens. The needs of low-income residents in inner-cities and rural communities will be particularly acute. These needs are reflected in record-level rates of unemployment, poverty, crime, delinquency, school dropouts, drug abuse, drug trafficking, AIDS, adolescent pregnancies, single-parent families, welfare dependence, etc.

America's colleges and universities will have to leave their insulated "ivory towers," and extend their services and support to low-income individuals and groups who traditionally have had little prospect of going to college. The type of outreach services that higher education will need to provide in the twenty-first century to the economically disadvantaged are:

- increasing the access of low-income youths and adults to postsecondary education, such as helping welfare recipients, adolescent fathers, incarcerated felons or ex-offenders to obtain two-year or four-year degrees;
- using grassroots leaders as instructors, consultants or experts on many "intractable" inner-city problems;
- enhancing the entrepreneurial skills of inner-city youths and adults and helping them to form their own businesses or cooperatives;
- shifting from conventional studies of the "deficits" or weaknesses of the poor to solution-oriented research that focuses on their strengths, assets and successes;
- assisting grassroots groups in documenting or evaluating the impact or effectiveness of their programs; and
- assisting low-income groups in preparing more effective proposals to obtain public or private funds to underwrite their programs and initiatives.

Historically black colleges and universities (HBCUs) should be viewed as special resources to address the needs of racially and economically disadvantaged groups. Since HBCUs are located disproportionately in low-income urban and rural communities, they are in a strategic position to play a major role in providing vital outreach services. Former HUD Secretary Jack Kemp provided important resources to HBCUs to enhance their community and economic development capacities through comprehensive HUD-HBCU federal initiatives.

Institutions such as Atlanta University have used such funds to form a local Community Development Corporation (CDC) and to move their faculty and students into the surrounding public housing dwellings that border their campus. Morgan State University has used HUD-Technical Assistance funds through its Community Development Resource Center (CDRC) to enhance the ability of grassroots groups to: a) prepare more effective proposals; b) use computers to access and analyze census data for program planning; c) strengthen the functioning of their organizations; and d) assist such groups in conducting solution-oriented research and program evaluations. Howard University's Small Business Development Center has assisted numerous inner-city individuals and groups to establish small businesses.

The example set by many HBCUs and other universities is a refreshing departure from the onslaught of "failure studies" conducted by universities. Academia spends billions of dollars annually on extensive research studies that assess the pathology and deficiencies of low-income Americans. In turn, these failure studies are used to substantiate the need for professionally managed programs to aid the poor. However, these pricey, top-down programs have not commensurately improved conditions for America's underclass.

As government, the news media and the public continue to value university-based studies, it is incumbent upon colleges and universities to acknowledge that strengths exist within low-income communities, to document those strengths and to develop approaches that build on them.🮲

Bibliography
John Gallagher

A good place to start would be *The Idea of the University* by Cardinal Newman (Christian Classics reprint edition, 1973). While many of the lectures that comprise the volume are concerned with theology and the Church's relationship to higher education, Newman's development of a philosophy of higher education remains the key portion of the lectures and is as strong a defense of learning for its own sake as has ever been made.

The Aims of Education by Alfred North Whitehead (Free Press, 1967) is also mandatory reading. Whitehead's subtle argument is still a sensible way to tie together the conflicting strains of liberal knowledge and practical learning.

The Higher Learning in America by Robert Hutchins (Yale University, 1936) reclaims the tradition of liberal education with a detailed, logical argument for it. See also Hutchins' *The Conflict in Education in a Democratic Society* (Harper & Row, 1953). For a spirited attack on professionalism and the business interests behind it, there is Thorstein Veblen's *The Higher Learning in America: A Memorandum on the Conduct of Universities by Business Men* (1918; August Kelly reprint ed., 1965).

An invaluable selection of American higher education documents exists in Richard Hofstadter and Wilson Smith's two volume edition, *American Higher Education: A Documentary History* (University of Chicago Press, 1961). Flexner, Wilson, Gilman, the Yale Report of 1828 and Jefferson are among those included in the work. The choices are, unfortunately, often excerpts, but the edition compensates for it with the chance to read a variety of related documents in a row. The brief introductions to each section are also helpful in putting the works in context.

Of particular interest, either in the volumes' selection or in their own editions, are The Harvard Report and the report of the Truman Commission. The latter runs to six volumes, of which the first is of primary importance for any discussion of higher education's purpose. Of use in understanding the historical flow of higher education are *The Academic Revolution* by Christopher Jencks and David Riesman (Doubleday, 1968), and, especially, *Higher Education in Transition: A History of American Colleges and Universities, 1636-1976* (Harper & Row, third ed., 1976).

Clark Kerr's *The Uses of the University* (Harvard University Press, 1964) is a relatively brief and clever analysis of the state of the university that says more about higher education than Kerr perhaps intended. Robert Paul Wolff's *The Ideal of the University* (Beacon Press, 1969) is a response to Kerr. Wolff is a cogent and witty writer, and while his proposals may seem naive, they are nonetheless provocative.

From the same period, *The American University: How it Runs, Where it is Going* (Harper & Row, 1968), by Jacques Barzun provides a more detailed critique of higher education from the same period, with particular detail to the increasingly corporate nature of higher education.

For a response to the student uprisings of the 1960s and 1970s, see *In Defense of Academic Freedom*, edited by Sidney Hook (Pegasus, 1971). It is, as the title implies, a rather defensive collection of essays supporting liberal learning under siege. Hook's earlier work *Education for Modern Man* (Dial Press, 1946) provides a fuller explanation of his philosophy of pragmatic liberal learning.

The State of the Nation and the Agenda for Higher Education by Howard Bowen (Jossey-Bass, 1982) is an interesting combination of educational philosophy and statistical analysis. Bowen tends to quantify anything he can—he presents eleven characteristics of the educated person—but he makes a strong case for reevaluating higher education's current role in society.

A reasoned approach to the renewal of education is to be found in College: The Undergraduate Experience in America by Ernest Boyer, president of the Carnegie Foundation for the Advancement of Teaching (Harper & Row, 1987). Boyer's report on the current state of that aspect of higher education, along with his even-handed discussion of the problems to be found there, allow for an intelligent analysis of higher education free from the polemics that have more usually characterized it of late.

Derek Bok's views are best represented by two books, Universities and the Future of America (Duke University, 1990) and Beyond the Ivory Tower: Social Responsibilities of the Modern University (Harvard, 1982). Both rely on an administrator's view in considering the purpose of the research university.

There is no shortage of books describing just how terrible the conditions are on campus now. The opening salvo was fired by Allan Bloom in The Closing of the American Mind: How Higher Education Has Failed Democracy and Impoverished the Souls of Today's Students (Simon and Schuster, 1987). Bloom's book is an amalgam of Nietzsche, Plato and unhappy remembrances of the 1960s that struck a national nerve and became a best-seller. A more damning, though no less belligerent, book is Dinesh D'Souza's Illiberal Education: The Politics of Race and Sex on Campus (Free Press, 1991), a compendium of every nightmare of political correctness imaginable. A liberal version of the battle on campus is provided by Julius Getman in In the Company of Scholars: The Struggle for the Soul of Higher Education (University of Texas Press, 1992), though it is no less hair-raising for its different political perspective. Page Smith, author of Killing the Spirit: Higher Education in America (Viking, 1990), is more thorough as history than Getman's personal reflections. A less detailed argument is put forth in Education with Impact: How our Universities Fail our Young (Birch Lane Press, 1992) by George Douglas, a professor of nonfiction writing at the University of Illinois.

Government education officials were no less interested in outlining the problems on campus. Of William Bennett's many sallies against higher education practices, perhaps the best is his speech at Harvard's 350th anniversary celebration (reprinted in The Chronicle of Higher Education, October 15, 1986). Lynne Cheney's reports often echo Bennett. Among the most interesting are Tyrannical Machines: A Report on Educational Practices Gone Wrong and Our Best Hopes for Setting Them Right (1985) and 50 Hours: A Core Curriculum for College Students (1989). (It is interesting to note that, with the exception of Cheney, most of the writing on the purpose of higher education in society has been done by men.)

Putting the current debate in perspective is A Free and Ordered Space: A Real World for the University (Norton, 1988), a collection of A. Bartlett Giamatti's speeches and essays. The most important of these is titled "The Academic Mission." ✝

Appendix E

The SCANS Agenda

In 1991 and 1992, the Secretary's Commission on Achieving Necessary Skills (SCANS) called on the American educational system, from pre-school through post-graduate, to attend to the responsibilities graduates assume as workers, parents, and citizens. Asserting that there is more to life than earning a living, SCANS also insisted that the following set of foundation skills and competences are essential for all in the modern world.

Foundation Skills

Competent individuals in the high-performance workplace need:

- **Basic Skills**—reading, writing, arithmetic and mathematics, speaking and listening.
- **Thinking Skills**—the ability to learn, to reason, to think creatively, to make decisions, and to solve problems.
- **Personal Qualities**—individual responsibility, self-esteem and self-management, sociability, and integrity.

Competences

Effective individuals can productively use:

- **Resources**—They know how to allocate time, money, materials, space, and staff.
- **Interpersonal skills**—They can work on teams, teaching others, serve customers, lead, negotiate, and work well with people from culturally diverse backgrounds.
- **Information**—They can acquire and evaluate data, organize and maintain files, interpret and communicate, and use computers to process information.
- **Systems**—They understand social, organizational, and technological systems; they can monitor and correct performance, and they can design or improve systems.
- **Technology**—They can select equipment and tools, apply technology to specific tasks, and maintain and troubleshoot equipment.

Notes